Fabian Bachrach

Charles Bohner

received his Ph.D. from The University of Pennsylvania and is currently a member of the Department of English and Director of the American Studies Program at The University of Delaware. The author has published articles in a variety of literary and historical journals.

JOHN PENDLETON KENNEDY
GENTLEMAN FROM BALTIMORE

John Pendleton Kennedy in 1846

From a portrait by Matthew Wilson; reproduced by permission of the owner, the Peabody Institute Library, Baltimore.

John Pendleton Kennedy

Gentleman from Baltimore

CHARLES H. BOHNER

THE JOHNS HOPKINS PRESS: BALTIMORE

© 1961 by The Johns Hopkins Press, Baltimore 18, Md.
Distributed in Great Britain by Oxford University Press, London
Printed in the United States of America
by H. Wolff Book Manufacturing Co., New York
Library of Congress Catalog Card Number 61-10735

This book has been brought to publication with the assistance of
a grant from the Ford Foundation.

**TO MY MOTHER
AND TO THE MEMORY OF
MY FATHER**

Preface

The American gentleman is less graceful than the Frenchman, and may be even less conventional in his air than the Englishman, but he is commonly gravely considerate of the feelings. Were he disposed to abuse his situation, his countrymen would not tolerate his airs. I have already told you that humanity is a distinctive feature of American intercourse. No man is kinder in all his feelings or habits.

—*James Fenimore Cooper,* Notions of the Americans *(1828)*

JOHN PENDLETON KENNEDY spent the morning of his fifty-ninth birthday in his library gathering pamphlets, articles, and manuscript odds and ends he believed worthy to be preserved in a volume of his collected writings. Essays in history, politics, economics, religion—they made a long and impressive list; and in 1854 the South could not boast of another living writer who had written on such a variety of topics with so much cogency and charm. Yet as the list of titles swelled to several manuscript pages, Kennedy was haunted by the disquieting doubt that his talent had been splintered away in trifles. Many of the speeches were doomed with the causes they championed and the formal orations were destined to go out of fashion. Anxious for his literary reputation, and prompted perhaps by the memories of past triumphs, he turned again to the writing of his autobiography.

Each time, Kennedy plunged into the task with fresh enthusiasm. Yet this project, like so many of his literary schemes in later life, was never completed, and the unfinished manuscript, broken off at his nineteenth year, was found among his papers at his death. What remains is a graceful evocation of his boyhood in post-revolutionary Baltimore, memoirs which, if completed, might have been a worthy addition to the distinguished American tradition of self-portraits in prose.

Kennedy, a sensitive and intelligent observer of his world, forged a distinguished prose style, unrivaled in the South at the time of the Civil War. Unfortunately, declining health, flagging creative energy, and the anguish of civil war all took their toll. The autobiography remained a brilliant fragment.

Kennedy, however, left abundant resources for his biographer. At the age of fifty-one, while gathering material for his biography of the lawyer and author William Wirt, Kennedy had been amazed to discover how little substantial evidence remained. "I am a little surprised to find," he wrote a friend, "how very little survives of the social and personal history of even the most eminent men. One might almost write as fully upon a hero of Plutarch's as upon a distinguished lawyer of twenty years gone by. A *statesman* may fare somewhat better . . . because you have a little of him pickled in the public records. But as to the social existence of any man, unless he have a Boswell at his heels, or that sort of wholesome vanity which may persuade him to keep a diary—and, by the by, I think every man owes that duty in some part to his friends—it has no chance whatever." [1] Kennedy possessed the requisite wholesome vanity, and he determined that what remained of his own life should not be lost to posterity through any lack of diaries or documents.

The papers that survive reveal a life story not devoid of drama. The reader interested in American history may well profit by following the course of Kennedy's career from the time when he was a soldier in the War of 1812 through his several roles as lawyer, man of letters, politician, railroad president, millowner, cabinet officer, and cultural ambassador from the New World to the Old. Also, he was one of those rare good travelers who possess the gifts of precise observation and genuine enthusiasm. He

Preface ix

traveled widely, filling his notebooks with pungent comments which form a valuable commentary upon the society in which he moved.

Kennedy was admired and loved because his career seemed to his contemporaries the epitome of what the great experiment in democracy could produce. Although he bore the name of one of the first families of Virginia, he had risen to wealth and influence from the slim legacy of a bankrupt father. Kennedy believed, as did most men of his generation, that politics was what really mattered. His career in public life spanned a half-century, from his first campaign for elective office in 1820, during the administration of James Monroe, to his last stump speech in 1868 supporting the candidacy of Ulysses S. Grant. Twelve times he entered the race to represent Baltimore, first in the House of Delegates, at Annapolis, and later in the House of Representatives, at Washington. Seven times he won. A vigorous campaigner, he could mount a whisky keg at a Whig barbecue to delight the electorate with broad humor and spread-eagle oratory. The climax of his political career came in 1852 when President Millard Fillmore appointed him Secretary of the Navy.

Throughout a versatile career, Kennedy remained a literary figure. He had written works which his countrymen were ready to believe challenged the masters of English prose. "His novels," wrote the elegist of the Old South, Thomas Nelson Page, "gave him a position among the leading novelists of the day, and placed him first among the Southern literary men of his time." [2] Kennedy's historical romances revealed America not as it had been but as it would have liked to be. The portrait was flattering, the blemishes retouched and the sharp edges softened. He expressed for Americans a view of their past commensurate with the prophecies the apostles of progress made for the future, and he adorned the present.

John Kennedy belonged to the generation that grew up with the century. He witnessed, and gloried in, the immense material development of the United States. He reaped a harvest for himself, and it is not surprising, considering the prosperity of the nation and his own and his neighbors' faith in progress, that he came to a sturdy belief in the grandeur and permanence of the Republic and its immunity from the ordinary mishaps of earthly empires. His faith endured throughout seven decades of the nineteenth century, surviving even the cataclysm of civil war. His story begins on the first day of that century.

January, 1961 *Charles H. Bohner*
Wilmington, Delaware

Contents

	Preface	vii
I	A Baltimore Boyhood	1
II	Heroic Years	16
III	Apprentice Years	33
IV	"A Right Merry Young Lawyer"	58
V	Virginia Revisited	72
VI	The Novelist as Historian	89
VII	"A Man of All Work"	115
VIII	A Whig in Harness	140
IX	"New Men, New Measures, New Country"	163
X	The Literary Life	178
XI	Cabinet Officer	199
XII	Elder Statesman	211
	Acknowledgments	237
	Sources	238
	Notes	243
	Index	259

JOHN PENDLETON KENNEDY
GENTLEMAN FROM BALTIMORE

CHAPTER I

A Baltimore Boyhood

AT SUNRISE on January 1, 1800, the artillery at Fort McHenry shattered the morning stillness with sixteen guns fired in quick succession, and throughout the day the dull thunder of cannon marked each half-hour. In the harbor, vessels flew their colors at half-mast, and in the city, church bells tolled continually. All business was suspended, and by nine o'clock the streets were jammed with people dressed in mourning, eager to see the military parade. George Washington had died at Mount Vernon on December 13, 1799, and the citizens of Baltimore had chosen the first day of the new century to honor his memory.

The body of Washington had been interred in the vault at Mount Vernon two weeks earlier. The ceremony at Baltimore was, therefore, a mock funeral procession, a hastily improvised tribute to the great man's memory. Yet that fact did not detract from the solemnity of the occasion. Volunteer regiments in full-dress uniform marched slowly up Baltimore Street to the dirge of a military band. Along the sidewalks spectators stood on tiptoe and elbowed through the crowd to catch sight of the bier borne by four sergeants. Behind the bier a soldier led the General's horse, the holsters and pistols slung across the saddle and the boots dangling in the stirrups, heels foremost, with the spurs glittering in the winter sunshine. Minute guns fired in the distance.

John Kennedy the elder rode with his company, a troop of light horse. He had been an enthusiastic partisan of the late President, and six years earlier had joined word to deed by marching out to help suppress the Whisky Rebellion in western Pennsylvania. And more important, he rode with the confidence of a prospering merchant in a city that respected commercial success. His whole personality responded to the pomp of military display, and his most famous son would later recall that his father's natural element seemed always the parade ground, not the market place.

The route of the procession passed the Kennedy home on Market Street and the merchant-soldier caught sight of his four-year-old son, John Pendleton, watching the parade from the window. The father made a sign of recognition, and the child, awed by the spectacle and pleased at being noticed by so important a figure, waved eagerly in return. He had never seen such an assembly before nor, for that matter, had most of the people who lined the streets of Baltimore that morning. The scene was John Pendleton Kennedy's earliest memory of childhood.[1]

The memory was significant. The revolutionary generation of George Washington cast a shadow over young Kennedy from which he never wholly escaped. He shared the great man's Virginia heritage, for his mother's family, the Pendletons, had been Virginians for generations. She did not allow her son to forget it; indeed, no Virginian ever forgot it. John's youth was passed in the America of the Virginia dynasty of Thomas Jefferson, James Madison, James Monroe. The giants of the revolutionary generation, and particularly the splendid sons of Virginia, seemed worthy models on which to pattern his own ambitions for distinction in public life, and from this background he formulated a code that shaped his destiny.

The memory of that mock funeral procession had still another, peculiarly appropriate, significance in the life of John Kennedy. The ceremony was a spontaneous tribute of a nation that did not yet have the symbols and rituals born of a long national tradition. To European eyes it would have seemed an amusing charade revealing nothing more than the thinness of the cultural atmosphere in America. But if the United States lacked feast days and national festivals, these must, like so much else the raw country needed, be manufactured. No one was more aware of this than John Kennedy, and in later life his novels were a conscious attempt to contribute to a national mythology. Baltimore in particular was a city without roots, a jerrybuilt, restless boom town in which a native, such as Kennedy, was something of a curiosity. But while men born on the seaboard were lured west in ever-increasing numbers, John Kennedy was bound to his birthplace by ties of memory and affection for three-quarters of a century.

John Kennedy was proud of his Virginia heritage. His mother, Nancy Clayton Pendleton, could trace her ancestry to Philip Pendleton, a schoolmaster of Norwich, England, who emigrated in 1674 and eventually settled in King and Queen County, Virginia.[2] From this beginning the clan multiplied and by the end of the Revolution boasted a distinguished Tidewater family that numbered among its sons a host of eminent patriots. Chief of these was Judge Edmund Pendleton, who led Virginia conservatives in support of the Revolution. Other sons found the Tidewater too constricting for talent and ambition, and moved inland toward the mountains. Henry Pendleton migrated to South Carolina, practiced law successfully, became a judge, and gave his name to a district of his adopted state. His brother, Nathaniel Pendleton, served as aide-de-camp to General Nathanael Greene during the Revolution and was Alexander Hamilton's second in the duel with Aaron Burr. A third brother, Philip Pendleton, married Agnes Patterson in 1772 and settled at his wife's estate in Berkeley County, Virginia (now West Virginia), at the foot of the Shenandoah Valley. Here, he turned to the practice of law, distinguished himself as a colonel in the Revolution, and served as a charter trustee of the town of Martinsburg. Nancy was the second of eight children born to Philip and Agnes Pendleton. On October 6, 1794, the Martinsburg *Potowmac Guardian* announced her marriage, four days earlier, to John Kennedy of Baltimore.[3] He had just returned from the wars, having volunteered to help put down the Whisky Rebellion. His company had got as far as Frederick in central Maryland when the quarrel was settled, so he continued on to Martinsburg and promptly took a wife.

Nancy Pendleton was seventeen years old when she married. Her sons often heard from their elders of her youthful beauty, and those who knew her later in life testified that she was still a handsome, even majestic, woman. She was intelligent and imperious, and she possessed, her son John observed, "a degree of command in her family which very decidedly directed its opinions, and from her possessing more intellect than my father, he has always quietly yielded to her influence." [4]

John Kennedy the elder had emigrated from the north of Ireland to Philadelphia in 1784 at the age of fifteen. Two brothers, Andrew and Anthony, had preceded him and had thrived as merchants. Andrew, evidently a man of fashion, lived lavishly in a house on Market Street which had been used as the presidential mansion in the days when Philadelphia was the nation's capital. Anthony, a misanthropic bachelor, lived a solitary life in Frankford, rebuking the follies of his townsmen and collecting his rents with all imaginable punctuality. About 1792 John Kennedy the elder established a branch of the family business in Baltimore, specializing in supplying copper to shipbuilders. Good times brought him prosperity. Ship merchants stood aloof from the internecine struggles of Europe and profited under a neutral flag. John Kennedy was gifted with wit and gaiety which remained even after old age had left him crippled and half-paralyzed. He cared nothing for amassing a fortune, kept a carriage even when he could not afford it, and insisted on spoiling his children. His son recalled, affectionately but candidly, that his father "never professed much talent and his cultivation was still less." [5]

John Pendleton Kennedy, the eldest of four sons, was born on October 25, 1795, in Baltimore. The following year the State of Maryland granted the city a charter. A community of about twenty thousand people, Baltimore was just awakening to the rich natural endowment which, in thirty years, would make it the third city of the Union. Like a fast-growing boy as yet but dimly conscious of his latent strength, Baltimore during John Kennedy's youth was awkward and ungainly. The names of families rising to prominence—Patterson, Hoffman, Dugan, Pascault—suggest the cosmopolitan atmosphere of the city, but its history would be stained with ugly brawls and brutal riots before the disparate national elements would be fused into a native character. Men successful in trade were building handsome brick homes, aloof behind spacious courtyards planted in locust trees, while the merchant princes established country residences and, aping the English fashion, gave them picturesque names like Mount Clare, Belvidere, and Homewood. The dingy courthouse overlooked the town from the summit of a small hill. Its windows afforded a pleasant view south over the harbor basin and the Patapsco River and north and west over rural streams and green meadows filled with grazing cattle. Before it stood the stocks and whipping post.

In this town John Kennedy played out the universal ritual of boyhood. "I drank water out of my hat," he later recalled, "carried tar in my pockets, eggs in my bosom, played at marbles with the negroes, skyed a copper with apprentice boys, hung kettles to dogs' tails, spread cobblers' wax on chairs, went to swim in March, followed a drum and fife about the town like the veriest rag-tag —in short, my habits were pure specimens of vagabondism." [6]

From these early days he remembered with special affection the veterans of the Revolution, leathery-faced campaigners with carefully cultivated martial brusqueness, a hint of swagger in their walk, and tales of derring-do calculated to entrance an impressionable youngster. Indifferent to the fashions of the new century in both politics and dress, they clung to their tiewig federalism as tenaciously as to their cocked hats, smallclothes, and powdered hair. It was a sight to see, and to remember, when one of these gallants greeted a lady on the street. There was a flourish of the cane, a scrape of the foot, and a sweeping bow which required the entire width of the sidewalk. The lady's responding curtsy brought her, with bridled chin and billowing skirts, halfway to the ground.[7] The bow and the curtsy, symbols of a courtly and gracious eighteenth-century world, seemed to young Kennedy archaic and musty. Yet he mourned their passing, for he was himself a child of that century. *The Spectator* and *The Rambler* supplied his vocabulary. *Gulliver's Travels* and *Tristram Shandy* inspired him to imitation. He was temperamentally attracted to men who praised moderation and stability, and his sympathies were clearly with the passion for order of the Age of Queen Anne and its faith in the sanative influence of society.

John must have often wandered down to the wharves at the

Basin, for there, surrounded by the acrid smells of tar and paint and fish, an alert boy could feel the heartbeat of a vigorous and ambitious city. Amid the clangor of mallets, the calkers, riggers, and copperers swarmed over the upturned hulls of boats and the scaffoldings of ships. Baltimore prosperity flowed in and out through its port. Oyster and wood pungies swung at the wharves, which jutted out from the shore in democratic disarray. The city's future was bound to the fisheries of the Chesapeake Bay and the commerce on the waterways. Wheat grown in the Piedmont of Maryland and the Susquehanna Valley of Pennsylvania was funneled through Baltimore to the West Indies and, later, South America. After the Revolution, the city throve. According to Hezekiah Niles, whose *Weekly Register* was published in Baltimore, the commerce of the city soared "from absolute insignificance, to a degree of commercial importance, which brought down upon it, the envy and the jealousy of all the great cities of the union." [8]

In this counting-house atmosphere it is not surprising that the metaphors of the market place became ingrained in the texture of John Kennedy's mind. He was fascinated by the intensity and novelty of urban life and from his youth he never doubted that the future of America lay with commerce and manufactures. Kennedy found the business life of Baltimore exciting and challenging. Within the life span of his contemporaries, Baltimore had been half farm and half forest. In 1750 it was a village of about two dozen houses, yet by 1800 it had taken on the appearance of a boom town. Great Conestoga wagons lumbered down Howard Street coming from the country, their axles creaking under loads of produce. Within the city, the manufacture of ships, cordage, and paper was prospering, as were the mills, furnaces, and forges in the adjoining countryside.

English craftsmen, Scottish merchants, and French traders, together with an admixture of Irish and Dutch, poured into the city. With its varied population, its flourishing economy, and its fever of speculation, the city's social lines were obliterated, indifference toward tradition was more potent than deference, and the city fathers occasionally found themselves unable to control the new forces set in motion. Murderers, arsonists, counterfeiters, and

A Baltimore Boyhood

pickpockets gave Baltimore the name of the "Sodom of America" and the "Headquarters of Mobocracy." Actually it was something of a frontier community that had sprung up in a mature land long under cultivation. Baltimore was unique, not only in the history of America, but, as travelers delighted to point out, in that of western civilization. "Among all the cities," wrote the editor of the *North American Review,* Jared Sparks, "whether of America or of the old world, in modern or in ancient times, there is no record of any one, which has sprung up so quickly to as high degree of importance as Baltimore." The reason, Sparks believed, was "the exuberance and quickening power of the commercial spirit." [9]

It is against this background that John Kennedy's life unfolds. Unlike his parents and brothers, all of whom returned to the Pendleton heartland in the Shenandoah Valley of Virginia, he cast his lot with the future of this restless, acquisitive, and cosmopolitan Baltimore.

Kennedy's mother, however, disliked Baltimore. A second son, christened Andrew after his father's brother and benefactor, was born two years after John in 1797, and each summer Nancy Kennedy and the two boys made the pilgrimage to western Virginia. Here Pendletons intermarried with Hunters, Cookes, and Dandridges; they gave names like "Clayton" and "Cassilis" to their homes to commemorate their ancestors; and they tried to preserve the leisurely and hospitable traditions of Tidewater society. It was a tight-knit community. Talent, pride in family, and the ties of marriage characterized this cohesive ruling class of staunch Federalists who looked with distrust, if not disdain, on the brash and heretical doctrines of Jeffersonian democracy.

In Virginia, young Kennedy observed at first hand a way of life that he was to weave into his fiction. Throughout long summer days he shared adventures with a host of cousins and innumerable slave children. The arrival of the Kennedy family was a jubilee. "The little negroes," Kennedy later recalled, could "be seen dodging round the stables, peeping through the corn cribs, stretched on dung hills, or mustered on the sunny side of a wall. . . . Whatever distinctions society may have created between the master and the slave, childhood abolishes all." [10]

From her father's home in Martinsburg, Nancy Kennedy visited her sisters and brothers on their estates in Jefferson and Berkeley counties. For John, the most attractive home was "Adam's Bower" in Jefferson County, the estate of his aunt and uncle, Sarah and Adam Stephen Dandridge. The Bower lingered in his memory as "a lively, gay establishment," for, like so many Virginia estates, it was a paradise for youngsters. John could race his pony over the hills or drive a team of four boys in twine harness across the fields. The boys would pause periodically, like good doctrinaire democrats, to elect a new driver, demoting a coachman to wheeler or promoting the leader to the box. The neighborhood was rich with historical places an imaginative boy could explore, such as "Greenway Court," the former home of Lord Fairfax, and the traces of the road cut by General Braddock on his ill-fated march to the west in 1755. On warm summer evenings there would be storytelling, perhaps a serenade by a Negro minstrel, impromptu theatricals, or, as a special treat, opossum-hunting by torchlight.

In this society there was a great deal to attract an intelligent and curious child. Life was leisurely and improvident. "We find dancing," a cousin wrote Kennedy from Martinsburg in 1812, "much more agreeable than settling the affairs of the nation. Taking a fort or getting a good partner for the *set*, is of equal importance to us." [11] The grace of this culture, its devotion to the good life, its delight in humor founded on the premise that in society one should make oneself agreeable—all this would charm a boy from Baltimore just as it would later charm the urbane New Yorker, Mark Littleton, the narrator of Kennedy's novel of plantation life, *Swallow Barn*.

Among John's relatives in western Virginia, his favorite was Philip Clayton Pendleton, Nancy Kennedy's brother. A Virginia lawyer addicted to politics but averse to the actual rough-and-tumble of office-seeking, "Uncle Phil" was the epitome of the Virginia character as his nephew interpreted it. Kennedy thought him "the first man in point of talents, acquirements and manners that I have ever been acquainted with." A natural aristocrat bred in the tiewig school of federalism, he lived out his life in his native Martinsburg, enjoying a local reputation as militia colonel and judge of the county court. A cordial and warm-hearted squire, called by Washington Irving "that rare old cavalier," his old-fashioned ways were uncorrupted by the innovations of the age and what he called the "fuss and fustian about the dignity of labor." Kennedy at eighteen thought him "as grave and dignified as the ghost of Hamlet's father." Fond of playing backgammon or accompanying a neighbor's flute with his violin, he could while away an evening with these amusements or merely sit musing in a political dream from which only the rustle of a newspaper or the chance for disputation could awaken him. Seldom venturing farther from his home than Richmond or Berkeley Springs, he judged everything by the exalted standard of Virginia, found Virginia invariably superior, and in its defense would cavil on the ninth part of a hair.[12]

Philip Pendleton was an eccentric who was understood and loved by his neighbors. He was the embodiment of the contrasts and peculiarities of the plantation world with its exaggerated deference and its niceties of conduct. His role as patriarch of the Pendleton clan made him generous and complacent. In his happiest mood he was courtly and charming, but when the spirit of disputation moved him, he could be peevish and arrogant. When his nephew wished to delineate a typical Virginia planter in *Swallow Barn*, he took Philip Pendleton for his model.

Powerful forces, however, were at work to leaven the provincialism of the society Philip Pendleton typified. Not only were the natural resources of western Virginia—mineral wealth, fertile pastures, and abundant streams—modifying the fixed ideas of men conditioned to the ideals of a slave empire, but German and Scotch-Irish immigrants, indifferent or hostile to things Virginian, were streaming westward from the great seaports of the middle states. Yet the scions of old Virginia families who had emigrated from the Tidewater, sensitive to the foreign element in their midst, carefully nurtured those very aspects of their heritage which they believed to be distinctly Virginian.

The Bower especially was a stronghold of the Old Order. In 1845 the historian of Virginia, Henry Howe, described the neighborhood of the Bower as settled "by old Virginian families from the eastern part of the state; and the inhabitants still retain that high, chivalrous spirit, and generous hospitality, for which that race was so remarkable in the palmy days of their prosperity." When the Civil War came, the Dandridge family at the Bower were ardently secessionist. During the war their home served for a brief season as headquarters for the dashing cavalryman, J. E. B. Stuart. The white tents of the troops were pitched in the grove of oaks that surrounded the mansion, the officers played to the hilt their role of heroes of romance fresh from the fields of glory, made love to Dandridge daughters and nieces, and in the dreary days of reconstruction recalled the interlude at the Bower as a "most remarkable combination of romance and real life." [13]

John Kennedy lived long enough to see his Virginia cousins go out of the Union, then openly snub him for his allegiance to his country. He lived, too, to see them pay a frightful retribution. But these events were a half century away. During the long summer vacations of his youth, he acquired his taste for the outdoor life, for horseback riding, trout-fishing, hunting wild turkeys and pheasants, and walking tours up into the Blue Ridge Mountains. He traveled over most of the middle region of Virginia, sometimes on foot, sometimes on horseback, but always alert to the beauty of Virginia scenery. He had a penchant for the picturesque and, never one to idle on a hillside inviting his soul, his retentive memory stored away pleasant landscapes which, he knew, would be a good capital investment that might bring a sizable return in a literary way.

Virginia vacations were only interludes in the education of John Kennedy. At the age of five he was sent to the dame school of Mrs. Coffey in Baltimore to learn his letters. "It was," he said, "a current opinion with all of us, who had no idea of the process by which life advanced, that she was born old." Her young scholars thought her "profoundly learned and extremely genteel, she was so starchy and keen and bitter looking and so glazed and rustling when she walked." She was a kindly, if eccentric, old lady who took snuff from a silver box and laughed immoderately at her own jokes. Clever children realized that it was politic to laugh too.[14]

In two years John advanced to Priestly's Academy. This school had gained some reputation in the city and had attracted the children of Baltimore's best families. Priestly himself was recalled by his students as a man of kindness and understanding, but the ample shadow his wife cast across the classroom terrified the pupils. Mrs. Priestly was a fat, short-winded lady, possessed of a masculine cast of character and a contempt for the minor courtesies of life that she believed indicated a vigorous mind. Priestly, according to rumor, had married her on the frontier and then educated her himself. Perhaps the students invented the story, current at the time, that she once swam the Ohio River with her son strapped to her back like a papoose while the Indians whooped in pursuit. True or not, she inspired such stories.

Mrs. Priestly could devise ingenious punishments for rebellious scholars. John was condemned to wear clumsy, blinker-like leather spectacles during a recitation as a penalty for restlessness, and for fighting he was made to sit back-to-back with his opponent in the doorway, their heads tied up in the same satchel with the string drawn tight about their chins. Mrs. Priestly had a thorough knowledge of those parts of the anatomy (the finger ends were a favorite) where the ferule could be applied for the improvement of the minds of her charges. Yet John's education was not neglected: "In Mr. Priestly's school, I entered upon that second journey, which, as Sterne says, lies between 'Criss Cross and Malachi,' the first attempt at writing and the last of the Old Testament, and thence into the realms of the Latins and the Greeks. Along with these I had as much as I could digest of figures, geometry, mathematics and algebra. At proper intervals came infusions of French and Spanish, and in short, my course ran through all the duly established highways by which it is supposed philosophy and letters were to be caught, appropriated and kept for a useful commerce with the world." [15]

In 1809, at the age of fourteen, John was ready to enter college and probably was thinking of Princeton, the choice of his Virginia cousins. But that same year disaster struck his father's copper business. Five years earlier he had become involved with his partner in unwise speculations. Hit by the hard times that followed the Embargo of 1807, he struggled to recoup his losses but plunged rapidly into bankruptcy. At this point his brother, choleric old Anthony Kennedy of Philadelphia, promptly came forward, to the astonishment of the family, and settled his younger brother's debts, which amounted to thirty or forty thousand dollars. These reverses in no way altered the elder Kennedy's determination that his son should have all the advantages of education. Accordingly, in the autumn of 1809 young John entered Baltimore College, founded that year by two Presbyterian clergymen, Samuel Knox and William Sinclair.[16]

Some years before, Knox had won a prize offered by the American Philosophical Society for a system of education and later was to gain a measure of recognition when Jefferson incorporated his ideas into the plan for the University of Virginia. Kennedy loathed this "great stall-fed presbyterian bull. He had a large round face with an angry eye, and a long shaggy eye-brow, a heavy double chin that lapped over his cravat and hid it from view. He was slovenly in his dress and unclean in his habits. His character was selfish, avaricious, and cruel, his opinions narrow and puritanical. . . . He was utterly destitute of any portion of taste or political acumen." There was an offensive despotism in his character which bred fear and hatred among his students. "We hurried through recitation before him at a gallop, saying what was set down for us, or seeming to say it, when he ran on ahead of us, unconsciously reading out the whole lesson sometimes, as if in a hurry to be done with it. He had no pleasantries by the way, no explanations, no appeals to our own perceptions of an author's merits. Thus we measured off Virgil and Homer *by the yard*, as rapidly and as recklessly as we should have measured so much tape." [17]

Baltimore College under such a pedant would have been stifling to a youngster gifted with intellectual curiosity and a growing awareness of the world of the mind, had it not been that Knox had joined with William Sinclair in the venture. Sinclair was an Irish clergyman of humor and sound learning. He was a Calvinist, yet his heart was not in Geneva but in the Athens of Pericles. He possessed the sort of honesty and simplicity of character which made his students ashamed to appear in his classes unprepared. The jolly and rotund Parson Chub of *Swallow Barn* was a portrait of Sinclair and an affectionate tribute from a grateful student.[18]

A Baltimore Boyhood

The year John Kennedy entered Baltimore College, 1809, his father moved the family to Shrub Hill, a house on the outskirts of Baltimore owned by his brother, Andrew. The change seems to have been the result of the elder Kennedy's business misfortunes, and to these were added the responsibility of a growing family. A third son, Philip Pendleton, was born in 1808 and a fourth, Anthony, followed in 1810. A fifth son died in infancy. Shrub Hill was bare and unadorned, consisting of one large room downstairs and a loft above. John shared a room under the eaves with his brother, Andrew.

Finding the college course of study "a long probation of Latin and Greek and a very superficial study of everything else," John read everything he could obtain with the help of the Baltimore Library. During his college years he sampled Locke, Hume, and Robertson; studied Burke, Taylor, and Barrow; and knew intimately the great essayists, Addison, Steele, and Johnson. Among English novelists, he read and reread Defoe, Goldsmith, and Sterne. For *Tristram Shandy* and the *Sentimental Journey* he had a special admiration. "I wrote a great many things in what I thought the same vein—the pages filled with dashes, and an imitation of that eccentric transition, and the parentheses, and the personal conjuration of the reader, which are to be found in all of Sterne's books." [19]

These first efforts at writing were undertaken in the privacy of his room in the loft of Shrub Hill. Locked in a crude desk was the jealously guarded "Budget," his collection of original essays, sermons, imaginary travels, abortive comedies, and embryo tragedies. He was secretly proud of his compositions, yet vaguely troubled when he measured his ambition against his achievement. In 1813 he scribbled on the back of a letter received from a Virginia cousin a brisk reprimand of his own desultory habits.

> Never was a person more than myself the sport of whim and caprice. Lately considering the number of literary enterprises I have in contemplation, I find the following, most of which are at present under my hand: Historical characters, Microcosm, Essay on Sympathy, Satire on Criticism, An Oration Exemplified, Opinion on Works of Mind, private memories, letters, Notes on Blair, Essay on Religion, System of Fortification, Portraits of

Nature, Diversions, Notes on Natural Law. About a year ago I burnt a collection I had made, called the Budget, which had swelled to a size sufficient to fill a volume. I'm sorry for having destroyed these, as nothing could give me more pleasure than to revise them.

Perhaps the war spirit which was rising in Baltimore, and to which Kennedy eagerly responded, caused him to destroy the collection. Such juvenilia must be sacrificed on the altar of manhood. Yet it was a rash act and he regretted it, not because of the intrinsic merit of the accumulation, "but because they were the footprints of my life up to that time, for I had scarcely any other life than in those cobwebs." [20]

These solitary studies, pursued in the loft of Shrub Hill, John Kennedy remembered in later days with much greater affection than the curriculum of Baltimore College. "In the four years of my college career, I went through the usual course of Latin and Greek authors; a short and imperfect system of mathematics, in which I took the smallest interest; some physical science done up in a very meagre volume; and along with these a barren and absurd scheme of logic in Latin, and some incomprehensible metaphysics. French, I acquired with considerable accuracy, could speak and write it tolerably well. I got some little Spanish also, though not much; and as an embellishment to this fund of *solid* learning I was taught to dance." [21]

Baltimore College unaccountably flourished for a brief season under the guidance of the two diverse Presbyterian divines. A lottery was granted by the state and in 1810 a building was raised on Mulberry Street out of the profits of Baltimore's gambling spirit. Two years later, on November 30, 1812, the first commencement took place under the new charter. Each of the three candidates for the degree of Bachelor of Arts delivered an address, John Kennedy speaking on "Criticism." Vice-President Sinclair outlined the course of study to the audience, and President Knox delivered what the newspaper called "an appropriate moral address." [22]

John Kennedy had waited impatiently for the college year to end, for he had determined upon his career. Six months earlier, in June 1812, the United States had gone to war with Great Britain.

Although he was careful to conceal his ambition from his mother and father, John had made up his mind; he would be a soldier: "At this period I was eighteen years old. Eighteen has always a susceptible heart. The war was the nurse of romance and kindled the conceit that drives youth into chivalric ideas of love. The young girls of Baltimore were very beautiful, and I was a passionate admirer with some violent preferences. Nothing is more natural than the association of youth, military ardor, and susceptibility to the charms of female society." [23]

CHAPTER II

Heroic Years

THE NEWS THAT the United States had declared war on England reached Baltimore on the evening of June 18, 1812, the same day that President Madison signed the bill. It had long been expected. Madison's embargo message sent to Congress two months earlier had indicated the drift of events. The embargo itself had not caught Baltimore shipowners unprepared. Warned in advance of the proposed action of the government, the ships lying in the Patapsco River swiftly took on cargo, spread their canvas, and cleared for the open sea. Baltimore traders feared war less than they feared embargo. Now that the administration at Washington had finally acted, the martial fever swept through the city like a contagion. In Baltimore the declaration strengthened the conviction, common throughout the South and West, that opposition to the war amounted to treason and should not be tolerated.

During the years that John Kennedy was struggling with the classics in Baltimore College, the city was smoldering with resentment toward England. The elder Kennedy could scarcely escape the inbred antipathy of his Scotch-Irish ancestry and this he communicated to his son. Furthermore, he probably recognized the cause of his recent and humiliating bankruptcy in the hard times resulting from British naval policy. The ships for which he had once supplied copper now swung idly at the quays in Baltimore

Basin. Business stagnated as the produce of the countryside rotted in crowded warehouses. And in this seaport community the Kennedys must have known personally sailors who were seized, handcuffed, and summarily impressed by British captains.

English society, interpreting Mr. Madison's War as the treachery of avarice committed at the moment civilized men were closing ranks against Napoleon, discovered a convenient focus for their hatred in this upstart city of Baltimore. "The turbulent inhabitants of Baltimore," said a London newspaper, "must be tamed with the weapon which shook the wooden turrets of Copenhagen," and it was common knowledge, as one traveler noted, that Baltimore "occupied the foremost ranks in deadly animosity toward England."[1] A single event, sordid and barbaric, proclaimed the city an incandescent symbol of war hysteria and nationalism run riot. The editors of the antiwar *Federal Republican*, their printing office already destroyed by a well-organized mob in June 1812, refused to be coerced by the rabble and on July 27 again issued a newspaper purported to be printed at a brick house on Charles Street which they promptly fortified. A savage mob formed from the dregs of society attacked that night. While the civil authorities stood by helplessly, an officer of the Revolution was brutally murdered and another crippled, and all the defenders who did not escape in the confusion were viciously tortured and beaten. The massacre recalled to men's minds the terror of the French Revolution, and it drew down bitter condemnation on the city.[2]

If mob rule shocked the sensibilities of John Kennedy, the colorful story of the privateers, and in particular the Baltimore Clippers which carried the war to England, contained all the elements needed to ignite his inflammable imagination. These graceful schooners, armed with letters of marque and bold seamen, brazenly challenged the sacred waters of British supremacy. About three score of these privateers out of Baltimore made prizes of some five hundred English vessels.[3] The *Weekly Register* of Hezekiah Niles faithfully reported these maritime escapades and ardently fanned the inflamed nationalism.

There were other forces at work in Baltimore to stimulate an impressionable boy given to scribbling romances and dreaming of literary fame. The deeds of the Revolution were fast acquiring the aura of myth, and a few of the heroes of that era might still be seen walking the streets of Baltimore. Luther Martin, the rollicking, convivial genius whom Jefferson called the bulldog of federalism, presided over Baltimore courts in the fashion of the Constitutional Convention, a curious anachronism in ruffles, flapping waistcoat, and buckled shoes. John Eager Howard, wounded in a bayonet charge at Eutaw Springs and decorated by Congress for heroism at Cowpens, lived rich and respected at Howard's Park north of the city. It was natural to romanticize these men and the memory of their glory, and John Kennedy was convinced that war must be "the sweetest remembrance which engages the attention of men." [4]

Having determined on a military career, John began to systematize his studies, and in the alcove at Shrub Hill he worked late into the night over fortifications and field engineering. Yet while he pored over these problems he was aware of a mortifying defect in his soldierly equipment—he was afraid of the dark. To conquer it he would steal out at midnight and wander through the woods near Shrub Hill, gaining courage by an occasional skirmish with nothing more hostile than a stray cow.[5] The incident in itself is trivial enough, but it reveals that facet of his character which found nothing more difficult to condone than personal weakness. Where he was generous with other men's faults, he was ruthless with his own. His early inclination toward solitary pursuits bred in the depths of his character a healthy contempt for dependence in any form. It was Kennedy's desire throughout his life to work out his destiny in isolation.

Unfortunately for Kennedy's daydreams of military glory, his father discouraged the army scheme, and he was forced to content himself with enlisting in the United Volunteers of the Fifth Regiment of Maryland Militia. It was the crack company of the city, the elite of Baltimore society. The company rolls glittered with distinguished names of merchants and lawyers who were secure in their prosperity, and young dandies of respectable families who were principally interested in the effect of a uniform on a Baltimore belle. Unlike the country militia, the United Volunteers could afford dashing blue and scarlet uniforms, and during

Elizabeth Gray Kennedy in 1835

From a portrait by William James Hubard; reproduced by permission of the owner, Sleepy Hollow Restorations, Tarrytown, New York.

John Pendleton Kennedy in 1825

From a portrait by Philip T. C. Tilyard; reproduced by permission of the owner, the Henry E. Huntington Library and Art Gallery, San Marino, California.

the summer mornings of 1813 they paraded for several hours to the delight of idle society, their shoulders aching beneath the weight of clumsy Harpers Ferry muskets.

Throughout the winter of 1814 and into spring, the militia stood sentinel at Fort McHenry and knew the war only through rumor or by the brief exaltation of a privateer capture. In the first flush of enthusiasm, Kennedy wrote what he believed to be stirring patriotic appeals and sent them anonymously to the newspapers. He had the satisfaction of seeing his writing in print for the first time and had his first experience with the mass indifference of a southern audience. It was his first lesson in the literary life in America. His temperament was too optimistic to be so easily discouraged, and only after a lifetime of assailing public apathy did he wearily admit "that fine writing falls on the business world like water on a duck's back." [6]

By spring of 1814 the young blades of the United Volunteers, restless from inaction, were beginning to fear that they were doomed to remain a parade-ground army. They were helpless before the wily Sir George Cockburn who threw the Tidewater into paroxysms of suspense and terror by his lightning attacks on undefended towns and forays against coastal plantations. The depradations of the enemy were relatively small but the countryside was kept in a state of perpetual alarm and the militia, continually under arms, was seething with rage. The British fleet bottled up the Chesapeake, and Maryland farmers watched their crops rot while the prices of necessities soared. Finally in June 1814, Baltimore was roused to an ecstasy of anticipation by rumors that British troops fresh from the Peninsular War were arming for America. The rumor materialized on August 19 when Major General Robert Ross, distinguished by campaigns in Egypt, France, and Spain, debarked his army at Benedict, Maryland, and began the march inland. Whether he meant to strike first at Baltimore or Washington, no one could know.

On Sunday, August 21, 1814, John Kennedy marched out of Baltimore with the Fifth Regiment to engage the British Army. The United Volunteers swung out of the city in full-dress uniform. Baltimore belles crowded the windows of every home waving handkerchiefs to the departing heroes, and friends rushed into the ranks to shout encouragement. It was real war and there was the assurance that the enemy was only marching distance away. For John Kennedy, not yet nineteen years old, the experience was pure romance, and as he stepped off at a brisk cadence, a fragment of poetry echoed and re-echoed in his mind and it spoke of his delight:

> It were worth ten years of peaceful life
> One glance at their array.

Confident of victory, he had even found a place in his knapsack for his dancing pumps in order to be prepared for the presidential ball which would surely follow the defeat of the invader.[7]

The young jingoes, loosely organized into a conglomerate army, at first seemed doomed to disappointment. They could not find the enemy. For three days they marched and countermarched about the countryside below Baltimore, demoralized by rumors and unnerved by irresolute commanders. On Wednesday, August 24, at two hours after midnight, an alarm called the troops to arms. In the confusion John lost his boots and hurried off to battle in his dancing pumps. At noon of the same day the American troops, exhausted by a forced march, took positions behind Bladensburg, a straggling hamlet eight miles northeast of Washington, and awaited the assault of the British Army.

The Fifth Regiment was drawn up on a hill behind the village, overlooking an orchard. Sweltering in the August sunshine, Kennedy lay in wait with his comrades as the British soldiers opened their attack. His ancient musket suddenly seemed no match for the showers of grape shot and the crazy roar of Congreve rockets fired by the British troops. The red-coated soldiers that he watched running from house to house too rapidly to form a target were the crack troops of a great nation, notorious for their dexterity with a bayonet. Men around him were petrified with fright.

The British professionals were contemptuous of this tatterdemalion American Army spread out before them. "A few companies only, perhaps two or at most three battalions," wrote a British officer who fought that day, "presented some appearance of regular troops. The rest seemed country people, who would have been more appropriately employed in attending to their agricultural occupations than in standing with muskets in their hands on the brow of a bare green hill." [8] In the lead a British light brigade dashed over a small bridge and took cover in an orchard. Suddenly the flaws of the American battle plan became agonizingly apparent, for the boughs of the trees in the orchard afforded cover for the British from the Americans firing from the hillside. At the first volley, the raw militia ran.

The Fifth Regiment held firm. Rolling with the first assault, they drove back the overconfident light brigade and then advanced to recover lost ground. The commanding general, a Baltimore lawyer named William Winder, galloped up to direct the Fifth, which almost alone still held the field. Winder ordered a retreat, then, in an agony of indecision, countermanded it. British regulars advanced rapidly and threatened to turn the American flank, harassing the troops with an enfilading fire. The Fifth held gallantly, behaving as firmly as the regular troops. But the situation was desperate. Winder again ordered a retreat. Then followed the ancient formula of military disaster: order, counterorder, disorder. Raw troops could not be expected to perform orderly movements in the face of an advancing enemy. The retreat turned into a headlong rout, and John Kennedy, bearing off a wounded corporal, ran with the rest.[9]

It was an inglorious moment but it was not the end. The people of Baltimore could see the fire at Washington glowing red against the night sky as the British put the torch to the public buildings, and it required no clairvoyance to realize that Baltimore, "the nest of pirates," was next. On August 29 John returned from Bladensburg with the remnant of the army. He was, he told his uncle Philip Pendleton in Martinsburg, "pretty much fatigued, and disposed to think more highly of British regulars." [10] He found the city in a frenzy of preparation, the citizens throwing up earthworks and digging out gun emplacements. On September 12, nineteen days after Bladensburg, scouts galloped in with news that General Ross had landed at North Point, a narrow neck of land extending below the city, and was marching on Baltimore. Again the United Volunteers marched out to meet the enemy and again

John Kennedy was among them, but if his mind was filled with the romance of war or scraps of heroic verse before this second battle, he left no record.

In the Battle of North Point, fought the afternoon of September 12, 1814, the United Volunteers again bore the brunt of the British assault and were commended for conspicuous gallantry by the commanding general.[11] Fifteen per cent of the company was killed or wounded and some others taken prisoner, but, as Kennedy said later, he did not get "so much as a scratch to brag of." [12] The Americans were routed but not without considerable loss to the British Army, which reported more killed and wounded than at Bladensburg. Among the dead was the British general, Robert Ross. The Americans fell back on Baltimore having fulfilled their purpose of fighting a delaying action, and the British, their advance checked by this brief but spirited battle, bivouacked on the field.

John returned to his home at Shrub Hill that evening and found his mother in the hall preparing to follow her younger children to Martinsburg.

"What, are you back?" she asked. "Where do you come from?"

"From North Point. We have had a battle today."

"Did you behave yourself well?"

"Yes. I believe so."

She anxiously inquired after his father, who had remained at the lines, then listened to the details of the day's battle. John spent the night at home and left for the lines at sunrise the following day. His mother gave him breakfast, helped him into his knapsack and crossbelt, and sent him off to what both believed was to be a general engagement of the two armies.

"Do not let me hear, my son," Nancy Kennedy said in parting, "of your turning your back disgracefully upon the enemy." It was the admonition of a Spartan lady. Forty years later, on receiving news of his mother's death, it was the memory of that September morning that came flooding back to John Kennedy.[13]

The British Army on September 13 slogged up the peninsula from North Point in a drenching rain until they came within sight of the bristling defenses of Baltimore. It would be a bloody assault and the prize would not be worth the sacrifice. A naval bombardment of Fort McHenry having failed to dislodge the Americans, the British withdrew rapidly to North Point and on September 14 embarked. For John Kennedy the war was over.

The crescendo of war hysteria which reached a climax at the Battle of North Point had raised a martial spirit that would not be exorcised simply by the withdrawal of the British Army. Red and blue uniforms were still conspicuous among the strollers on the Market Street promenade, and the militia still donned crossbelts and cartridge boxes to make saber-rattling charges across undisputed fields. Two months after the British invasion John Kennedy was elected a corporal in the United Volunteers, and in the following year he applied for and received the command of a rifle company, the colonel of the Fifth Regiment testifying to his "courage and firmness" [14] at Bladensburg and North Point.

Although this blaze of enthusiasm for a military career soon faded in the light of common day, Kennedy always recalled with nostalgia these years of anxiety and danger. The experience was unique. Like the men he idolized in the revolutionary generation, he had gone forth to fight the common enemy invading native shores. His consciousness of re-enacting a drama that was already hallowed in the country's folklore imbued the war for him with an emotional impact out of all proportion to its practical results. "The Bladensburg Races" have so long been the jest of historians that it is easy to overlook the effect the battle had on the men who that day endured their baptism by fire. In comparison to the slaughter that would stain Maryland soil a half-century later at Antietam, the battles at Bladensburg and North Point were only meadow and pasture skirmishes. But for John Kennedy the battles were a test of physical courage more terrible than any he would ever face again, and he grew increasingly aware of the experience as the threshold of his manhood.

On the other hand, the whole affair had been a disillusionment. Bladensburg, for all the valor of individuals, was a national disgrace, a microcosm of the blunders of the War of 1812: political bickering, state jealousies, and, stemming from these, the fatal error of failing to appoint a commander-in-chief. Even the United Volunteers had signed a resolution in March 1813 refusing to serve outside of Maryland.¹⁵ The Battle of Bladensburg had been a ludicrous example of command by committee. Baltimore, by contrast, owed its safety only to the prompt action of a group of citizens who, in defiance of the channels of command, delegated complete authority to a hard-bitten old soldier of the Revolution, General Samuel Smith. It was an object lesson in the problems of democracy in crisis, and Kennedy emerged from the experience with a new vision of the future of the Union.

Having helped to overawe the British Army before Baltimore, Kennedy began to look beyond state lines to a more comprehensive view of national destiny. Nationalism, like character, is forged in adversity, and for a young war hawk, chastened by humiliating defeat and then flushed with victory, it was not difficult to foresee a manifest destiny opening before the United States. A change in the intellectual climate was immediately sensed by perceptive observers. Hezekiah Niles wrote in his *Weekly Register* in 1815 that "the people begin to assume, more and more, a NATIONAL CHARACTER." ¹⁶ Kennedy shared this nationalism—he could scarcely do otherwise—but for him the major impact of the war was profoundly personal. Of that stirring time, he could later say: "We have had nothing like it since. It is the glory of my life, the vivid point." ¹⁷

The return of peace abruptly ended seven lean years of embargo and blockade. Like the opening of a flood gate, the Treaty of Ghent released for market harvests of three seasons and, swept along by this sudden sluice of prosperity, the people turned from international issues and passions which had furnished controversy for a generation to new and equally vital questions at home. For John Kennedy, twenty years old in 1815, peace meant a reluctant return to the study of the "dense thicket of the law."

It is perhaps inevitable that Kennedy in his search for a vocation should have chosen the law. Certainly the arduous quest for precedents and the untangling of legal principles held little attraction for him. But the Pendletons had been lawyers for generations, and the law might be a springboard to political preferment and eventually provide the leisure for writing. "Kennedy was too much addicted to politics and literature," wrote his friend, the

Baltimore attorney John H. B. Latrobe, "to make a distinguished lawyer. He spoke well and fluently, but he disliked the labors of the profession. Whatever he did, he did well, but it was pride, not fondness for the work, that urged him to effort." [18] Not only pride, but ambition. Even the merchant princes of Baltimore did not enjoy the prestige that an eminent lawyer did. The French critic de Tocqueville had observed, and most Americans were ready to agree, that if the United States had an aristocracy, it occupied the judicial bench and bar.

The Baltimore bar in the generation following the War of 1812 was indeed an aristocracy, an imperious fraternity of talent and intellect. In retrospect it seemed the golden age of Maryland lawyers, and any listing was certain to be invidious. William Pinkney, sometime minister to the Court of St. James, militia major wounded at Bladensburg, attorney-general of the United States under Madison and later senator from Maryland, was perhaps the best known among his peers. A man of enormous vanity with an insatiable appetite for applause, he was dreaded in the courtroom as an arrogant and crushing opponent. He expected no quarter and gave none. His courtesy was perfunctory and tended to encourage conflict rather than avoid it. His oratory was florid and affected. Many Baltimoreans, particularly young lawyers not yet within the pale of rivalry, worshipped him; others, notably his opponents before the bar, detested him. Contemporaries enjoyed making a Plutarchian contrast between William Pinkney and his chief rival, William Wirt. The genial Wirt, attorney-general under Monroe and Adams, was in temperament the exact opposite of Pinkney. The most tolerant and benevolent of men, he valued the courtroom as a stage for his dramatic gifts, and his low-keyed performances were so effective that ladies often crowded the courtroom when he spoke. At the conclusion of one speech, famous in Baltimore legal annals, the audience broke into spontaneous applause which even the judges were too spellbound to check. Both Wirt and Pinkney befriended John Kennedy, and, as will be seen, their influence, exerted at crucial moments, materially forwarded his career.

Forgotten by history, but a towering figure in his time, was punctilious and autocratic General Robert Goodloe Harper. In his blue coat, buff waistcoat, and highly polished boots, the old soldier reviewed his law students as a commander would his troops. A man of sound learning and polished style, he advised his students to temper Blackstone with Spenser's *Faerie Queene* and to culivate facility by translating Latin verse and writing poetry. Others, unknown to fame, lent color and humanity to the profession. "The witty, learned, profligate and accomplished" Charles Mitchell was such a man, "an impulsive speaker, an able lawyer, and in curious knowledge a learned man. He was ambidextrous and unprincipled, witty and cowardly." Mitchell was the perfect companion with whom to share a tureen of oysters and a bottle or two of wine. Kennedy thought him "a prince of wit" and a living representation of Falstaff.[19]

Roger Brooke Taney, the Baltimore lawyer of that era destined for fame as Chief Justice of the Supreme Court, in old age recalled his associates with affection: "It was my good fortune to commence the practice of the law when they were all in the prime of life, and to become familiarly acquainted with all of them, and to be engaged in the practice in the same courts. They were all gentlemen of high attainments, courteous and kind in their intercourse with each other, and of unblemished honor. They have now all passed away; and I can truly say, when the recollection of them has come back freshly to my memory, that each one of them would have been eminent at any bar or in any court of justice." [20] But Taney was one of the initiated. At least one candidate who stormed the heights of the Baltimore bar only to be icily rebuffed, the exuberant Yankee John Neal, recalled it as "the ablest of our country and by far the haughtiest." [21]

In the winter of 1813 when Kennedy was not drilling with the militia, he began reading law under his uncle, Edmund Pendleton. John found it stifling. A young clerk on sufferance in the hushed sanctum of a law office, he set about the tasks of drafting briefs and inditing in longhand the interminable declarations and pleas. Traditionally the apprentice at law unearthed the first principles for himself, and John plunged unaided into the tortuous legal phrasing and the opaque verbiage that filled the law books then in use. He read attentively, referring to the authorities cited, sifting and searching, collating and digesting passages from all the

Heroic Years

works within reach. The library of Edmund Pendleton contained, in large part, the books once belonging to the celebrated Federalist judge, Samuel Chase, a signer of the Declaration of Independence and a justice of the Supreme Court. John found some stimulus to his ambition by getting his first lessons from volumes which bore the autograph of the distinguished jurist. He said later: "Many of these books were, in after years, given to me by my uncle, by me at a later period given to my nephew Andrew. Among these I read Rutherford, Blackstone and Justinian, and worked with a vigor of application and perseverance which, if it had been seconded by anything like a proportionate capacity to understand, would have made me the wonder of the street. This law—what an intricate, inscrutable, dreary mystification it is to the young student in his first endeavors to get into and out of the fog—the dense fog —that fills its whole atmosphere." [22]

Since from the first John found the study of the law dull, his choice of a vocation may have been owing only to a paucity of alternatives. His father would not allow him to enter the army and could not assist him in trade, and John had little inclination toward medicine or the church. To become a writer would have suited his inclination, but the times were not propitious. "Your authors are mostly low people," he was soon to write, "and till some of our fashionables shall make it the mode—which is unlikely to happen in this generation," a man might as lief confess himself a bankrupt as an author.[23] So he diligently pursued the "repulsive studies" of the law, struggling with the *Maryland Reports* and *Acts of Assembly*, Cruise's *Digest*, and "the flinty highway of Coke and Littleton." When Edmund Pendleton left Baltimore, John continued his preparation under Judge Walter Dorsey and in 1816 was admitted to the bar. He had worked without enthusiasm, and the achievement brought him little satisfaction. Still, Baltimore offered compensations. For during these years of study, his interest in literature continued to grow under the stimulus of Baltimore's increasing cultural awareness.

With the coming of peace in 1815, Baltimore enjoyed a short-lived but exciting period of literary activity, the result of the sudden influx of immigrants following the Treaty of Ghent. John

Pierpont, a graduate of Yale who had come to Baltimore to seek his fortune in trade, wrote during the intervals of shopkeeping his *Airs of Palestine*, a poem in praise of sacred music which placed him in the front rank of American poets of the time. His partner in the dry goods business, John Neal, a native of Portland, Maine, was reading law, writing poetry and fiction at fever pitch, brawling in Market Street with Irish shopkeepers, and being posted as a coward by Edward Coote Pinkney for refusing to fight a duel. The volatile Pinkney, son of the great lawyer, was himself engaged in writing some of the best romantic poetry produced in the South before Poe, who called him "the first of American lyrists." [24] Henry Marie Brackenridge, son of the author of the American satire *Modern Chivalry*, published in Baltimore in 1816 his *History of the Late War* and was trying to combine a career in literature with law and service in the House of Delegates. William Wirt, in active practice before the Baltimore bar, was equally famed as the author of *The British Spy* and *The Old Bachelor*. The aging Wirt, his contemporaries believed, was not only a great lawyer but (such was the state of American literature) the first man of letters in the Union.

The literary center of Baltimore was the Delphian Club. Founded in 1816 and limited in membership to nine men who styled themselves the consorts of the muses, the society included at one time or another the commanding general of the Bladensburg fiasco, several newspaper editors, and assorted merchants, lawyers, and physicians addicted to literature. There was not, of course, a professional man of letters among them simply because the profession did not exist. The club was a survival of the London coffee-house tradition, but the founders also had homebred models on which they might draw for inspiration, notably the New York coterie of Washington Irving and James Kirke Paulding, "The Nine Muses," whose devotion to the arts was tempered by an equally fervid allegiance to Bacchus. The Delphians attracted such men as John Neal, Henry Marie Brackenridge, and Kennedy's beloved schoolmaster, William Sinclair. Characteristically, Neal squabbled with the Delphians when they blackballed a friend he had proposed for membership, but he recalled the association with pleasure: "High-minded, generous, unselfish men, they were intellectual and companionable, indulgent, and, with all their whims and freaks, original, and clearly stamped with the idiosyncracies that distinguish one superior man from another." [25]

The Delphians were responsible for *The Portico*, a monthly magazine which began publication in January 1816. Beginning with the second number, John Kennedy contributed a series of sketches entitled "The Swiss Traveller." [26] Except for a few contributions to newspapers made during the war, these essays marked his debut as a man of letters. Kennedy adopted the venerable device of introducing a foreigner into the native scene in order that he might comment satirically on manners and customs. Imitative in manner and derivative in thought, the essays reveal only that Kennedy had given his days and nights to the study of Addison. A sentimental paean of rural life, a rhapsody on the glories of war, the dangers of "The Lethargick of Peace," the essays were predominantly jingo in tone and revealed the martial spirit still lingering in Baltimore society.

In two of the five essays Kennedy dealt with the obligation of American parents to instill in their children the virtues of republican simplicity. Perhaps remembering his father's veneration of George Washington, Kennedy advised each American father to inculcate in his son reverence for the first President. The child should be made "intimately acquainted with the history of the American hero. He should read of his difficulties and his sufferings, and they would never fail to enlist his most ardent sympathy. He should contemplate his courage, his disinterestedness, and his magnanimity, and in each he would find all the comeliness and dignity of a hero. He should love him as his father, and speak of him as the father of his country." Kennedy's own mature judgment of these essays as "very trashy and verbose, and full of pretension" is harsh but hardly inaccurate: "They serve to show how green and insufficient was the mind of their author at that age. They show views of life distorted and exaggerated by an enthusiastic complexion of character, and a style of writing full of the redundant rhetoric of a school boy." [27] Certainly there is nothing in them to foreshadow the keen eye for character and delightful sense of humor which distinguish Kennedy's best writing.

The chauvinism of "The Swiss Traveller," however, anticipated the characteristic attitude of mind in much of Kennedy's later work and was in accord with the prevailing tendencies of the time. In the two decades following 1815 an unmistakable note of nationalism permeated American literature, a counterpart in the nation's cultural life to the Era of Good Feelings in politics. During these years at least three major authors—Cooper, Irving, and Bryant—achieved a substantial measure of both critical and popular success. All three developed national themes from native materials, and each struck a note more or less national in tone. By the late 1830's whatever cultural cohesion these years possessed was shattered, for the disputes over slavery and the tariff clearly revealed lines of sectional cleavage. Kennedy's apprenticeship as a writer was passed during this generation of literary nationalism, and it was during the 1830's that his four novels, all dealing with native materials and all national in tone, were written.

The Portico soon became exclusively Delphian, for the editor, Tobias Watkins, was a member, and he conducted the journal in the interests of the society. John Kennedy was never a member of the Delphians,[28] and there is no record that he was ever asked to join. He was only twenty years old when the club was organized in 1816, while the founders were older men established in the community. Excluded from this elect, Kennedy founded his own literary group, the Belles Lettres Society, a club which was soon decidedly anti-Delphian. The society, reflecting the tastes of its founder, was equally divided between political and literary interests. The members split into factions and argued questions, entering into intrigues and combinations after the fashion of their elders. Topics for debate were assigned, and Kennedy eventually acquired a bulging portfolio of resolutions, constitutions, protests, and remonstrances. The election of a president meant weeks of party cabals, perhaps an angry resignation, and, on at least one occasion, a challenge to a duel.[29]

An account of these verbal combats and paper wars deserves but a footnote in literary history, but to John Kennedy, at the beginning of his career, they were exciting skirmishes, and he later credited them with inspiring his own efforts at literature. The Baltimore societies survive only in faded minutes of the meetings or in the casual allusions of the members. They produced no man

Heroic Years 31

equal to James Fenimore Cooper of New York's Bread and Cheese Club, and they but dimly foreshadowed Boston's olympian Saturday Club. Yet in a climate in which literature was not so much despised as ignored, they did service by providing a forum for aspiring authors and by challenging the complacency of merchant royalty.

The activity in literary circles was but one aspect of the general ferment of Baltimore society. By 1820 the city with a population of over sixty thousand had outstripped Boston in size and had grown to be the third largest city of the Union. Charles Carroll, last surviving signer of the Declaration of Independence, delighted to tell visitors that he could recall when this city of sixty thousand souls was a village of but seven houses.[30] The first view of the skyline of domes, spires, and columns seldom failed to impress a traveler, and although here and there a sidewalk might be blocked by a pig searching for garbage, even the critics who were prepared to find fault were disarmed by Baltimore hospitality. No American city was reputed to be so gay and warmhearted; none was graced by so many beautiful women. Henry Marie Brackenridge, backtrailing from the Ohio in 1808, was intoxicated by his first glimpse of the city's activity after a boyhood on the frontier. "Although I could see but little," he wrote, "except the glare of the lights in every direction, the illuminated shops, and the crowds hastening along the sidewalks, nor could hear anything but the mingled rumbling composed of a thousand different sounds, I was lost in amazement." [31] When Kennedy made his first journey to a frontier settlement in 1819, he found it rude and brutish and returned to Baltimore with a fresh appreciation of the advantages he enjoyed and a stock of sage observations on frontier barbarism to astonish city-bred young ladies.[32]

John Kennedy's youth was lived against the background of this city which was itself young. "The youth of a city, like the youth of a man," he said later, "has a keener zest for enjoyment and finds more resource for it than mature age." [33] Improvident, boisterous, cocksure, Baltimore most certainly was, but on the other hand it was no cultural waste land. The book sellers and the theaters thrived. *Waverley* was the most popular fare, but American authors—Cooper, Irving, Paulding, Neal—were granted a hearing. At the Holliday Street Theater, *the* theater in Baltimore, "How to Grow Rich" and "The Toothache" played to crowded houses, but so did "Richard III," "Hamlet," and "Othello." Kennedy and his friends were ardent theatergoers, and they saw and admired George Frederick Cooke, William Burke Warner, and Joseph Jefferson; and, as he said, "we remembered them in every wink, shrug, poke in the ribs, or caper of any kind whatever which they had ever made in a play we had seen; and we, of course, acted all such gesticulations over again until the fountain of our mirth had gone dry from the excessive draughts upon it." [34]

But the Holliday Street Theater, the Belles Lettres Society, the command of a militia company, all were diversions from the law, the "crabbed, unamiable, and indigestible law." The more he studied it, the more sure he was that the law was but a dreary treadmill of precedent, a discipline that cramped the mind and warped the perceptions. In its zeal for authority, its worship of established forms, its quibbles over phrases, the law failed to make a distinction between questions great and small. Yet he doggedly pressed on, for, as Edmund Pendleton, the uncle who was his preceptor at law, was quick to remind him, a man must make a living. "As to poetical emminence [sic]," wrote Edmund Pendleton, "I deem it of no great value in this state of ours." [35]

CHAPTER III

Apprentice Years

JOHN KENNEDY, at the age of twenty-one, could look back with some measure of satisfaction on a childhood singularly tranquil and happy, and throughout life he clung with more than ordinary fondness to the memory of youth. He had profited by the friendship of at least one stimulating teacher, he had defended his country against invasion, and by 1816, upon his admission to the bar, he had been launched in a profession that offered a chance for wealth and recognition. With the artist's instinct for form, he consciously tried to order the pattern of his destiny, confident that a life lived fully and richly was itself a work of art. Yet he was vaguely dissatisfied. He had no special fondness for the law, and he may well have felt uneasy with the new friends he was making in Baltimore. The young men who had been his companions in the United Volunteers had come from wealthy families in Gay Street, and he may have envied them the studied carelessness of their manner and their easy entrance into society. Kennedy was ambitious, but the false starts and uncertain aims of these early years suggest that he yearned chiefly for recognition and was careless of the means in his eagerness for the goal. The decade 1816–1826 marks a distinct period in his life, years in which he achieved a series of remarkable social and political triumphs, triumphs ending in disaster and personal tragedy.

Having gained admission to the Baltimore bar, a young man

was faced with the necessity of driving an entering wedge into a profession jealous of its prerogatives and ruthlessly competitive. Every embryo lawyer soon discovered the engaging irony that he needed clients to build a reputation but he needed a reputation to attract clients. A handful of prominent lawyers dominated the bar while a host of hangers-on mingled at the edge of the courtroom hoping to force an entry into the inner chambers. So Kennedy joined the throng who burned candles at their offices in the Athenaeum late into the night, walked with unnecessary haste to court each morning, and affected to be quite besieged with clients. His father, who had already made great sacrifices for him, could help no further. After his business failure in 1809, the elder Kennedy tried again to re-establish his copper business with the aid of his son Andrew but without success.

John grasped at straws. In 1819 he sailed from New York to Charleston, South Carolina, to investigate a land claim which was put in his hands with the assurance of a considerable interest if he were successful.[1] There was probably little substance to the scheme and it came to nothing, but the trip was not without incident. In a frontier cabin he met an old woodsman, James Robinson, who awed this rather green young man with tales of the Revolution which, freely embellished, became the core of Kennedy's best known novel, *Horse-Shoe Robinson* (1835).[2] John returned overland from Savannah to Augusta, through Raleigh and Richmond to Chesapeake Bay, getting his first close look at tidewater Virginia. He was exhilarated by this excursion to the frontier, for he had a natural taste for forest and wilderness acquired during his boyhood exploring trips around Martinsburg.

The return to Baltimore meant a return to the law. Ambitious for social distinction, he quickly discovered that invitations to fashionable balls at the Assembly Rooms did not add to his list of clients. As militia captain, he was more apt to come into contact with the class of men likely to employ untried lawyers. Politics, too, was a means of noising a young lawyer's name abroad. But Kennedy's initial successes seem to have been owing largely to influential friends. He was one of those young men endowed with masculine good looks, a sense of humor, and natural charm, whom elder statesmen are quick to single out for favor and

Apprentice Years 35

patronage. Chief among these patrons was a judge of the Baltimore county court and original city councilman of Baltimore named Zebulon Hollingsworth. The judge had acquired a local reputation as a wit and *bon vivant*. Flattered perhaps by the hero worship of a talented youth, he undertook the task of mentor to Kennedy. Hollingsworth communicated his own enthusiasm for the Roman poets to Kennedy, and, his interests kindled, sent him back to a fresh examination of the ancients. The judge could breathe life into those marble men. A tall, gaunt figure with an impassioned, quixotic manner, he would recite Terence in the Latin text while striding across the porch of his country estate, magniloquently declaiming the verses, his long arms flailing the air. The judge had two sons with whom Kennedy became good friends, and he soon found himself entering Baltimore society through frequent invitations to "Upton," the Hollingsworth estate situated not far from the Kennedys' Shrub Hill.[3]

John had a second patron in these years, the flamboyant William Pinkney. To be singled out by Pinkney was a stroke of fortune that probably determined Kennedy on a political career. Pinkney was the first man in Baltimore and one of the first men in the Union. In December 1821 his unanimous election to the United States Senate from Maryland was the final triumph in a long career as lawyer, diplomat, and politician. In early life Pinkney had cultivated popularity by mingling freely with his constituents, but later he became punctilious and reserved, affecting what he considered to be the manner of a gentleman. He was a superb self-dramatist. He adopted extreme British fashions and appeared in court in amber-colored doeskin gloves, having carefully prepared his speech by long practice before a mirror. "I never heard him allow," a friend said, "that any man was his superior in anything"—and summed him up exactly.[4]

Pinkney found the company of talented young people attractive, and he was anxious to accommodate them. Kennedy's intimacy with the great man and his family led in 1820 to his engagement to Pinkney's daughter, Charlotte. The engagement was soon broken off, but the disagreement apparently made no breach between the two men.[5] In fact, Kennedy's rise in politics dates from the beginning of his friendship with Pinkney.

But this is to anticipate. John's engagement to the eminently eligible Miss Pinkney indicates how rapid had been his ascent in Baltimore society. He was undergoing the transformation from a studious and rather shy youngster to a poised and self-assured young man of considerable charm. As though to proclaim his independence, he established bachelor quarters in St. Paul Street with several other young lawyers. One was the droll and genial Josias Pennington, who had served with John in the United Volunteers in 1814. Later they built homes side by side in fashionable Mount Vernon Place near the Washington Monument and for forty years were associated in innumerable civic and social enterprises. Another, Grafton Dulany, a member of a distinguished Maryland family, was destined for a successful career at the Baltimore bar. The third was John's closest friend, Peter Hoffman Cruse.

During the long, idle evenings, Kennedy and Cruse began to project a periodical to be called *The Red Book*, a satiric potpourri in the *Spectator* tradition. Josias Pennington recalled the two friends during the years in St. Paul Street as about "equally fond of literature and ladies," and the idea for a periodical was probably inspired less by the thought of unselfish service to the muse than by a hope for drawing-room notoriety.

Kennedy and Cruse were inseparable. Whether attracting attention at a masked ball as palmers from the Holy Land or dominating the table talk at the dinner of a wealthy merchant, their combined wit could transform a gathering into an occasion. John H. B. Latrobe, son of the designer of the Capitol and a friend of both Kennedy and Cruse, called them "the Damon and Pythias of society in Baltimore. . . . Both had humor; but while Cruse was full of it, Kennedy was overflowing." "We have associated so long together," Kennedy wrote in the first number of *The Red Book*, "that all our habits and notions have become completely identified, and it not infrequently happens from this very cause, that one of us is eternally appropriating, as the peculiar figment of his brain, the schemes and projects of the other." [6]

Cruse had a ready facility for brilliant conversation, and his law office in the Athenaeum was a center of good literary talk in Baltimore. He had a volatile temper and could be moody and irritable when depressed by what he considered the world's neglect. A defeat at chess would throw him into "an infernal passion." With a sweep of his arm, he would pettishly scatter the chessmen about the room; and having sworn never to play again, in two hours' time he would sheepishly offer to renew the game. In later years, Kennedy said of Cruse: "He is preeminently the most scrupulous and delicate man in his judgments that I ever knew, and one who . . . would not hesitate to speak to me in such a tone as suited my honour and reputation without the least bias from friendship." [7] In *The Red Book*, Cruse penned a self-portrait in verse:

> Meanwhile,—that doughty men may know
> What doughtier hero is their foe,—
>   My height's five feet eleven,
>   My courage fair, my temper hot,
>   My hand not bad at pistol shot
>   My age scant twenty-seven.

Cruse did not share Kennedy's inclination for public life, for he longed to be a poet in a world where the vocation did not exist. His ill-starred career leaves the impression of a man whose wit was a defense against a hostile environment that valued him below his merits. The two men illustrate the paths open to an ambitious author in the early nineteenth century. A man could, as Kennedy did, enter the law and go on to politics, considering literature as a by-product and ornament of an "elegant leisure." This was a role society readily sanctioned. Cruse, on the other hand, drifted out of the law, which he found uncongenial, and into journalism, writing an occasional review for the *North American*, and eventually becoming editor of the Baltimore *American* and later the *Patriot*, where he seldom transcended the limits of a newspaper column. Wracked by ill health and depressed by the drudgery of hack writing, he grew increasingly waspish. "Were I to follow my inclination, I should hardly ever shut my book, or leave my chamber. It is not that I am morose, but I can neither bear the same temperature nor enter into the same topics that others can." [8] Cruse fell victim of a cholera epidemic in Baltimore on September 7, 1832, his early promise unfulfilled, and he is unknown to literary history except for his association with Kennedy in *The Red Book*.

The Red Book was brought out by a local printer, Joseph Robinson. His "Circulating Library" at the corner of Market and Belvidere streets was a flourishing Baltimore institution owing to its imaginative proprietor. Robinson had a thorough acquaintance with the vagaries of the genus author, and he brought to his work experience as an enterprising publisher, literary critic, and unflinching counselor to ambitious writers. When the first printing of *The Red Book* rapidly sold out, he hastened to deflate the vanity of these young authors by assuring them that all depended on the second number, curiosity alone having sold the first. True, the town was in a ferment. But he attributed this, with more truth than tact, to the mystery surrounding the publication and the thinly veiled allusions to personalities rather than to any intrinsic merit. "A word," he cautioned, "about *concealment*. I have commenced the publication of several works under the plan of concealment—but unfortunately the success and popularity of the first efforts has generally tickled the authors into an avowal to a few particular friends, who soon made it publick. It is against this vanity of authorship that I caution you, as I know from experience that curiosity is the ruling passion in the publick, the gratification of which is the principal incitement to purchase a Book." Robinson also acted as censor: "As you promise *not to offend*, I hope there will be nothing offered that will have such a tendency, which (should there be) I must have the privilege of returning for amendment." [9]

Robinson was a past master of merchandising. He contrived to keep a crowd at the Circulating Library all day by refusing to let copies of *The Red Book* out to other book sellers, for, he remarked dryly, "nothing sells a book so well as the *apparent* demand." He confided to the fledgling authors that "I have rather the publick should believe they could get a copy with difficulty and intend to have the first edition *out of print* before it's half sold, in order to induce a belief that the work is in great demand—a second edition looks so very respectable." His advertisements were exercises in subtlety. Shunning the blurb as too obvious, he informed his customers through the newspapers of the progress

Apprentice Years

of a forthcoming number and of the exact hour of the day it would be offered for sale, apologized for his failure to meet public demand, and advised purchasers to have the "ready change," so that he might "accommodate them quicker."[10] It was perhaps Robinson who suggested whetting the curiosity of the town wits by inserting the following "puzzle" in the Baltimore *Federal Gazette* on October 21, 1819, two days before the publication of the first issue of *The Red Book*.

> There will appear in a few days a phenomenon, which its inventors, but for their modesty, would call a prodigy. It will not be seen in the heavens, though it is believed it will *take air*. It will be of a small size, (the philosopher who has predicted its advent, having determined it to be eighteen times less than his *folio*) and of a red color. It is not, however, of the comet family, though it is of a fiery complexion, and of a devious course, and will be somewhat irregular in its returns. It will be full of black spots like the sun, which it is expected the curious will often be found gazing at; but what is singular, it is these only which will make it *shine*. There will no earthquakes attend its appearance, indeed judicious thinkers believe it will do good, though it will no doubt create some consternation among silly and ignorant persons, and set all *light bodies* and *mere vapors* in a flame. It will exert, perhaps, some influence on the approaching *season;* but it will be very opposite to that which is sometimes experienced from the Moon; and astrologers say it will have the singular property of setting the young men to reading, and the young women to guessing. Its *right ascension* is not yet determined, but it will look for all the world like Sagittarius shooting the *goose*. We are inclined to believe it does not shine with borrowed light; but there will be some very shrewd Philosophers of a contrary opinion. It resembles *Saturn* least of all the planets, and is certainly no *satellite*.
>
> It may now be expected in a few days, and we recommend to all persons, as is customary on the appearance of a new moon, by all means, to have some silver in their pockets.

The reference to silver was particularly appropriate, for Robinson's aims were refreshingly clear. "The object is profit," he announced of one new periodical. It would "be issued *when* the publisher pleases, as *often* as he pleases, and *contain* what he pleases." Similarly, *The Red Book* would appear "varying with the inclination of the publisher." He was so inclined, for it was a popular, and presumably a financial, success. The hand presses could not keep up with demand. It was "talked of at every dinner and tea drinking in town," and by March 1820 Robinson was advertising a bound volume of the first six numbers.[11]

The Red Book faithfully mirrored Baltimore society, for Cruse and Kennedy had observed closely and reported accurately. The pamphlets had all the exuberance and brash insolence of youth, and like any young man's book, tried to sound a hundred years old. The authors began with the classic stereotype of the satirist: "The World in our opinion needs correction, and we have essayed to use the weapons placed in our hands." Although Robinson warned them that the barbs of their wit struck too close to home, in all probability it was the personal tone that gave the paper its notoriety. Allusion to angry protests and insulted victims, probably imaginary, was a technique borrowed from the *Salmagundi* of Washington Irving's New York coterie. The town eagerly scanned a new issue, each person searching for a reflection of his own likeness. Frivolous coquettes, fops and dandies, the pompous new rich; all were roundly abused.

The first issue warned Baltimore what to expect: "Baltimore, it is said abroad, is celebrated for three things—its *music*,—its *churches* and its *military*. In each of these, are strange anomalies. Music is patronized by those who have the least *ear* and the most *money* (which is only another name for discord.) The best *churches* are built by the worst christians; and in the *military* department, it is observed, that all logick is set at defiance in making *majors* of *minors*." Fashions in humor change and today this doubtless sounds fatuous, but in 1819 Baltimore laughed and tried to guess the identity of the wags who wrote it. *The Red Book* revealed this society as it was, increasingly self-conscious and increasingly sophisticated, for the satiric spirit invariably accompanies such growth. The authors were ready to admit what the success of their pamphlets implied—Baltimore's awakening interest in literature. "Letters are now of such repute," Kennedy has his old philosopher, Mr. Bronze, observe, "that I am not bold in saying that most of our gentlemen read the Reviews, and our ladies Waverly—only skipping the Scotch."

Since Kennedy and Cruse had "promised to rectify all abuses,"

Apprentice Years

they "found it necessary from time to time to stroll through the principal haunts of our fashionables, in order to ascertain the precise condition of the body politick at each period: It seemed particularly necessary, that Market-street should be accurately inspected from either extreme—first, because Market-street is a perfect epitome of the whole city, and secondly, because it is the perfect prize fighting ground to which every patrician and plebian is referred for contest."

> In this motley assemblage, the sourest face I saw, belonged to an old maid who had in her youth been a toast. The most cheerful looking man, was a bankrupt. The busiest matron, a widow who had a young friend about to be married—the wisest looking man was a bank director—the prettiest girl was a young quaker. The most egregious fool—here I am at a loss,—this honor was divided among several candidates. The most out-landish man was a dandy—the most gossiping was a lounger—the most dogmatick, a parson—the most pompous, a lawyer—the most learned, in his own opinion, a doctor—the most dignified, a dancing master. The happiest of the whole group was the ash-man, lording it over his mound of the decomposed essences of mortality—dust and ashes; careless and contented, whistling in the cloud that enveloped him, as little affected by the din and clamour and vanity and folly of the scene around him, as the Mohawk chief in Drury-Lane.

The Red Book incorporated many of the stock devices and comic conventions of the English periodical essay which had already been naturalized in *Salmagundi*. The mock epistles, counterfeit erudition, and essays on sentiment were couched in a style that persistently echoed Addison and Steele. Allegories and parodies were varied with sketches after the manner of the seventeenth-century "character" ("A Full Length Portrait of Mr. Dunder") and with efforts to temper wit with morality ("Letter to a Young Lady"). The old philosopher Mr. Bronze, endowed by Kennedy with a sentimental past and a quaint air of detachment, was a lineal descendant of Sir Roger de Coverley, but was influenced perhaps by William Wirt's *Old Bachelor*. An imaginary travel sketch such as "Voyage to the Underworld" not only was reminiscent of *Gulliver's Travels* stylistically, but also coolly borrowed several Swiftian episodes in describing a Laputa-like subterranean country.

Cruse contributed a series of spirited verse satires under the title "Horace in Baltimore." Cruse knew his Roman poetry, but he was also acquainted with James and Horace Smith's *Horace in London*. Even though the topical and personal allusions are lost, the odes retain considerable verve and wit. The ode "To Fashion," in the first number of *The Red Book*, is characteristic:

> Bright dame! who sweep'st with Cashmere vest
>   Thro' halls another's cash has furnish'd,
> My *plumed* lance is in the rest,
>   And my satirick armour burnish'd.
> I cannot see without a frown
>   Knaves, fools and coxcombs all thy passion;
> Fast as some rogue of note goes down,
>   Some ass of merit takes his station.
>
>   . . . . .
>
> Shall Wealth and Thou to Chloe bring
>   A score of beaux the dunce to flatter?
> Shall Delia round the bowing ring
>   Deal out impertinence for satire?
> Shall Bauble from his empty pate
>   Unmark'd his windy trifles vent,
> And wealthy Dunder walk sedate
>   In all the pride of "cent. per cent.?"
>
> No! if to me the Red Book yield
>   A place upon its honest pages,
> My Quixote muse shall take the field
>   Careless what *windmill* she engages.
> Mere windmills all thy doughtiest sons,
>   That veer with every veering blast:
> The noisy thing its circle runs,
>   But bursts too oft its sails at last.

Kennedy wrote the prose and Cruse the poetry: "Horace [Cruse] disdains to speak save in rhyme; looking down on us *prosers* with the same sort of tranquil scorn with which a wholesale man contemplates a retailer in Market Street. He is indeed a veritable poet, 'married to immortal verse,' unlikely to adventure on any other sort of matrimony." Many of the puns and epigrams, however, were probably the result of literary communism, a collaboration of youth, wine, and cigars at stag revels in St. Paul Street.

In the literary career of John Kennedy, *The Red Book* marks a summit of youthful high spirits. It did not really matter if the wisdom was merely aphorism and the humor only impudence. The young author had captured an audience and had experienced the ecstasy of print. If the scope of the papers was narrow and the characters only types, what Kennedy did was accomplished with vivacity, and if his achievement was modest, he could reply that he had aimed at nothing more. *The Red Book* revealed how steeped was Kennedy in the literature of coffee-house London and how sedulously he had aped his models. The picture of Baltimore society was limited but authentic, circumscribed by a literary convention and without interpretative depth. Except for an occasional comic thrust at the depressed financial condition of the country owing to the financial panic of 1819, the authors did not venture beyond the confining walls of a Gay Street drawing room or the fashionable section of the Market Street promenade. Yet, and the fact is not without significance, there was no trace of the anti-Anglican bias and arrogant assertion of cultural independence which vitiated so much periodical writing of the time like a neurosis of inferiority. Men like James Kirke Paulding complained to Kennedy that "our literary taste is but the reaction, the mere echo across the Atlantic." [12] Kennedy, however, seems not to have felt it necessary to challenge the British sneer "who reads an American book?" and the fact argues the independence and brash self-assurance, rather than the insularity, of the Baltimore intellectual climate.

It did matter, however, if Boston read Baltimore books, and the young men rushed the first volume of *The Red Book* to that city for review. From the heights of the New England Parnassus, Andrews Norton, professor in the Harvard Divinity School, confessed himself faintly troubled by the irreverent tone he discovered in its allusions to scripture and grumbled over the impurities of its Greek but, all things considered, he managed to "pronounce a favorable judgment." Edward Everett, editor of the *North American Review*, found the little volume bursting with talent and regretted that it was not the policy of his journal to review periodicals. Everett envied them the growing size of Baltimore, for, he complained, in Boston a writer must be more prudent lest he offend an acquaintance.[13]

A Baltimore lawyer sent a copy to William Wirt, the attorney-general of the United States, and that amiable gentleman, as famed for his law as for his surreptitious "scribbling," wrote a rather weighty opinion.

> I am much obliged to you for the Red-Book—which I have read throughout—it is written with great ease and sprightliness, and displays some fine strokes both of conception & execution—the moral being every where I think unimpeachable—with the exception, perhaps, of the attacks upon old maids, whose state, not being a voluntary one, is a misfortune & therefore not lawful game for the satirist—his proper objects are follies and vices —but they, ought, perhaps, to be attacked only in the abstract, or exhibited perhaps in a *really* fictitious character—I heard it said in Balto. that this book was a tissue of *personalities*—but I do not know enough of the secret history of the town to apply it—Neither the moralist nor the satirist can, in my opinion, justify an anonymous personal attack, on *private* individuals, and least of all on ladies—it is not necessary to his purpose that he should thus stoop to individuals—because there are vices & faults enough, of an epidemick character, to give him full employment—Hence if the Red Book be personal in its attacks, I should condemn it—but if it attacks vices, prejudices, follies, *en groupe* I should consider its purpose not only legitimate but highly laudable.
>
> Pray was not the Red Book written by the author or authors of "Keep Cool," [14] which I understood, originated in your town? I think there is a family likeness in the style both of thought and expression—Keep Cool with a *quantum sufficit* of proving and drollery, has, now and then, some vivid touches which are very pretty—This *quaere*, however, and these remarks are *entre nous*, for if the Red Book, be, as some represent it, a scandalous chronicle, I have not the least disposition to provoke its resentment— [15]

Cruse and Kennedy announced twelve numbers of *The Red Book*, and after the appearance of the sixth in January 1820, they promised to resume following a six-week vacation. The first issue of the second volume duly appeared for sale at the Circulating Library March 3, 1820, and was followed by two more at intervals of about a month, but there was a noticeable decline in quality. Alas, these two young men really did not have much to say, and they had exhausted their heavy ammunition in the first volleys. A year passed without further publication, but so intense was the interest aroused that speculation persisted as to the identity of the authors. Finally, the publisher, Joseph Robinson, suggested issuing a tenth number in which the authors should take a half-merry, half-grave leave of their public, momentarily rekindle enthusiasm, alarm their foes, and end with the promised explosion. Then with the sudden unmasking of the authors, "we may," Cruse reminded Kennedy, "live a little day of bagatelle glory once more." [16]

Kennedy agreed, for he was growing bored with the scheme. *The Red Book*, he knew, had slight claim to immortality even though, as these punsters boasted, "it possesses the advantage, that let the world slight it as it may, it will always be *red*." Kennedy had, however, another enthusiasm; he had embarked on a new career. On October 4, 1820, three weeks before his twenty-fifth birthday, he was elected a representative from Baltimore to the Maryland House of Delegates on the Republican ticket.[17] Politics was a novelty and its rewards were more tangible than the baubles of bagatelle glory among Baltimore's litterateurs. Cruse, also, believed "it is certainly time for us to be doing something better than writing R. Books." [18] The tenth and last number, made up chiefly of poems by Cruse, appeared March 16, 1821, and it was Cruse who wrote the valedictory of *The Red Book*.

> But go! you idle, insect thing;
> You brought some honey with your sting,
>   More merriment than trouble:
> Like other things that aim at *style*,
> 'Twas yours to soar and shine awhile,
>   A breath-inflated bubble.

Like many men of his time interested in writing and impatient with a profession he found dry and tedious, John Kennedy hitched his ambition to politics as well as to literature. He entered politics during a period of intense stability. Jefferson's familiar phrase—we are all Federalists, all Republicans—was, in

Baltimore in 1820, more truth than rhetoric. James Monroe was in the White House about to begin his second term in office, and during his stewardship only twice was the tranquillity ruffled. The economic crisis of 1819 momentarily roused the country, and the next year the slavery question flared up briefly in the Missouri controversy. Kennedy would later look back upon the period as a halcyon interlude in the annals of partisan warfare: "All men exulted in this peace; and those at the head of affairs enjoyed the rare good fortune of witnessing an honest and patriotic appreciation by the people, of their own honest and patriotic endeavours to advance the public welfare. Party spirit had in a great degree disappeared; faction was disarmed; no venal press was subsidized to conceal truth or stamp a fair seeming upon falsehood. Demagogues, the curse of free government, found no mart wherein to ply their seditious trade. So profound was this peace, so beneficent the spirit of the time, that, in 1821, Mr. Monroe was elected to a second term without an opponent in the field." [19]

Maryland shared the surface harmony of the Era of Good Feelings, but the sessions of the legislature at Annapolis revealed divisive forces at work. Chesapeake Bay divided the state into two distinct sections, provoking suspicion and hostility between dwellers on the Eastern and Western shores. This conflict within Maryland was magnified by its position as a border state. The lower counties were southern in sympathies, while the northern and western counties were drawn toward the North. These geographical forces were further complicated by the steady shifting of the Maryland economic center toward Baltimore. The city's magnificent natural advantages, a superb harbor and natural waterways, spurred industrial growth. On the Western Shore deserted farms stood rotting on soils depleted by successive plantings of tobacco, while north and west of Baltimore, the mineral wealth of the Alleghenys was beginning to be tapped and the hilly regions offered natural waterpower for factories.

Within the city of Baltimore, all was not sweetness and light. On the local political scene, astute observers could detect faint lines of cleavage. Kennedy was generally believed to belong to

Apprentice Years

the faction called "Pinkneyites" from its allegiance to that Maryland statesman.[20] Since Kennedy had become engaged to Charlotte Pinkney during the autumn of 1820 when he was making his first campaign for office, it was probably William Pinkney who introduced him to state politics at Annapolis. Kennedy's first election victory was a popularity contest among seven contestants, most of them young lawyers. If any significant issues were raised, they were not reported in the press.

Statesmanship at Annapolis was largely a humdrum routine of presenting claims, charters, and petitions or unsnarling the tangled laws for divorce, laws for insolvent debtors, and laws for Negro slaves. Like young men in every generation, Kennedy rushed into public life, confident that at last government would be purified and politics refined. With enthusiasm generated by an optimistic temperament and political naivete, he plunged into the task, obviously relishing his role as *enfant terrible* of the legislature. With a fine sense of theater, he created an immediate sensation by introducing a bill liberalizing the laws concerning imprisonment for debt. This was an impulsive gesture and the Federalists threw up their hands in dismay at such antics. They groaned aloud over "his youth, his inexperience, and the enthusiastic ardor of his temperament." But the Federalists, after all, were a political minority in Baltimore. And even though the bill failed to pass, Kennedy, with a daring stroke, had dramatically identified himself with the working men of the city.[21]

While the tempest roared in Baltimore, at Annapolis Kennedy was speaking often and effectively. Backing a free turnpike road, he vigorously endorsed internal improvements at government expense. On slavery he was equally explicit. No sane man could deny that the Negro, "the persecuted child of misfortune," was downtrodden, and it was the responsibility of Maryland to ameliorate his condition. But compare him with the freedman, condemned to a limbo scorned by whites and envied by slaves. The problem was, Kennedy argued, an economic one. Manumission would come only when the density of population should force whites to enter into competition with slave labor and thereby render it valueless. Such views in 1821 were scarcely original, but in the South they clearly placed him in the camp of the moderates and just as clearly separated him from those who yearned for the blessings of a slave empire. Privately, he accepted the characteristic southern view of the Negro as a parasite, incapable of freedom. Traveling to the North, he was slow to reconcile himself to Negro freedom. It rankled this scion of Pendleton stock to be ordered by a Yankee stagecoach driver to relinquish his seat to a Negro woman. On one occasion in Philadelphia he came near being thrashed by the husband of a Negress for imprudently suggesting that she make room in the coach for a white woman. "[I] would have apologized," he fumed, "even if the gentleman had required it. In this City of Brotherly Love and black freedom—for I don't think the Goddess is white here —I would not be thought a violator of the rules of *bienseance*. I should have done the same thing in Constantinople if a Musselman had called me a Christian dog—both of these cities are said to be extremely well ordered." [22]

Yet Kennedy was a man of tolerance and generous sympathies, and at Annapolis he began to acquire a reputation for championing the government's responsibility toward humanitarian causes. It satisfied the latent idealism of his nature and became the passion of a lifetime. During the first session of the legislature he supported appropriations to aid hospitals and the penitentiary, and personally guided through a bill to subsidize the University of Maryland. And he was laying the foundation for the next campaign. On several local issues arising from the hostility between the growing urban interests of Baltimore and the rural counties, Kennedy made several fire-eating speeches which were so effectively publicized at home by his claque that he returned from Annapolis to find himself a local hero.[23] In three months he had spoken out unequivocally on the crucial issues of the day. He was on record. That record would stand with remarkable consistency for a lifetime.

John Kennedy's star was in the ascendant. Perhaps never again throughout a long lifetime would he feel such complete mastery of his environment. He stood for re-election in the autumn of 1821 and won by a gratifying majority, leading a field of five

Apprentice Years

candidates and doubling his vote of the previous year. In 1822 he was returned to Annapolis by practically the unanimous vote of Baltimore.[24] His position was unique. He possessed the first qualification for office—a distinguished record in the "late war." He could command the franchise of the best classes, for he was coming to be accepted as one of them. On the other hand, his father had failed in business, and John Kennedy was known to have built his career without special advantages, a role he took some pains to dramatize.

From the first he identified himself with the commercial and manufacturing interests of Baltimore. His reward was the chairmanship of the Committee on Internal Improvements in the House of Delegates, a post he filled with characteristic energy. His report was a call to arms. The present generation, he declared, must expect to exert an aggressive and positive force in stimulating the American economy. His program was neither provincial nor narrowly partisan. He would lay the groundwork for co-operation with Virginia and Pennsylvania in order to make navigable the Potomac and Susquehanna rivers. He outlined the advantages of a canal between the Chesapeake and Delaware bays. Profiting by a peaceful Europe, a tranquil political scene in America, and the brisk rise of competition, the United States should channel its natural resources and labor force into manufacturing. The rhetoric of his report suggested a sentimental basis for his nationalism, but it was, in fact, economic.[25] Here was a point of view that, developed and ramified, would become the total political structure of his matured Whig philosophy. He thought of his program as a dynamic plan for economic nationalism.

The tension of political maneuver and countermaneuver at Annapolis was a heady stimulus. It was hard work, often drudgery, but the experience left John Kennedy with an insatiable taste for public life. Society at the state capital during the winter session was predominately masculine. In the evening the representatives would gather in the antique apartments with their lofty ceilings and gaping bow windows, rooms which a Negro servant kept heated by continually feeding bonfires roaring in the cavernous and battered old fireplaces. Here, fortified by brandy and cigars, and secluded from the northwesters that swept over the dreary sand hills and pines around the old city, the politicians exchanged coarse jokes and rusty anecdotes and settled the affairs of Maryland late into the night.

John Kennedy was immediately initiated into this select circle, for at twenty-five he already had a gift for friendship and a talent for society. He was handsome, about five feet ten inches tall, and he carried himself erect as befitted the captain of a militia rifle company. He was exacting in his dress, and while not inclined to attitudinize, he had a flair for bright colors and slightly exaggerated fashions. Perhaps the more homespun legislators from the western counties privately labeled this young man a coxcomb who obviously enjoyed the effect produced by a brilliant scarlet lining in his greatcoat. His forehead was high, his chin slightly aggressive, and his lean, oval face was redeemed from an ascetic quality by a faint glint of humor in his eyes. This last, the reflection of a tranquil and sunny temperament, was admirably caught in the portrait by Philip Tilyard [26] and was not altogether submerged even in the murky daguerreotypes. His were the eyes of a man who scrutinized life and found it inexpressibly droll.

Kennedy had every reason to be cocksure, for he was riding on the crest of a wave of popularity and had yet to discover how close a politician dared sail to the wind without capsizing. In the political calm that prevailed, he found himself praised by men of diverse persuasions, and in the sessions at Annapolis he was emerging as an influential leader in counsel and debate. It was flattering to have his uncle and former preceptor at law, Edmund Pendleton, baffled by his "magical influence" over his fellow townsmen and to hear that his Virginia cousins pronounced him the most distinguished young man in Maryland. On one occasion he appeared at a Baltimore theater after effecting a popular reform at Annapolis to be greeted by spontaneous cheers.[27] He was riding high—too high—for he unhappily overestimated his political influence.

In 1823, his third year at the state capital, the question of a Potomac canal was introduced. The idea immediately appealed to Kennedy. He envisioned the Potomac River as a major chan-

Apprentice Years

nel of commerce, tapping the western markets and funneling prosperity into Baltimore. The canal would stimulate the coal trade, and the banks of the river would eventually develop into one long manufacturing village. Such projects would bind the Union with economic ties. He had taken the long-range view of the question, but his constituents were not so farsighted. They were less absorbed than he in the pageant of national destiny; their eyes were fixed steadily on Baltimore realities. They cast covetous eyes on western produce, but the commerce the great National Road now carried to the city might be siphoned off to the city of Washington by a Potomac canal. As early as 1784 Baltimore interests had blocked the canal project, and they were not disposed to change. Overnight the bubble of Kennedy's popularity burst.

The news that Kennedy had voted to subscribe stock in the Potomac canal company was greeted with mixed anger and unbelief.[28] The bill was interpreted as a victory for the agricultural counties bordering the river which had earned the city's hostility by repeatedly frustrating legislation favorable to Baltimore. There was talk of burning Kennedy in effigy, and there were demands that the mayor call the council into extraordinary session. The cry went up for a town meeting to censure Kennedy, since he now apparently represented not the city but the central government. In self-defense Kennedy wrote a letter to the newspapers outlining his position, and, as the outcry grew louder, he defined his views in a series of tightly reasoned articles.[29] But the damage was done. Moreover, a rumor persisted that Kennedy's father owned property on the Potomac and that his son had acted out of self-interest. What appeared to lend substance to this slander was the general knowledge that Kennedy had received a diplomatic post early in the session,[30] and with his appointment in his pocket, he could afford to treat the voters with contempt.

Months preceding his third canvass for the legislature, Kennedy had applied for a post in the diplomatic corps.[31] The idea appealed to him: the prestige of an appointment, the opportunity for travel, the release from truckling to the electorate, and perhaps the leisure to return to writing. With the exception of several short and trivial letters to the press concerning Annapolis gossip, he had written nothing since *The Red Book.* Fortunately for his ambition, several new posts were created in May 1822 when President Monroe signed a bill appropriating funds to send ministers to the recently organized republics in South America. As with William Pinkney in 1820, Kennedy could again count on the influence of a friend in high places. His law practice had brought him into association with the attorney-general in Monroe's cabinet, William Wirt. Kennedy greatly admired Wirt and was ambitious for fame in the three fields in which Wirt was popularly conceded to excel all other men in the Union: law, literature, and oratory. Wirt, in short, was a most valuable friend to have. He liked Kennedy and exerted influence with President Monroe, and on January 21, 1823, Kennedy was named Secretary of Legation to Chile.[32] This was a debt Kennedy was amply to repay twenty-six years later when he published his two-volume *Life of William Wirt* in 1849.

Even before the appointment was confirmed, Kennedy was beginning to repent of his application. From the first, Baltimore had been a center of enthusiasm for the Spanish colonies anxious to identify their revolts with the causes of the American Revolution, and the youthful Kennedy, ardent and impressionable, may have warmed to their propaganda. But as the time grew near to leave his native Baltimore for Chile, the mission came to look to him increasingly like political exile. He may have shared the common view that the populace of Spanish America was an ignorant rabble, brutalized and miscegenated, suppressed by the combined tyranny of church and state. A young diplomat could not be sure that such a people were capable of self-government. The Maryland House of Delegates conferred no tenure, but a fickle Baltimore electorate was no less uncertain than the untried government of Chile. Also, he would have to forfeit a law practice which had been the painstaking work of seven years.

When he called at the State Department for instructions from John Quincy Adams, the Secretary could tell him nothing. Adams impatiently shrugged off all questions, gave Kennedy only a design for a diplomat's uniform, and advised him to find a tailor. The disillusionment was complete. Against the advice of

Apprentice Years 53

William Wirt, Kennedy resigned the mission before it sailed. John C. Calhoun, the Secretary of War, wrote to him from Washington that it was a wise decision, for now that the revolutionary generation had passed from the stage and the younger men had still to determine their relative merits, the fairest opportunities were at home.[33] The choice, however, was no longer entirely Kennedy's own, for in the late spring of 1823 he became engaged to be married.

On January 20, 1824, John Kennedy married Mary Tenant, the daughter of one of the wealthiest merchants in Baltimore. Thomas Tenant was a militia colonel whose Federalist proclivities in Republican Baltimore had kept him from becoming a general officer. His imposing mansion on Gay Street was one of the show places of the city. The friends of Kennedy's bachelor days at the rooms in St. Paul Street were in the wedding party, and Peter Cruse mentioned them all in some verses entitled "Some Sublime Doggerel on the Late Happy Occasion of the Marriage of Mr. John Pendleton Kennedy and Miss Mary Tenant." [34]

>   Now I'm out of the squeeze, and again at my ease,
>   And have room for my elbows, I'll try to rehearse
>   What efforts we made at the bridal to please,
>   And tell all that happened in elegant verse.
>   The Groom and the Bride we will just put aside.
>   Their case is too serious to make fun about;
>   Besides all their praise should I sing in my lays
>   My verse and your patience might chance to run out.

>   . . . . .

>   And then for the Groomsmen—the first on the scene
>   Was Pennington, with his fine figure and air,
>   In life as genteel as he is in a reel,
>   And who tells such a wonderful "tale of a bear."
>   What talents divine in his person combine!
>   What more in a spouse could a fair lady wish!
>   He's great at a jig and at running a rig,
>   But his wittiest joke was purloining a fish.

>   . . . . .

> As for Dulany, that man in the moon
>   One cannot but like that original sinner,
> Although he's so absent he looks like a loon,
>   And even while eating forgets he's at dinner.
> As for Cruse I must leave him to speak for himself;
>   A man who tags verses and doggerel chimes
> And thinks, I suppose, he's a wonderful elf,
>   Because he has written these very bad rhymes.

John's marriage to Mary, so gaily launched, was destined for tragedy. On October 16, 1824, in the first year of her marriage, Mary Kennedy died while giving birth to a son. She was twenty-two years old. Her son, Tenant Pendleton, survived her but eleven months. Of Mary Tenant nothing is known but her brief obituary, couched in the formal rhetoric that was the fashion.[35] When she died, a door in John Kennedy's life closed forever, and whatever his feelings, they were his alone. In the bound volumes of his letters, he tore out every vestige of their life together. Wealth and honors came to John Kennedy, age came also, and looking back over the years, this brief interlude of his youth may have seemed almost unreal as the memory of it dimmed. Perhaps at times he wondered whether she had ever existed. Twenty-eight years after her death, he alluded in his journal to his first marriage—his only surviving reference to that event. The passage spoke poignantly of his sorrow.[36]

> I have to note that in the course of last winter, the burial ground of Christ Church was broken up, and the remains of those buried there removed—amongst the rest, those of one who is associated in my early affections with a fond memory, and whose short career belonged to a period of my life which was greatly endeared by her gentle and loving devotion—my first wife Mary .... A brief space wife, still briefer mother—a woman of kind and virtuous nature; true, just and noble in character, with a spirit all devotion, cheerfulness and trust.
>   Although I set no value upon a tablet to mark the resting place of human remains, holding it to be an idle and useless custom, yet in deference to common opinion I mean to place some unostentatious and simple monument over the mother and child, whose brief fortunes will never interest the world, and will never need a memorial for my remembrance. I must attend to this, and get a stone prepared with such inscription as custom

ordains, to tell to those who may seek such a record hereafter, how little is left of that natural structure which was once the temporary lodgment of a spirit as pure and gentle as that of the good into whose companionship she has long since entered, and with whom she now abides.

In the months immediately following his wife's death, Kennedy thought again of entering the diplomatic corps. When rumors reached Baltimore that the office of chargé d'affairs at Brussels was soon to be vacant, he hurriedly wrote his friends at Washington to ask that they exert their influence in his behalf. Perhaps the administration suspected he was fickle of purpose after his refusal of the post at Chile, but whatever the reason, he was passed over for the appointment.[37] Thus disappointed, he turned again to politics and in 1826 entered the race for a seat from Baltimore in the House of Representatives at Washington.

The uncertain state of parties after 1820 had enabled Kennedy's personal popularity to return him repeatedly to the Maryland House of Delegates, but by 1826, although no clear-cut opposition had emerged, the National Republicans had begun to count on a certain amount of party regularity and to muster some sort of party discipline. For Kennedy at this time to challenge the present administration was to put himself in an anomalous position in regard to his past actions. He had, after all, recently sought a diplomatic appointment, and the two representatives at Washington, both seeking re-election, had only a year before endorsed him for the post at Brussels.[38] Moreover, it developed in the course of the canvass that although Kennedy had taken no part in the presidential campaign of 1824 because of the death of his wife in October of that year, he had not voted for John Quincy Adams, from whose administration he had sought preferment. He had voted for Andrew Jackson.

Jackson immediately became the central issue of the Baltimore campaign. The election of Adams in 1824, through the support of Henry Clay, followed by the appointment of the latter as Secretary of State (at the time the equivalent of heir apparent) had carried the suspicion of a "corrupt bargain," a suspicion which for many had crystallized into a conviction. Although the people of Maryland had given the majority of their electoral votes to Jackson, in the House of Representatives the state had defected to Adams. Kennedy had found his issue. Should the next presidential election be thrown into the House as had the last, he assured the citizens that a vote for him was a vote for Jackson. There would be no corrupt bargain. In 1826 there was, of course, no inconsistency in standing for internal improvements, a national bank, the manufacturing interests, and Old Hickory. Jackson was politically an unknown quantity and was prized for his freedom from sectarian political principles, his integrity of character, and the cohesive effect his personal popularity would have upon the alarming growth of sectionalism. Even such a die-hard Maryland Federalist as Charles Carroll of Carrollton, bitterly antagonistic to Jefferson and Madison, favored Andrew Jackson.

The campaign was vicious. The press was uniformly hostile to Kennedy. It did not attack this upstart but, what was worse, it ignored him. The Baltimore newspapers refused to accept his political articles except on the terms of a common advertisement, and Kennedy was forced to resort to handbills printed at his own expense.[39] The specter of the Potomac canal rose to haunt him. Only three years ago, his critics recalled, John "Potomac" Kennedy, his passage safely booked for Chile, had voted for the project in open violation of the known wishes of his constituents. The opposition had another trump. A diligent search revealed that in one of Kennedy's articles of 1823 defending his vote on the canal, he had remarked that Baltimoreans were "not the most remarkable for their reading propensities."[40] The choice of language was fatal, and it provided a field day for those who envied his rocket-like rise and would gladly injure this *Red Book* dandy with that portion of the people who, in fact, did not read.

The election came, and Kennedy was hopelessly routed.[41] Although he had believed that he would win, in retrospect he could see how ill-judged had been his decision to run. The campaign set his political ambitions back at least a decade and left him one thousand dollars in debt.[42] Following as it did the death of his wife and son and the wreckage of his plans for a diplomatic career, the defeat was a personal catastrophe. From the high tide of his fortunes in the winter of 1821 when he had been reveling in the masquerade of *Red Book* authorship and experiencing the first delights of success at Annapolis, he reached low ebb in the autumn of 1826. Yet his resiliency of temper sustained him. Although his spirits sank at the thought of returning to the full-time practice of the law, within two years his fortunes were again spectacularly on the rise.

CHAPTER IV

"A Right Merry Young Lawyer"

LATE IN LIFE John Kennedy observed, half in jest and half in earnest, that his career as a Baltimore lawyer was not of his own choosing but the inexorable force of destiny. "It was fixed fate," he said. "I came along to the verge of the bar as a cork upon a stream bobs along towards the eddy which catches it on its way, and bears it upon its own perpetual circle."[1] In 1826, surveying the wreckage of his plans for elective office and diplomatic preferment, and contemplating a return to his sole means of dependence, the law, he may have felt like the hero of a Sophoclean tragedy—though he might rage at the oracle's prophecy, his destiny was sealed.

Despite Kennedy's distaste for his vocation, his law practice flourished. He entered into formal connections with several local business houses and was retained as counsel by the Union Bank of Baltimore. His father-in-law, Colonel Thomas Tenant, a Baltimore merchant, frequently retained him. After the death of Mary Kennedy in 1824, the two men remained friends, vacationing together at the western springs of Virginia, and the old colonel showed his confidence in the younger man by appointing him executor of his estate. John's uncle, Anthony Kennedy of Philadelphia, died in 1828, and his will named his nephew executor of an estate made up largely of Pennsylvania real estate. John came in for a share of the inheritance, but he did not profit greatly. Cash was needed to pay off old debts of his father, and the details of overlooking the extensive properties proved a burden.

By the winter of 1827 Kennedy was again mingling in society. Preoccupation with his law practice had begun to divert his mind from the numbing loss of his young wife and infant son. Caught up in the diversions of the Baltimore "season," he began to regain his customary high spirits and his reputation for being what William Wirt called him, "a right merry young lawyer." [2] He was appointed to the committee which organized the dances at the Assembly Rooms, a duty traditionally required of Baltimore's most eligible young men. During the autumn of 1827 he met and fell in love with Elizabeth Gray, the daughter of a prosperous textile manufacturer. Elizabeth was strikingly beautiful. Her portrait by William Hubard which hangs now at Washington Irving's home on the Hudson River, "Sunnyside," confirms the contemporary praise of her flawless features and dark, candid eyes. In June 1828 John and Elizabeth became engaged, and on February 5 of the following year they were married. Allowing for the usual ups and downs of domestic life, there were to be no serious difficulties in their married life.

Elizabeth Gray was twenty years old when she married, thirteen years younger than John Kennedy, and her personality seems to have been submerged in the more forceful character of her husband. "She takes amazingly deep root in her household," Kennedy said; "as for me, being a perfect cork—a fishing float—I am ready to bob in any water that runs briskly and sparkles." [3] Gracious in manner and possessed of a quiet charm, Elizabeth was eager for her husband's success in his career but unobtrusive in her efforts to forward it. She was a competent, if not brilliant, mistress of a fashionable home. Kennedy soon discovered that his bride was incurably superstitious, inclined to be apprehensive of the future, and, on occasion, delightfully ineffectual. She cultivated, if she did not naturally share, her husband's passion for politics and his thirst for public recognition, and he sought and valued her advice concerning decisions, great and small, of his career. The glimpses in Kennedy's journals of their life together are oblique and matter-of-fact, for he seldom betrayed his feelings in personal matters. "These pages," he once remarked in passing, "are intended as a loose chronicle of ordinary events—not of feelings." On his nineteenth wedding anniversary, however, he allowed himself a rare moment of sentiment: "No man was ever happier in wedlock than I have been through all this lapse of time—no man had ever more reason to be grateful for the blessings of a truly good wife." [4]

It is not in the journals but among the letters that John Kennedy wrote to Elizabeth, "my dear Puss," that the secret of their happiness together is revealed. It was quite simple. Kennedy's courtship never ended. During the months of their engagement, he played the distraught and impatient lover, his letters gaily parodying the conventional rhetoric of romance: "I have vowed myself to your service and would perform my vow with the deep and earnest and respectful devotion of Sir Kenneth of Scotland." Later the letters became more natural in tone, even boyish, as for example Kennedy's description of breaking the news of his engagement to his mother: "I came out and told her everything—and how good you were, and how sensible, and how educated; how pretty, and how much I loved you—I couldn't tell her how much—and then I let her into all my plans, and I could see in her eyes, while I spoke to her, that joyous lustre that comes from a mother's sympathy." [5]

During the early years of his marriage, Kennedy's law practice, and later his election to Congress, took him often to Philadelphia, Annapolis, and Washington. He tried and generally succeeded in keeping to his resolution to write a daily letter to Elizabeth, letters carefully composed in a bare and drafty hotel room, letters scribbled in the courtroom while the opposition droned on well past the dinner hour, or cryptic notes hastily scrawled from his desk in the House of Representatives while a colleague was "crowing about the glories of the Western Waters, five feet from my right ear, in a most thundering gutteral slangwang." [6] Frequently the contents recorded only the comings and goings of a busy and successful man: business transactions, victory or defeat in court, gossip overheard at a boardinghouse table. Occasionally the letters were novel and clever, sometimes in rhyme, and witty with extravagant coinages and outrageous puns—the brisk and

"A Right Merry Young Lawyer" 61

playful talk of a disarming and ingenuous man deeply in love with his wife and impatient of separation. A few letters communicate a rare epistolary charm, the illusion of a moment of true intimacy.

> Think of your unfortunate lord [Kennedy wrote from Philadelphia] pent up in the third story of Mrs. Sword's back building, looking out westwardly upon a buckwheat-batter sky, with a pewter sun shining through it like a kitchen plate—no minstrel's music to beguile his captivity, except the clink of trowels chucking in mortar upon the foundation stones of Mrs. Sword's new house that is building next door; no wild ocean roar to lullaby his free soul into forgetfulness, except the roar of a cart that is now passing along with ashes, over the pebbly bottom of chestnut street; no warder's tramp except the heavy, fat-ankled footfall of John A. Morton of Bordeaux, father of Alfred Morton who deals in wines—as he steps ponderously along the lengthened corridor in a pair of indiscriminate boots, fire-bricketish and meal-baggish; no chieftain's horn to raise up visions of the woodland chase, but the huge, prolonged, proboscal blast of Doctor Caldwell (next room) as he ever and anon puts down his pen and, for a second, ceases to illuminate the world, while he revivifies his brain with snuff and twangs his nose so loud and clear that all Mrs. Sword's boarders, among them is Mrs. Otis, acknowledge it the herald and harbinger of learned tidings to the world of reading dunces. Such and so barren is the thraldom of your poor husband.[7]

John Kennedy deftly and humorously sketched the jolting stages, the drafty railroad cars, and the interminable canal boats, but he begrudged the duties that took him so often from his home. For after 1834 his life, more than ever before, was centered in his native Baltimore. That year, the fifth year of his marriage, he splendidly launched himself and his wife into society by building a home in Mount Vernon Place near the Washington Monument. The monument, a towering marble shaft, but a few years before had stood isolated in the countryside north of the city, "indescribably striking," William Wirt thought, "from the touching solitude of the scene from which it lifts its head." [8] Kennedy guessed correctly that Howard's Park, as it was then called, would soon become the court end of the city. The house and lot cost twelve thousand dollars, indicating both increasing success at law and (considering the mortgage) confidence in the future. He built for permanence: a substantial dwelling, four stories high, with an ample flight of white marble steps leading to a small but elegant portico. The spacious rooms, equipped with bell pulls to summon the Negro servants, furnished a handsome setting for the Kennedys' frequent and elaborate entertaining.

Since they had no children of their own, John and Elizabeth surrounded themselves with young cousins from the extensive Pendleton clan of western Virginia. Kennedy also became adept at attracting celebrities to his new home, for he was Virginian enough to delight in a prodigal hospitality. The English traveler Harriet Martineau dined at Mount Vernon Place, the guests finding it an unsettling experience to converse by shouting across the dinner table into her ear trumpet. Philip Hone, the affluent New York man about town, visited the Kennedys and noted in his diary, "a fine library and a charming little wife." [9] Kennedy's early passion for the theater had not abated with time, and actors could always find a welcome. Tyrone Power and Sheriden Knowles dined with him as did the young and talented Charles Kean, who, after the cloth was drawn, entertained the guests with an impromptu mad scene.

Professional success accompanied social success, and Kennedy's reputation as a rising young lawyer continued to grow. In 1835, his first year in his new home, he was admitted to practice before the Supreme Court, defending a cause of Colonel Thomas Tenant. "My debut in the Supreme Court," he wrote Elizabeth, "was quite an interesting event, as I, very much against any previous calculation, found myself *a little* (but a little) frightened at the first meet. I believe, considering all things I did very well, and certainly tomorrow hope to do better." [10]

He won the case. Indeed that year he seemed to be winning them all, and he began to receive tempting offers from other cities. Prominent Philadelphians hinted that banking interests in that city presented greater opportunities than Baltimore could hope to offer. A group of New York merchants suggested he come to that city, assuring him that he could immediately command a business of five or six thousand dollars a year. In a moment of despondency brought on by an outbreak of civic knavery

"*A Right Merry Young Lawyer*" 63

and mob violence in Baltimore, he wrote Elizabeth: "I could almost find it in my heart to cut my cable and make for New York." But on second thought he added sententiously: "The truth is this is a wicked world and the rogues have the majority I believe in every nook upon its surface. One may be reconciled to the iniquity around him by the reflection that the whole lump is leavened with the same material in pretty equal proportions." [11] Kennedy noted rather wistfully in his journal such opportunities as came his way, for although he became exasperated with his native city and railed against it, he knew he would never leave. He could not. He was bound to Baltimore by indissoluble ties, none more tenacious than the tie of marriage.

John Kennedy's marriage introduced him to a tightly knit family circle whose influence on his career was intangible but pervasive. Elizabeth's parents and her sister Martha lived on the Patapsco River about eight miles west of Baltimore where her father, Edward Gray, owned a cotton-spinning factory. After the Kennedys built their Mount Vernon Place home in 1834, the Grays spent more and more time visiting in Baltimore, and after the death of Elizabeth's mother in 1845, Edward Gray and Martha came to live permanently with John and Elizabeth. Each June both families removed to the Gray cottage by the Patapsco River to escape the heat of the Baltimore summer. Kennedy seems to have welcomed this domestic arrangement, and it is only against this background that his career after his marriage can be properly understood. It explains much about his waning ties with the South and his financial conservatism.

It is the image of Elizabeth's father, Edward Gray, which looms large in the life of John Kennedy. Gray's life was in the best tradition of Horatio Alger. Emigrating from Londonderry about 1794, he was a fervent admirer of the heroes of the Revolution, particularly George Washington. Gray never wearied of telling how he arrived at the Philadelphia wharf on a Sunday morning and passed the great man as he walked up Chestnut Street. By a second coincidence he took lodgings where Alexander Hamilton was staying at the moment, and Gray's first job as messenger for a commercial house brought him frequently into the presence of both men. After a series of ventures in trade, successes and failures, Gray gained control of a cotton-spinning factory on the Patapsco River. After the passage of the tariff of 1824 the mill prospered, and by 1847 Kennedy estimated its value at about three hundred thousand dollars. Four years later Kennedy noted that Gray was enjoying an income of about seventy thousand dollars a year.[12]

The factory was a feudal domain over which Gray ruled with a benevolent paternalism. In the little community the workers, some of them sent from the north of Ireland "upon an order," dealt at the company store and, when times were hard and spindles idle, received supplies dispensed by Gray's foreman. Every six months Gray and Kennedy met to perform the ritual of a stockholders' meeting, declaring to themselves the usual dividend of five per cent.

Edward Gray was impulsive and emotional, easily irritated and just as easily moved to tears. He might in a sudden rage order his pet dog shot, only to be plunged into a fit of despondency once the rash act was done. Intensely devoted to the welfare of the factory, he still relished the good things of life. He enjoyed choice food and drink, a weekly musicale with a few select friends, or an evening at the Holliday Street Theater. And he became expansive under the influence of the brilliant guests his son-in-law entertained: men like the great unionists Daniel Webster and John Quincy Adams; or the President-elect, William Henry Harrison, whose ideas on the economy were reputedly sound and conservative; and of course Henry Clay, who certainly should be President, and who was so everlastingly right on the tariff. For Clay, although born in Virginia, was no southern firebrand. Edward Gray was suspicious of Southerners, although he knew nothing of them at first hand except as he found them in Baltimore. His own financial success was linked to the tariff program of the North, and he condemned John C. Calhoun and the disciples of free trade as willful obstructionists or visionaries. Slavery he opposed on principle, and he shared the common prejudice that the South was a land of extravagant idlers.

Kennedy was on the best of terms with Gray: "I would not say to his face what I think of him—the tenderest, lovingest, most considerate man, full of the finest impulses and most generous qualities I have ever found in any man." [13] Kennedy had the complete confidence of his father-in-law, who began to defer to the younger man's judgment in matters of policy concerning the factory. But Gray's disposition soured with age. He demanded the constant attention of his two daughters, and met any fancied neglect with a fresh recital of his symptoms. When he complained that his asthma made it difficult for him to climb the hill to Mount Vernon Place, John and Elizabeth dutifully moved in 1840 to William Wirt's former home on fashionable Monument Square. During Gray's last lingering illness he filled the house with his groans and clung tenaciously to life while daily foretelling his death. In the final weeks before his death in the spring of 1856, he grew inordinately concerned about distribution of his money and almost daily pressed a discussion of the terms of his will on his reluctant son-in-law.

Gray's invalidism forced Kennedy to restrict his political activities to Baltimore and Washington, for he was devoted to his wife and she would not leave her father after his health began to fail. In 1848 Daniel Webster, who nursed a fondness for literary men and was anxious to foster their interests, seemed disposed to offer Kennedy a diplomatic post, and two years later Henry Clay suggested that he be sent to Berlin.[14] Kennedy was eager to travel and was suited by temperament for the diplomatic corps, but Gray's health put it out of the question. For Kennedy's interest in literature Gray had little sympathy. What he did appreciate was Kennedy's vigorous reply in 1830 to a report of the Committee of Commerce of the House of Representatives attacking the protective system. Kennedy's pamphlet, a witty and ironic assault on free trade, created a stir in its time and was widely circulated as a campaign document. It so pleased Gray that he gave his son-in-law a present of a hundred dollars and paid the printing bill.[15]

Of the literary men Gray met, he preferred Washington Irving. Irving, to Gray's sorrow, had once served a Jackson administration, but he had repented of this heresy, and in conversation was unlikely to begin canting about the common man. Also, Irving was familiar with the stock market, had on occasion lost as much as a gentleman ought to lose, and could be, if he were in the mood, an attentive listener to the intricacies of textile prices or the supremacy of Maryland-cured hams. Irving sincerely liked this "capital specimen of the old Irish gentleman—warmhearted, benevolent, well informed, and, like myself, very fond of music and pretty faces, so that our humors jump together completely." [16]

Vernon L. Parrington's charge [17] that Kennedy shifted his opinions with a cold-blooded opportunism after he married the daughter of the "masterful" Edward Gray fails to do justice to Kennedy. In the years immediately before and after the tariff of 1824 while Edward Gray was a struggling and obscure textile operator on the Patapsco River, Kennedy was already becoming known as a staunch friend of protection for home manufactures. While serving his political novitiate in the Maryland House of Delegates during the early 1820's, he had subscribed to the doctrines of economic nationalism which another Baltimorean, Hezekiah Niles, was popularizing in his *Weekly Register* and which Henry Clay was championing on the national scene as the American System. Besides serving as chairman of the Committee on Internal Improvements in the House of Delegates, Kennedy had backed legislation favorable to the Union Bank of Baltimore. As for Kennedy's early Jacksonism, his campaign for a seat in Congress in 1826 had revealed that his allegiance to Andrew Jackson was based largely on the Old Hero's glamour and his apparent freedom from the trammels of party. As will be seen hereafter, Kennedy broke sharply with Jackson when the drift of his fiscal policies became apparent.

Therefore, when John Kennedy married Elizabeth Gray in February 1829, far from undergoing a change in political or economic philosophy, his reputation as a spokesman for Baltimore's financial and manufacturing community increased his eligibility as a son-in-law in the eyes of Edward Gray. Neither is it quite fair to assert that "the family income was dependent on tariff favors," for Kennedy's law practice was paying him handsomely. If he were pressed, however, Gray was always there. "By the by," Kennedy wrote him from Saratoga Springs, "regarding the expenses I am not sure, although I live in hopes, that

"A Right Merry Young Lawyer" 67

my purse will hold out. So to be on the safe side I wish you would remit me a fee of fifty or a hundred dollars, whichever is most convenient, for my invaluable services in postponing the mill dam case until low water for you." [18]

Kennedy had cast his lot irretrievably with his native city, but there was no reason why he should regret the choice. He was constantly reassured of his eminence in his world by the flattering offers which poured in upon him. Would he allow himself to be put in nomination for a judgeship in the Baltimore County Court? Would he assist in editing the Baltimore *Republican* at fifteen hundred dollars a year? Would he accept an offer from the noted journalist Duff Green to edit a new periodical devoted to jurisprudence to be published at Washington? He was manifestly pleased, but he resolutely declined each offer.[19]

Soon after his marriage to Elizabeth, Kennedy had his portrait painted by William Hubard. He looks directly from the canvas, faintly amused at what he sees. His expression is engaging and assured, the look of a man who will make an effort to please and who knows from experience that he will succeed. His hair is dark, cropped rather shorter than the fashion, and brushed carelessly back from his forehead. He looks boyish, scarcely his thirty-five years. But the fashionable and poised Baltimore gentleman of the Hubard portrait is clearly not the diffident youth who had at first tried to swim against the current of Baltimore society. Kennedy had discovered that the tribute society exacted, particularly from an ambitious lawyer, was "the duty of a gentleman and good policy, too." It was a maxim with him, born of experience, that "success depends so much upon present manners and tact in the affairs of life, and often, so little upon scholarship and acquirement." [20] Kennedy was gifted with tact in abundance, he had acquired flawless manners and sufficient scholarship, and he was possessed of a young and pretty wife. It is not surprising, therefore, that John and Elizabeth found themselves in constant demand at Baltimore social functions.

The city itself had begun to provide an appropriate setting for the proverbial gaiety of its society. The architect Robert Mills, designer of Baltimore's Washington Monument, lined the streets of the city with houses of Adamesque gentility. Toward the outskirts were elaborate mansions. Belvidere in Howard's Park had been built by John Eager Howard, a revolutionary hero who had grown rich in real estate speculation. Farther out was Homewood, one of the finest homes of the period, the estate of Charles Carroll, son and namesake of the last surviving signer of the Declaration of Independence. Many of these lords of the manor kept open house, rode to hounds, filled their evenings with whist and dancing, and believed themselves as richly blessed as any English country squire.

Josiah Quincy of Boston, a guest at one of these family homes, was captivated: "Any social meeting more hearty, easy, friendly, and in all respects agreeable than those which characterized the Baltimore society of 1826 it has never been my fortune to attend. My stay seemed like a long English Christmas,—such a one, I mean as we read of in books. The beauty and grace of the ladies and the charming ease of their manners were very taking to one reared among the grave proprieties of Boston." Nor could a visitor forget that, notwithstanding Baltimore's dependence on commerce and manufacturing and its many emigrants from New England, a large segment of its society claimed a quixotic allegiance to the South. Quincy was sharply reminded: "I was engaged to dine with Mr. ———, one of the principal citizens, but received a polite note from him regretting that the party must be postponed, as his nephew had just been shot in a duel." [21]

The attractions of Baltimore society and the demands of a thriving law practice did not consume all Kennedy's energy, and in the years immediately following his marriage to Elizabeth he plunged into a round of activities aimed at raising the cultural level of Baltimore. In 1830 he helped to organize a phrenological society, offering his home as a meeting place. At its inception the movement was composed not of quacks but of intelligent men using the best scientific methods of their day. The Baltimore Phrenological Society included the leaders of the city's intellectual life and became, in 1830, the nucleus of the group that organized the faculty of arts and science in the University of Maryland. This latter project was also a favorite of Kennedy's. Among the newly appointed faculty, Peter Hoffman Cruse, Kennedy's collaborator on *The Red Book,* was named professor of belles lettres, and Kennedy himself was appointed professor of history and vice-president of the faculty. He began reading for a course of lectures and delivered the address at the formal opening of the college on January 3, 1831, using the occasion to outline an elaborate program for degree and nondegree students. The failure of these high hopes was clearly foreshadowed, for the professors were serving without "any hope of emolument to themselves." [22] Kennedy journeyed to Annapolis to persuade the Maryland legislature to subscribe funds for the support of the new college, but without success. In addition to these pet schemes, Kennedy began to gain local repute as an occasional orator. He was always ready to address his fellow townsmen on the merits of industrial development, the spirit of the age, and the gospel of progress.[23]

One more of Kennedy's activities during these first years of married life remains to be told, "The Monday Club." Soon after his establishment in his Mount Vernon Place home, Kennedy "set on foot a little weekly meeting or *reunion* of the gentlemen of Baltimore. The object proposed was, by this periodical concourse, not only to cultivate intimate acquaintance and friendship amongst the members, but also to afford strangers who might casually be in the city an opportunity to gain some knowledge of our Society." The Monday Club met once a week for an evening of conversation. Its aim was to stimulate the intellect, not the appetite, and the members agreed, but with only indifferent success, to keep refreshments at a spartan level. At the inaugural meeting, Kennedy interpreted this to mean a tureen of stewed oysters, turkey salad, and ice cream.

The group began as a pure democracy functioning only through "understandings," but grew eventually to about twenty-five members, adopting on the way some outward trappings of formal organization. Before disbanding in 1841, the club had included at one time or another the most influential leaders of the city's business, professional, and intellectual life. In all, thirty-seven Baltimoreans belonged to the Club during the six years of its existence, including ten lawyers, eight physicians, six merchants or bankers, the Archbishop of the Roman Catholic Church, the postmaster, the editor of the *American*, two professors in the University of Maryland, a judge, and Baltimore's representative in Congress. The Monday Club was certain to command the presence of any distinguished stranger, and one visitor, James Wynne, thought it "the most agreeable reunion in Baltimore" and remembered Kennedy as, with one exception, "the best talker." [24]

It is in the Monday Club that the life of John Kennedy in these years finds its most perfect symbol. The Club represented an aspect of American culture that was patrician yet robust and masculine, not consciously literary but actively interested in the arts, a way of life still vivified by a vigorous infusion of economic and political thought and not yet withdrawn into an aloof and fastidious gentility. Some of these men had come to Baltimore as restless youths to seek their fortunes in a new city. Others had shipped as seamen from Baltimore to the West Indies, South America, or Europe. A few were men of narrow sensibilities, such as Kennedy's father-in-law by his first marriage, Colonel Thomas Tenant, a hard-fisted martinet who boasted he had read but one book in his life.

But there were also men such as the urbane Robert Gilmor, the Club's president for a time, who filled his home in Water Street with works of art and whose culture was too humane to be corrupted by Baltimore's blatant materialism. These men had opportunities for broad experience, and life as they found it was good. Living in a new city where men had come to piece together a new social fabric, they spoke glibly of "progress" but in practice were wary of meddling with the status quo. Being men of means, they felt that property and freedom were inextricably bound. They had a horror of leveling by law and clung to the belief that the only real equality was equality of opportunity. Most would agree with Kennedy that "the war is and shall forever be between the ignorant, the idle, the dissolute and their antagonists in the social frame." [25]

The Monday Club recognized this antagonism, its very organization implied as much, and it formed a cohesive, convivial unit. It was a stable society, one in which John Kennedy felt secure, and within its boundaries he formulated a clearly defined philos-

"A Right Merry Young Lawyer"

ophy. It was a philosophy that had been conditioned in the twilight of the eighteenth century, for he subscribed to a view of life and letters which by the middle of the nineteenth century would be a quaint anachronism. It was a philosophy that called on men of background, talent, and education to assume leadership of public affairs as a sacred duty. Its essence was not adequately expressed in the word *aristocrat* but in the word *gentleman*.

And Kennedy's philosophy had a second responsibility: the nurturing of the arts, either through performance or patronage. For despite the manifold distractions of his life, Kennedy had not forgotten his resolution to be a writer made years ago in the loft of Shrub Hill. Although *The Red Book* was all but forgotten by the 1830's, Kennedy continued to keep his reputation alive locally by writing an occasional political pamphlet. When a letter was required for the press, men turned to Kennedy to "put it into good English." [26] With the publication of his first book in May 1832, *Swallow Barn, A Sojourn in the Old Dominion*, his reputation became more than merely local. In Philadelphia on Christmas Day, 1832, Kennedy described to Elizabeth a minor triumph in the metropolis. "Do you know they make a great parade here about Swallow Barn; and everybody who is introduced to me forthwith begins to talk of Ned Hazard, Mike Brown, &c. . . . A gentleman said to me, 'I have waded through it.' 'No sir, that's impossible,' I replied. 'It is out of your depth my good friend. You got over your head.' I think I had him there, and here he and all the bystanders—some dozen—set up a great laugh."

Kennedy made his bid for serious consideration as a writer at a fortunate moment, for in the 1830's his countrymen were eager to bestow praise. American literature was something of a rarity, and the applause of a handful of reviewers was enough to bestow fame. Kennedy carefully clipped from the newspapers and pasted in his scrapbook thirty-three reviews of *Swallow Barn*, most worthless as criticism but all generally favorable. It was an auspicious beginning to his new career as man of letters.[27]

CHAPTER V

Virginia Revisited

JOHN KENNEDY began in earnest to write *Swallow Barn* on October 19, 1829, eight months after his marriage to Elizabeth. At least four years earlier he had been planning a novel dealing with life in Virginia, and during the summer preceding his marriage he had written to Elizabeth from Winchester that he was gathering notes and impressions for the projected work. These earlier plans came to nothing. But after his marriage he found, in the domestic routine provided by Elizabeth, the atmosphere conducive to sustained creative work. Devoting an hour in the afternoon and an occasional evening to writing, in six weeks he had completed five chapters. At intervals from his law practice and the distractions of Baltimore society, he worked at the novel, and on December 31, 1831 he wrote triumphantly in his journal, "Finished Swallow Barn." [1]

Kennedy's friend of *Red Book* days, Peter Hoffman Cruse, hurried off to Philadelphia to offer the manuscript to Henry C. Carey of the firm of Carey and Lea. Carey was possessed of critical intelligence and taste and was sincerely interested in the development of an American literature. He immediately recognized the merits of *Swallow Barn* and agreed to bring out an edition of two thousand copies. It appeared in May 1832, "the worst possible time" according to Carey, for a month after publication a cholera epidemic forced many shops to close their doors. By

February 1833, nine months after publication, about one quarter of the first printing remained to be sold. The novel was immediately pirated in London, but Carey interpreted this as a good omen: "The most important thing is to have it published even if the author should receive little advantage from it, as it will enable him to make better terms for the next." [2] Subsequently, *Swallow Barn* was translated into Swedish and published in Stockholm in 1835.[3]

Kennedy's intent in *Swallow Barn* was clear. "My design in this work," he wrote in the preface, "has been simply to paint in true colors the scenes of domestic life as I have found them in Virginia." Both contemporary reviewers and literary historians have readily acknowledged how thoroughly he realized his aim. George Henry Calvert, a fellow member of Kennedy's Monday Club, noted in the Baltimore *Times* "the striking correctness of the portrait" and immediately recognized the value of the work as social history. James Kirke Paulding, the Knickerbocker author who in 1817 had published his own description of plantation life in *Letters from the South,* found "the sketches of character, manners and scenery so fresh and agreeable that one cannot help feeling that they are all drawn from nature." Some years later the Charleston novelist and editor, William Gilmore Simms, told Kennedy that *Swallow Barn*'s "genial and natural pictures of Virginia life, are equally true of Southern life generally among the old and wealthy families." And the most recent and best informed historian of southern literature, Professor Jay B. Hubbell, has called the novel "the best picture of Virginia life in the early nineteenth century." [4]

If *Swallow Barn* deserves attention as an authentic document in the social history of the South, it also holds a significant place in literary history as the prototype of a persistent and influential theme in American literature—the southern plantation tradition. *Swallow Barn* stands at the head of a long stream of novels of the Old South, novels that increasingly romanticized their materials until they all but lost their anchorages in reality and became, like a buoy floating where there is no shoal, a pastoral and feudal mythology. The ante-bellum South, to be sure, had its legend-makers, planters who styled themselves the lineal descendants of the Virginia Cavaliers and who prided themselves on perpetuating the aristocratic tradition. But the legend of a southern Golden Age before the Civil War which has captured the popular imagination was primarily the work of the novelists of the post-bellum South.

Writers such as Thomas Nelson Page and Mary Johnston were themselves descendants of distinguished Virginia families, and they created for their heroes and heroines genealogies as distinguished as their own. In the remote and romantic world of plantation novels, gallant and debonair young men ride home from the wars to find waiting for them supernally beautiful heroines in farthingales. The flirtations and courtships, the duels and dances, which fill the idle days of these charming men and women seem always to be set against a scene of manorial splendor dominated by a mansion with a glistening white portico overlooking green lawns sloping down to a placid river. In the cottonfields the darkies, too numerous ever to be counted, sing contentedly at their work. This tableau is familiar to everyone today, owing chiefly to the phenomenal popularity of Margaret Mitchell's *Gone With the Wind* and the motion picture made from the novel—certainly the apogee of the plantation tradition. So in returning to *Swallow Barn*, it is necessary to disencumber ourselves of the aura of romantic idealism of the fully evolved plantation tradition, and to recall that Kennedy's contemporaries considered his novel a faithful transcript from life.

It is not difficult to account for the authenticity of *Swallow Barn*, for Kennedy was admirably equipped for the task he set himself. His boyhood summers had been spent among the scenes he wished to describe, and as the years passed he had not severed his ties with Virginia. In 1820 his parents and three brothers—Andrew, Philip, and Anthony—had left Baltimore and settled at "Clayton," a farm near Charles Town, Virginia, which Nancy Kennedy had inherited from her father. John, busy with his law practice and politics, remained in Baltimore, but each August he returned to western Virginia to visit his family and the Pendleton circle in Jefferson and Berkeley counties.

He looked forward to these tours, for vacationing in Virginia was an improvident, vagabond existence. He found himself "obliged to attend riding parties and talking coteries and dances from morning until bedtime."[5] To his friends Kennedy wrote witty accounts of a society markedly different from that of his native Baltimore. In the midst of a letter of family gossip written from Winchester in 1828, he distilled in a casual paragraph Virginia society at its most quixotic:

> They have belles and beauties here [Winchester], and coquettes too, and scores of flirtations. . . . Society is tolerably large and gay. I must be in the parlour presently as one of the best specimens I could desire is to be there this morning—a Miss Hebe Carter—a perfect Hebe they tell me in complexion and figure and very much caressed. I remember hearing of her that a son of Mr. Stanley of North Carolina two or three years ago took laudanum on her account, which failing he tried to cut his throat with a pen knife, but the knife was too [*several words illegible*] married to another lady—which it is supposed has cured him of this foolish passion. I almost tremble at the thought of meeting this terrible lady. They say half of Winchester is mad for her now.[6]

These excursions had something of the nature of a triumphal tour, for, as he told Elizabeth, "I am like the stray sheep of the Scripture whose return gives more joy than the safety of the whole flock."[7] Actually the coming of this Baltimore politician and lawyer may have seemed to his Virginia relatives more like the return of the prodigal son, so alien were his ideas to their own. Kennedy tactfully moderated his views to please them, but the division of his loyalties explains the curious combination of ironic detachment and affectionate sympathy which characterizes the tone of *Swallow Barn*. Like the novel's narrator, Mark Littleton, who came from New York to see plantation life at first hand, Kennedy was sufficiently detached from Virginia to see it objectively.

In setting out to picture the life of a Virginia plantation, Kennedy quite naturally drew on his knowledge of society at the foot of the Shenandoah Valley, and particularly his extensive backlog of boyhood associations. Roseate memories of summer vacations—the delicious applejack made by an old Negro mammy, the bitter home remedies for the ague, the country school at

Martinsburg—supplied a vast reservoir of raw materials on which to draw.[8] Since many of these recollections were associated with "Adam's Bower" in Jefferson County, the estate of his aunt and uncle, Sarah and Adam Stephen Dandridge, Kennedy turned first to it for inspiration. Moreover, in 1825, five years after leaving Baltimore to take up residence at Clayton, Kennedy's parents moved again, this time to make their home at The Bower. During the years *Swallow Barn* was being planned and written, Kennedy had before him as a model the society of The Bower. It was this society he chose to chronicle.

The evidence for believing The Bower to be the prototype for *Swallow Barn* is strengthened by the existence of an early draft of the novel in which Kennedy proposed to take Mark Littleton directly to western Virginia.[9] In the final draft, however, Kennedy shifted his scene to the south shore of the James River. There were several reasons for the change. The "lordly James" evoked rich historical connotations which contributed to the total effect. Kennedy may have decided, after looking over his manuscript, that scenes drawn so closely from life needed the additional disguise of a shift in locale. Also, he sensed the change that was overtaking the Valley and rapidly altering what he believed to be its distinctive Virginian quality. A new influx of German and Scotch-Irish settlers had modified the character of the region. Kennedy noted the change in a letter written in 1828 to Elizabeth:

> One thing I should like your father to see in this country—you know his prejudice (I think I may call it one) against Virginia, for its loose manners and thriftless mode of life—I should like him to travel through this upper region at least to see how completely the elegancies of society and the best points of a luxurious mode of living, have been invaded by a sort of stiff, awkward, and *churchly* morality, that seems to have attacked every seal of grace in gesture, speech, "affections of delight" (as Shakespeare calls them) with everything that made Old Virginia once the seat of noblemen, but not of pennysaving presbyterians.[10]

Kennedy's use of his experiences in the Valley to picture Tidewater society did not, as might be expected, mar the accuracy of the portrait. Rather the old Virginia families who had settled in

Virginia Revisited

the Valley, sensitive to the foreign element in their midst, were intent on preserving the tradition their ancestors had established on the Tidewater.

Kennedy's experience of life in Virginia extended beyond the neighborhood of The Bower. In 1819 he had made a leisurely journey through eastern Virginia, chiefly to see the sights. Again in May 1830 he and Peter Hoffman Cruse toured much of the state, visiting the university at Charlottesville and making a pilgrimage to Monticello. The two friends eventually made their way to Richmond, talking meanwhile of working up their experiences into a book.

As for his knowledge of the Tidewater gentry, Kennedy had been an attentive student of this genus at the western springs of Virginia. At White Sulphur and at Berkeley he mingled with the planters who came thirsting for the purgative waters and for the companionship of their fellow man. Each day at the springs began with two hours of conversation, the guests leaning far back in cane chairs with their feet balanced precariously on the ground porch railing. After a hearty breakfast and a tepid bath, the guests continued to talk on the second porch until dinner. This meal was the high point of the day, for in peak season about two hundred visitors sat shoulder to shoulder at long tables eating ham, chicken, and boiled onions. After dinner the talk droned on until time for tea. Kennedy dutifully accounted for his time to Elizabeth: "Total eating 3 hours—sleeping 8; reading, 9 pages—writing, one letter—walking, one mountain; drinking, 7 tumblers—philosophy 5 minutes—bathing, one plunge; nihilology, nonsense, &c. about 12 hours. Time bravely spent." [11] The confabulations were endless and, for Kennedy, illuminating. The anecdotes and impressions were literary capital which, he knew, would pay dividends to a clever speculator in literature like himself.

So rich and varied were the materials on which Kennedy could draw that as the book took shape in his imagination, he despaired of reducing the whole to the organic unity of a novel and intended instead a series of essays unified only by setting and atmosphere. His first plan was subtitled "Studies from Nature by a Young Artist," and Mark Littleton, provided with portfolio, bristol boards, and crayons, had in mind nothing more elaborate than a sketch book of Virginia scenes collected at random. "The original idea of Swallow Barn," Kennedy wrote later to his publisher, George P. Putnam, "was connected with a plan to write a sort of Headlong Hall Story—rather of the comic and satirical kind. I meant to represent an old decayed place with odd and crotchety people inhabiting it. . . . The plan was changed afterwards." [12]

The original plan for *Swallow Barn* derived from Washington Irving, for Kennedy, a literary amateur, had followed the lead of the reigning American man of letters. Perceptive reviewers like Alexander H. Everett and Edgar Allan Poe, although praising the work, were quick to note and condemn the imitation.[13] The resemblance to Irving's *Bracebridge Hall* was particularly striking. The centering of interest in a large and hospitable country estate, the concern with eccentric character, and the structural device of having the inhabitants tell stories were parallels too obvious to be overlooked. There are other similarities in subject matter, superficial but unmistakable, such as the pampered old servant, the romantic trappings of falconry, and the satire of knight errantry in a sentimental love affair. Kennedy apparently tried to mold his materials to a preconceived form out of admiration for Irving, but a talent for sustained narrative, noticeably slight in Irving, kept rising to the surface and threatening to run away with his plan. "I have had great difficulty," the preface begins, "to prevent myself from writing a novel." The difficulty proved insuperable. As the events of the story gained momentum, Kennedy admitted that "unawares, and without any premeditated purpose, a few desultory sketches of the Old Dominion have fallen into a regular jog trot, novel-like narrative." Some years after, in outlining his literary career for the anthologist Rufus Griswold, Kennedy wrote of *Swallow Barn* that it "was originally intended for a series of detached sketches of the customs, opinions, and habits of the tidewater region of Virginia, but gradually taking the character of a connected story, it was thrown into the shape in which it now appears before the public." [14]

In a preface written for the revised edition of 1851, Kennedy still insisted that "Swallow Barn is not a novel. . . . It is, therefore, utterly unartistic in plot and structure." This diffidence is one aspect of a pose that is sustained throughout the book. The author who proceeds "half venturing, half shrinking, surprised at his own good fortune and wondering at his own temerity," [15] apologizing for his slender powers and demurring to the reader's superior judgment, was a role Kennedy learned from Washington Irving. It was a role particularly evident in the South, for as Thomas Nelson Page observed in *The Old South*, "where literature was indulged in it was a half apologetic way, as if it were not altogether compatible with the social dignity of the author." Whether a defense mechanism to disarm criticism, subtle flattery to ingratiate the author, or simply the adoption of the ageless convention of the humble author, this pose has fostered the belief that as an artist Kennedy was careless or indifferent toward his materials. Nothing could be further from the truth.

Among Kennedy's papers as many as five drafts of a chapter still survive to bear witness to his care in composition. A day-by-day time scheme for the entire novel has been preserved, which contradicts his assertion that the book merely "was linked together by the hooks and eyes of a traveller's notes." As early as August 1828 he was devoting a summer vacation from the law to writing, under the stimulus of a visit to The Bower. Some of the material incorporated into *Swallow Barn* was written as early as 1825—seven years before its publication—and when, on September 21, 1830, he began to write out the final impression, he had an extensive portfolio of notes. John H. B. Latrobe, who maintained a law office in the same building with Kennedy and who heard each chapter as it was completed, testified that portions of the work were heavily revised. Kennedy also submitted chapters for criticism to friends whose judgment he respected, and he occasionally adopted their suggestions.

Every scrap of evidence points to the fact that, eager for literary success, Kennedy was a painstaking craftsman.[16] In 1851 he revised and republished *Swallow Barn* with a manifest desire for the good opinion of posterity. He wrote in his journal: "I have determined to revise and correct the book, leaving out what was especially applicable to *the date* at which I wrote it." In a new preface he informed the reader that the book had been "carelessly consigned by the author to that oblivion which is common to books and men—out of sight, out of mind." This was nonsense. From the first he had exerted his influence to have a new edition printed, but his publisher had discouraged the plan as unlikely to be profitable.[17]

Two interrelated plots bind the episodes of *Swallow Barn* together: a lawsuit and a love suit. The first is an ancient and silly dispute between two planters, Frank Meriwether and Isaac Tracy, over a few worthless acres of land lying between their plantations, Swallow Barn and The Brakes. The second is a comic series of misunderstandings in which the boyish and impetuous Ned Hazard, Meriwether's brother-in-law and heir to Swallow Barn, tries to play Captain Absolute to the Virginia Lydia Languish, Bel Tracy. The feud over the boundary line is marked by many ludicrous episodes, a simple compromise being impossible since the affair has been magnified into a question of a Virginia gentleman's honor. Both litigants are "apt to be impatient of contradiction" and "always very touchy on the point of honor." The love affair goes forward haltingly owing to Ned Hazard's fumbling efforts to conform to the sentimental Bel's ideal of a lover "like the hero of a novel." The two threads of narrative are woven against a background of plantation life which is charming without being idealized. Both suits will only be happily resolved when, as the oracle Mammy Diana foresees, "Swallow Barn shall wed The Brakes."

But it is superb characterization rather than plot which gives *Swallow Barn* its continuing interest and charm. In the unhurried and graciously formal manner of this society, Kennedy introduces the reader to a cast of memorable Virginians as sharply realized as a dry-point etching: the country gentleman, Ned Hazard, characterized by the "half swagger with which he strikes his boot with his riding whip, or keeps at bay a beautiful spaniel"; the spinster of uncertain years, Prudence Meriwether, who manifests "a little too much girlishness, which betrays a suspicion of its opposite"; the two lawyers, Philly Wart and Taliaferro Hedges—the first canny, convivial, venerated for a lifetime of wise, if impromptu, justice, and the second raffish, slightly alcoholic, substituting for a thorough grounding in the law a lightning intuition concerning county juries. Kennedy plainly relished these last two characters, for without much reverence for the vocation of the law, he had boundless affection for its practitioners. In the character of Singleton Swansdown, still another lawyer who had forsaken his calling to write mawkish poetry, Kennedy satirized the sentimental tradition of the South at its most maudlin.

It is a safe surmise that in these characters Kennedy was working from living models, for, in the dedication to William Wirt, he remarked, "you may recognize, perhaps, some old friends, or, at least, some of their customary haunts." Wirt may have detected a resemblance to himself in Philly Wart, for there is a striking similarity in both name and character. In other cases it is possible to identify within close limits the living counterparts of the ménage at Swallow Barn. Lucretia Meriwether, the mistress of Swallow Barn, is reminiscent of Kennedy's great aunt, Mrs. Ferguson, who took pride in her home remedies for the ague.[18] The original of Mammy Diana was probably Mammy Lucy, an old Negress who, in Kennedy's boyhood, was famous for conjuring up interpretations of dreams. Kennedy mentioned her in a letter written from western Virginia when he was eighteen years old.[19]

Several characters were drawn from Kennedy's recollections of Baltimore school days. In 1825 he had written what he entitled an autobiographical sketch but what was actually a series of essays after the manner of the Theophrastian characters of the seventeenth century.[20] Four of these characterizations were incorporated into *Swallow Barn*. Kennedy's beloved teacher at Baltimore College, William Sinclair, was the model for the schoolmaster at Swallow Barn, Parson Chub. "He is a plump, rosy old gentleman, rather short and thick set, with the blood-vessels meandering over his face like rivulets,—a pair of prominent blue eyes, and a head of silky hair, not unlike the covering of a white spaniel. . . . His beard is grizzled with silver stubble, which the parson reaps about twice a week,—if the weather be fair." "I wrote the chapter describing him," Kennedy said later, "on the day after his death. The picture of the person and manner is entirely after the life."[21] The original of Rip Meriwether, the scapegrace son of the master of Swallow Barn, was a schoolmate of Kennedy's, Carruthers Swann, who had shipped from Baltimore as a cabin boy and was later lost at sea. Mr. and Mrs. Priestly, directors of the Baltimore academy which Kennedy attended, appear as Mr. and Mrs. Crab, teachers of Ned Hazard. Mrs. Coffey, mistress of Kennedy's dame school, became Barbara Winkle, supervisor of the "little infantry."

The prototype of Frank Meriwether, master of Swallow Barn, was undoubtedly Nancy Kennedy's brother, Philip Clayton Pendleton. Both model and fictional counterpart were Virginia lawyers and judges of the county court. Like Meriwether, Philip Pendleton was "a landed proprietor, with a good house and a host of servants." Guests were a necessity of life, and his house was open to everybody as freely almost as an inn. "But to see him when he has had the good fortune to pick up an intelligent, educated gentleman,—and particularly one who listens well!—a respectable, assentatious stranger!—All the better if he has been in the Legislature, or better still, if in Congress. Such a person caught within the purlieus of Swallow Barn, may set down one week's entertainment as certain—inevitable, and as many more as he likes—the more the merrier. He will know something of the quality of Meriwether's rhetoric before he is gone." Patriotic and provincial, inflexible in opinion, Philip Pendleton was, as Kennedy's biographer, Henry T. Tuckerman, described him, "a genuine specimen of the old school Virginia gentleman."[22] In short, Kennedy's beloved "Uncle Phil" was just such a man as Frank Meriwether of Swallow Barn.

> Meriwether is not much of a traveller. He has never been in New England, and very seldom beyond the confines of Virginia. He makes now and then a winter excursion to Richmond, which, I rather think, he considers as the centre of civilization; and towards autumn, it is his custom to journey over the mountain to the Springs, which he is obliged to do to avoid the unhealthy season in the tide-water region. But the upper country is not much to his taste, and would not be endured by him if it were not for the crowds that resort there for the same reason which operates upon him; and I may add,—though he would not

confess it—for the opportunity this concourse affords him for discussion of opinions.

Such a man as Frank Meriwether would naturally find it difficult to reach agreement with the master of The Brakes, Isaac Tracy, "a bad listener and a painful talker." Tracy is a cantankerous old Tory so absorbed in the boundary-line controversy that when he wins the case, he loses his zest for life.

Kennedy skillfully evoked the atmosphere of the plantation. He captured "the mellow, bland, and sunny luxuriance of her [Virginia's] old time society—its good fellowship, its hearty and constitutional *companionableness*, the thriftless gayety of the people, their dogged but amiable invincibility of opinion, and that overflowing hospitality which knew no ebb." What was so attractive in this civilization was its rural simplicity, a blend of rustic open-heartedness and naive parochialism which permeates this comic pastoral. Kennedy described his book as "in the mirthful mood," and the sustained high spirits light up the landscape of the novel, suffusing it with a genial warmth. The satiric tone is skillfully maintained, the author laughing at personal idiosyncracies without sarcasm and criticizing institutions without malice. The style is well adapted to the material—leisurely in pace, unobtrusively didactic, and on occasion brilliantly epigrammatic.

The revision of a description of Frank Meriwether, chosen from the interlineations in the final draft of the manuscript, reveals Kennedy's sureness of touch.

> In this temper, he has of late leaped into the mill pond of country affairs, keeping the peace as if he commanded a garrison, and administering justice like a cadi, notwithstanding his amiable republicanism.

This became in the final draft:

> In this temper, he has of late embarked upon the mill pond of country affairs, and notwithstanding his amiable and respectable republicanism, I am told he keeps the peace as if he commanded a garrison, and administers justice like a cadi.

The substitution of *embarked* for *leaped* is not only more appriate to Meriwether, who was inclined to look rather than leap, but the rearrangement reveals an eye for the subordination of ideas and an ear for the rhythms of the English sentence. In the revised edition of 1851, less tolerant of the tendencies of Virginia republicanism, Kennedy struck out "amiable and respectable"; he now found it "doctrinary."

Kennedy had a tendency to prefer the quaint word to the apt one. James Fenimore Cooper pointed this out when *Swallow Barn* first appeared: "Its faults are affectations of style and a want of interest, of which there is enough, however, to make us wish it had more, handled in the same clever manner. The writer has too great a command of language to abuse himself with hard words. Style should be, like the dress of a handsome woman, felt, but not perceived, and Mr. Kennedy has too much matter to attend to his manner, beyond the point that is necessary to illustrate the first. Au reste, it is unquestionably the work of one of our ablest men." [23]

William Wirt, whose taste in literature as in food inclined toward substance rather than sauce, found the style affected. He wrote to Dabney Carr on May 23, 1832:

> Pray have you seen a new work called 'Swallow Barn' which is dedicated *to me*. It is said to be by John P. Kennedy, a right merry young lawyer of this place. It is a *sort* of a novel, of which the scene is laid in Virginia—but it is a *non descript* sort of a novel—very little incident—& a great deal of what is called sketches of characters—It is said to be much puffed in Philadelphia—But it is too much like Paulding's conceited style—flippant & smart enough—but no deep and strong drawing or solemnising [?]—This is *entre nous*—for as I am complimented by the dedication, it wd. seem ungrateful in me to decry the work—but to you I say whatever comes uppermost.[24]

On the same day Wirt wrote to Kennedy:

> My Dear Sir:—If you should chance to know a certain Mark Littleton, author of "a righte merrie and conceited work," called "Swallow Barn," which is occupying all the attention that can be spared from politics, I would thank you to make my respects and acknowledgements to him for a handsome copy of the work, and the well-turned dedication with which he has complimented me. He might have chosen a patron more auspicious for himself, but no one with kinder and warmer feelings

and wishes for his success. The dedication proves his ability to give interest to trifles. With regard to the book itself, I have been so engaged as to have been able to make but little progress in it. But so far as I have read, it is full of gayety and goodness of heart, and the author trips it along, on "light fantastic toe," with all the imaginable ease and grace. The characters are well sketched and grouped, and the plan as well as the incidents are new and fresh so far as I have gone.

But I have read too little of it to play the critic on its merits. The object of this note is simply to convey my thanks to the author, without delay, for the present of the book and the honor of the dedication, and I trouble you with this agency, because of the *on dits* that the author is in the circle of your acquaintance. Good night.[25]

Swallow Barn abounds with memorable vignettes of plantation life—moonlight serenades by an old Negro minstrel, opossum-hunting by torchlight, Independence Day festivals, impromptu theatricals, planters carousing over their cups until dawn breaks through the shutters. Kennedy lingered over these descriptions of country amusements with the loving attention of a connoisseur. They could be savored as an exotic, but not regarded with unmixed praise. On the contrary, *Swallow Barn*, far from a nostalgic lament for a vanishing golden age, is permeated by a genial but nonetheless penetrating irony.

Kennedy shared the admiration of Virginians for their history and their splendid sons of the Revolution. But their homebred notions and pride in place seemed comic and their insularity dangerous. In 1825 Kennedy was warning against the tendency of Virginia to exalt state above nation. This exaggerated provincialism, he predicted, "will one day sever our bonds. When that unhappy crisis shall come Virginia, if I mistake not, will be seen in the van of those who foster the treason."[26] Kennedy's narrator, Mark Littleton, found the planters to be boon companions, but their self-sufficiency had made them indifferent, even contemptuous, of the outside world. And lurking about the plantation, on the fringes of this society, was a substratum of humanity that implicitly rebuked southern complacency. Loafers, tipplers, failures, they lounged at the crossroads, hating the rich planter, and occasionally daring to taunt him openly. When Littleton recorded their political discussions, the satire was heavy-handed

—rural buffoons with plodding minds parroting the empty shibboleths of state rights and nullification. A true gentleman lost caste if he even recognized their existence, but on occasion, as Ned Hazard believed, they must be taught a wholesome lesson by a pommeling with a planter's fists.

Although Kennedy did not wish to romanticize his materials, and insisted that his book was "a faithful picture of the people," he wanted to show the South in its best light. A hint of his intent is revealed in a letter from his publisher, Henry C. Carey, written in February, 1832. "If it [*Swallow Barn*] should produce such a feeling as you desire," Carey wrote, "you will have rendered a great service to the nation. Each portion of the Union looks with a feeling of dislike towards the other, when it requires only to know them better to see the admirable qualities in every portion. The Yankee dislikes the Virginian and the Virginian despises the Yankee, when a stranger would find good reason to admire both." [27]

There were aspects of Virginia society which Kennedy, on second thought, chose not to reveal. A scene involving Mark Littleton's grand uncle, Edward Hazard, a choleric old planter whose slave was so impolitic as to grin "saucily and good-humoredly" at his master's stupidity, is a case in point. "It is said, that my grand uncle looked up at the black with the most awful face he ever put on in his life. It was blood red with anger. But bethinking himself for a moment he remained silent, as if to subdue his temper. *He did not speak one word. If he had not constrained himself by this silence, he would probably have attacked his slave with his stick.*" Such realism is hardly to be expected to occur in the southern literature of the time, and especially in a domestic idyll like *Swallow Barn*. As a matter of fact, it does not occur. In the final revision before sending the manuscript off to the printer, Kennedy reconsidered and struck out the last two sentences.

Negro slavery is relegated to the background in *Swallow Barn*, chiefly because in the Valley it was less important than in the Tidewater. One chapter, "The Quarter," is devoted to the subject. The monologue of Frank Meriwether, a benevolent and generous master, "may serve to explain the feelings of an intelligent slave holder on this subject [Negro slavery]." The slaves, Meriwether believed, were incapable at present of freedom, and the typical Southerner, far from desiring to perpetuate the institution, favored a pragmatic "wise and beneficent consideration of the case as it exists." Historically, Meriwether argued, slavery was a temporary phase in human evolution. He entertained a vague notion of colonization and even hinted, half in earnest, at a scheme that would establish feudal ranks among the slaves whereby the state would recognize levels of merit. What Meriwether chiefly deplored was the fanaticism that inflamed moderates and practical men into doctrinaires. It was a regional problem and should be met by men who understood its complex domestic implications. The average slaveholder did not regard slavery as a good. The most that could be said for the institution was that, as matters stood, it was the best auxiliary within reach. At Swallow Barn the slaves held their master "in most affectionate reverence," and were "not only contented, but happy under his dominion."

The reception of *Swallow Barn* was all that a first novelist could desire. Edgar Allan Poe in the *Southern Literary Messenger* praised "the rich simplicity of diction—the manliness of tone —the admirable traits of Virginian manners, and the striking pictures of still life, to be found in Swallow Barn." [28] Alexander H. Everett, editor of the *North American Review*, advised the author to "withdraw his attention from other objects, and devote himself entirely to the elegant pursuits of polite literature, for which his taste and talent are so well adapted . . . ." [29] The *New England Magazine* remarked: "We could almost have sworn that Dean Swift had come alive again. . . . With ten times the talent of any but one or two of our best writers, there is scarcely anything in the literary way, that we deem the author incompetent to achieve." [30]

And it was the *New England Magazine* that noted the ironic tone which pervades the novel:

If we may hazard a conjecture, at variance with the opinions of the newspaper critics, we will say, that we think it was intended for a satire, a gentle satire on the pride, aristocratic feeling, and ignorance of a certain class, rather numerous in the South. The farther we read, the more strongly are we convinced that the author intended to "show up" the Virginians. His principal characters are humorously conceited, pompous, ignorant and dogmatic. He has succeeded admirably in showing them in a ridiculous light . . . . The gentlemen of Swallow Barn are the most ordinary, trifling, useless generation the world ever saw.[31]

This Yankee reviewer was, of course, gleefully overstating his case, but it is Kennedy's ironic tone which accounts for the novel's accurate portrayal of Virginia society. It was left for the generation of Thomas Nelson Page and those following him to write the elegy of this vanished civilization. For although *Swallow Barn* is the first important novel in the plantation tradition, it stands apart from the novels that come after it by virtue of its authenticity. Unlike the elegant mansions that later authors reared all over the South, Swallow Barn was spacious but hardly luxurious. A burdensome mortgage and other "gentlemanlike incumbrances" had been lifted only by a fortunate marriage; the old walnut door sagged on wornout hinges furrowing the floor in a quadrant; the massive wooden columns of the portico were split by the sun; and the slave quarters were rude hovels or unfinished log cabins. Kennedy had sought authenticity, and that is what he achieved; he is one of the pioneers in our literature in the use of local color. John H. B. Latrobe declared that "the distinguishing feature of Swallow Barn is its pure Americanism; and there are certain institutions, and modes of thought and feeling, which have never been so well described." James Kirke Paulding wrote Kennedy that he considered the book "a valuable addition to our little, very little, stock of really national literature." [32]

A half-century after the novel's appearance, John Esten Cooke, a novelist in the plantation tradition and the historian of Virginia, a native of Martinsburg who spent his boyhood among the scenes Kennedy described and knew at first hand many of the models for the portraits, declared *Swallow Barn* "the best picture of Virginia country life in literature." And as Vernon L. Parrington observed, it is well worth remembering by later generations who have forgotten how to live so genially.[33]

CHAPTER VI

The Novelist as Historian

JOHN KENNEDY had every reason to be encouraged in his career as author by the critical reception of *Swallow Barn*. Both James Fenimore Cooper and Washington Irving reported favorably on the book to its publisher, Henry C. Carey, and Edgar Allan Poe and James Kirke Paulding praised it in print. Applause rang agreeably in Kennedy's ears. "No man," he said later, "ever wrote a successful book without contemplating another. The frequent fillip to personal vanity which is given by the notice of the press, magnifying into matter of public importance the conceits of one's brain and rendering his thoughts a commodity in the market—these things are not unrelished by the modest craft,—but straightaway set the wits again at work to redouble the echo and its accompaniments." [1]

The literary tendencies of the time inclined Kennedy toward the historical romance, and his next two novels, *Horse-Shoe Robinson* (1835) and *Rob of the Bowl* (1838) were both in the prevailing genre. In perspective it appears that events conspired to popularize the historical romance in the United States during the 1820's and 1830's. With the rise of nationalism following the second war with Great Britain, a sentiment Kennedy enthusiastically shared, the historical romance was close to the mood of the public. It seemed a steppingstone to literary nationalism. American authors, unwilling apprentices to British masters, searched for a mode to express their individuality. A new form, relatively free from conventions, could be readily adapted to the needs of a raw country eager to experiment and neither blessed nor hampered by tradition. Also, the vogue of Walter Scott was at its height. In Baltimore John Kennedy, turning over in his mind the possibility of a career as man of letters, read and admired Scott's novels as they appeared, and he absorbed techniques which he would later incorporate into his own fiction. As for subject matter, if the new nation had no moldering ruins or shrines old in story, as Nathaniel Hawthorne lamented, it did have the Indians and the Revolution, certainly fit subjects for romance.

The historical novel in the United States dates from the publication of Cooper's *The Spy* in 1821. In the wake of his success, a multitude of imitators embarked on the literary seas, more often than not in vessels of less trustworthy structure than that of their acknowledged master. The publication of these native productions gathered momentum during the 1820's, reaching a climax in the year of the semicentennial, 1826. The impetus occasioned by the anniversary was recognized by Kennedy in the preface to *Horse-Shoe Robinson:* "An opinion had heretofore prevailed that the Revolution was too recent an affair for our story-telling craft to lay hands upon it. But this objection, ever since the fiftieth anniversary, has been nullified by common consent,—that being deemed the fair poetical limit which converts tradition into truth, and takes away all right of contradiction from a surviving actor in the scene."

In the preface Kennedy was careful to point out that he had been scrupulous to preserve the utmost historical accuracy in the narrative. More of an antiquary than Cooper, Kennedy took delight in searching the records for authentic detail. Yet in turning to the American past, he would be faithful not only to the surviving documents, "the dry timbers of a vast old edifice," but also to the spirit of the time, to the truth of the historical imagination. It was a theory of history that owed a debt to Walter Scott and Thomas Carlyle, both of whom Kennedy had read with profit.

> That which makes history the richest of philosophies and the most genial pursuit of humanity is the spirit that is breathed into it by the thoughts and feelings of former generations, inter-

preted in actions and incidents that disclose the passions, motives, and ambitions of men, and open to us a view of the actual life of our forefathers. When we contemplate the people of a past age employed in their own occupations, observe their habits and manners, comprehend their policy and their methods of pursuing it, our imagination is quick to clothe them with the flesh and blood of human brotherhood, and to bring them into full sympathy with our individual nature. History then becomes a world of living figures,—a theatre that presents to us a majestic drama, varied by alternate scenes of the grandest achievements and the most touching episodes of human existence.[2]

For the setting of *Horse-Shoe Robinson* Kennedy chose Virginia and the Carolinas during the closing years of the Revolution. Early in the war active fighting had been carried on largely in the North—Lexington, Bunker Hill, Saratoga, Monmouth, Princeton. As hostilities ground to a stalemate, the British began to look southward. Perhaps southern Tories would prove more belligerent than their northern brethren. The South was more sparsely settled and inaccessible to patriot reinforcements by land, yet there existed easily navigable sea routes for the invader. In the winter of 1778-1779 Savannah and Augusta fell to the British, and Georgia was again under the rule of a royal governor. On May 12, 1780, Charleston fell in one of the major defeats of the war, and, following Colonel Banastre Tarleton's victory at the Waxhaw on May 29, 1780, South Carolina was in British hands. Dispirited citizens, offered a choice between spoliation and taking an oath of allegiance to the King, pledged their loyalty to George III by the hundreds. Yet there were grounds for patriot hopes. Lines of communication, mainly along rivers, were long, outposts few and scattered, and Whigs numerous. At this moment in the "Tory Ascendency," *Horse-Shoe Robinson* opens.

The plot follows the conventional pattern of costume romance. Kennedy's heroine, Mildred Lindsay, is torn between love of the hero, Arthur Butler, a major in the Continental Army enjoying "a handsome fortune," and loyalty to her father, Philip Lindsay, "one of the most opulent and considerable gentlemen of the Old Dominion." The theme of lovers imperiled by war is introduced as Butler leaves for southern battlefields guided by the resourceful scout, Sergeant Galbraith or "Horse-Shoe" Robinson. The trip through Virginia and the Carolinas follows the familiar picaresque formula of the gentleman traveler and his doughty companion. The hero is hurried off stage through his capture by the Tories, and interest is focused on the comic ruses and ingenious devices of the titular hero as he schemes for the escape of Butler. All plans are foiled by a wily British officer, St. Jermyn, who, in disguise, is not only trying to persuade Philip Lindsay to advocate openly His Majesty's cause but is also lusting after Mildred. Unable to free Butler, Horse-Shoe skillfully guides Mildred through the lines to plead for her lover's life before Cornwallis. In counterpoint to this main theme is the subplot of a rustic maiden, Mary Musgrave, and her "patriotic" lover, John Ramsay. His fate (no surprise to the seasoned reader of romance) is heroic death in the service of Arthur Butler. The climax of the novel is a full-dress reconstruction of the Battle of King's Mountain. With a nice regard for poetic justice, Kennedy has Philip Lindsay pay for his Tory heresy by death from an American bullet, while Horse-Shoe dispatches the villain, St. Jermyn, on the field of glory.

Just as the structure of *Swallow Barn* owes a debt to Irving's *Bracebridge Hall*, so *Horse-Shoe Robinson* is broadly patterned after *The Spy*. Like Harvey Birch, Cooper's spy, Horse-Shoe Robinson is the fictional counterpart of an authentic hero of the Revolution drawn from the lower orders of society who plays out his part against a conventional love story of the gentry. Both books are set in 1780, and the action in each case is concerned with the guerrilla warfare of hard-riding bands of Tory renegades and Whig troopers. Similar scenes, such as a drumhead court martial of the hero in which strict military punctilio results in an unjust verdict, a rustic funeral, and woodland roistering of the soldiers, emphasize the parallel. Kennedy incorporated other devices effectively employed by Cooper: the escape and pursuit motif, the division of family loyalties, the overheard conversation, the celebrity traveling incognito, and the almost pendulum-like swing between broad comedy and stark tragedy. In each novel there is a memorable characterization of a comic old Negro retainer. And finally, Cooper's bluff, hearty Virginia campaigner,

Captain Jack Lawton, bears a remarkable resemblance to Horse-Shoe Robinson.

Although the structure of Kennedy's novel is derivative, it is the exuberant individualist Horse-Shoe himself, an epic original, who made the book a success on its appearance and who has kept it alive until the present day. Horse-Shoe, like Harvey Birch, could outwit the British by a clever disguise or an extemporaneous lie of heroic proportions. His earthy speech and malaprop humor set the novel apart from the deluge of insipid and hackneyed romances that flooded the country. An example is this explanation, which its hearer found neither "grammar, English, nor sense": "When I observed, just now that I couldn't be instigated, I meant to be comprehended as laying down a kind of general doctrine that I was a man not given to quarrels; but still, if I suspicioned a bamboozlement, which I am not far from at this present speaking, if it but come up to the conflagrating of only the tenth part of the wink of the eye, in a project to play me off, 'fore God, I confess myself to be as weak in the flesh as e'er a rumbunctious fellow you mought meet on the road."

Kennedy may have shared the faintly patronizing attitude of his imperious hero, Major Arthur Butler, toward the uncouth and undignified Horse-Shoe. He seems not to have fully appreciated the fact that it is the intrepid woodsman who brings the book alive. For months he considered calling the novel "Mildred Lindsay" after the heroine, and in at least one early plan Horse-Shoe was dropped.[3] Kennedy valued the bluff frontiersman as a dramatic foil to Butler and for his Falstaffian antics, which were taboo for a genteel hero of romance, while later generations find Butler a prig and admire the woodsman's practical democracy and his jaunty readiness to judge men on their merits.

In *Horse-Shoe Robinson* Kennedy was perhaps conscious of doing for the South what Cooper had done for the New York frontier and James Kirke Paulding for the Dutch Knickerbockers. The sections had begun to turn their attention to the untilled, though narrower, lands of local history. Revolutionary South Carolina was as yet untapped by the romancer. As described by Kennedy, it was a no-man's land where tightlipped yeomen changed the color of their coats simply to survive. This made for dramatic effectiveness, for the suspense engendered by the possible treachery of every man met on the highway enabled the author to create an atmosphere of constant tension. "The whole country," Horse-Shoe remarked, "was full of tories, and it wasn't safe to meet a man on the road: you couldn't tell whether he was friend or enemy." Walter Scott had achieved the same effect in his tales of border warfare.

Whig foresters bivouacking in the Carolina woodlands, moving silently in the flickering glare of campfires, provided materials ready-made for the romancer. The broad expanse of the South, its marshes, rice paddies, scrub forests, fields, and meadows, furnished natural fortresses for patriots who rallied to the guerrilla bands of Thomas Sumter, Francis Marion, and Andrew Pickens. Kennedy chronicled a war of sneak attacks and lightning onslaughts in which the fighting, especially when rival militia units met, often assumed the nature of a grudge feud—violent, bloody, and merciless.

The American romancers whose novels Kennedy read—Cooper, Paulding, Neal—all felt the need to be national, that is, to give expression to what they believed was noble in the American past and unique in the American character. Kennedy agreed, and as *Horse-Shoe Robinson* reveals, for him the great formative factor in the shaping of national character had been the Revolution. As early as his "Swiss Traveller" essays, written twenty years before *Horse-Shoe Robinson*, Kennedy had defined the cohesive force generated by the memory of the War for Independence. "In that remembrance is found a more agreeable substitute for the real existence of war, and the greatest stimulus to honorable action. 'My father fell, on board the Constitution,' would cry the tar of a future day, while he prepared to fight. The tear of memory would steal down his cheek, and his father's spirit would conduct the animated son to victory and triumph." Kennedy's own experience under arms at Bladensburg and North Point had confirmed this view. Thus in writing *Horse-Shoe Robinson* Kennedy saw himself as not unlike a latter-day epic bard singing of national wars and national glory.

He nevertheless rigorously checked the temptation to idealize his national heroes, a temptation few of his contemporaries could resist. When he introduced such men as General Francis Marion, "The Swamp Fox," he refused to draw them larger than life-size. He was less successful in his use of documentary evidence. In his notes for the novel he prepared a table of dates and actions relating to the war in the South from the fall of Savannah in 1778 until General Horatio Gates was named head of the Southern Army in June 1780. In plotting the narrative, he was careful to parallel his story with the historical record, but the history was only partially assimilated and tended to mire the sweep of the action. At the conclusion Kennedy's desire to relate all the threads of narrative necessary for fidelity to history played him false, for he had to introduce himself into the story and terminate with a rush. Perhaps Kennedy became bored with the book and was anxious to finish it, for in the final draft there was some indecision evident as to how loose ends were to be tied, and the manuscript itself showed signs of haste in composition.

Kennedy's special gifts led him to deviate from the traditional formula of historical romance. His style, reflecting sensitivity to sense impressions and inclining toward prolixity, was suited to rendering detail rather than to painting with broad strokes. He had in abundance what Henry James thought a peculiarly American trait, "a hungry passion for the picturesque." [4] Kennedy recognized the tendency in himself. "I have always had such a vivid relish for country scenery, such a keen perception of the beauty of landscape, that . . . for years afterward I could sketch pretty well, from memory alone, the scenes I had witnessed." [5] The opening chapter of *Horse-Shoe Robinson*, for example, was devoted to describing with Baedeker exactness the scenes and prospects of the South Garden in western Virginia, a lovely valley in the Blue Ridge Mountains which Kennedy had visited in 1831 and which he had chosen as the setting for Philip Lindsay's plantation, "The Dove Cote."

In the character of Philip Lindsay, Kennedy described a Virginia gentleman of a generation earlier than Frank Meriwether of *Swallow Barn*. It was a study in nostalgia, for Lindsay was the epitome "of a refined and polished civilization, which no after day in the history of this empire has yet surpassed—perhaps, not equalled." In the description of Lindsay's library, Kennedy may have had in mind his own library in his new home in Mount Vernon Place, and he allowed to obtrude his belief in gentility as the chief requisite of the good life.

> It was only in the library that evidence might be seen of large expense. Here the books were ranged from the floor to the ceiling, with scarcely an interval, except where a few choice paintings had found space, or the bust of some ancient worthy . . . .
> I have trespassed on the patience of my reader to give him a somewhat minute description of the Dove Cote, principally because I hope thereby to open his mind to a more adequate conception of the character of Philip Lindsay. By looking at a man in his own dwelling, and observing his domestic habits, I will venture to affirm, it shall scarcely in any instance fail to be true, that, if there be seen a tasteful arrangement of matters necessary to his comfort; if his household be well ordered, and his walks clean and well rolled, and his grassplots neat; and if there be no slovenly inattention to repairs, but thrift against waste, and plenty for all; and, if to these be added habits of early rising and comely attire—and, above all, if there be books, many books, well turned and carefully tended—that man is one to warm up at the coming of a gentleman; to open his doors to him; to take him to his heart, and to do him the kindnesses of life. He is a man to hate what is base, and to stand apart from the mass, as one who will not have his virtue tainted.

Horse-Shoe Robinson bears all the earmarks of having been written for popular success. Kennedy had thought of variations on the familiar themes, perhaps having his hero, Butler, killed in battle and then, in a series of letters, revealing an unconsummated marriage. But, on second thought, he decided, "I don't think I can afford to kill Butler." [6] Kennedy deliberately grouped the characters into rascally Tories and noble patriots, an indulgence which, while assuring his success in the American market, cost him the total failure of the English edition which the London publisher Richard Bentley brought out upon the recommendation of Washington Irving.[7]

Irving wrote Kennedy from New York that he had read the work "with great gusto." He predicted correctly that Horse-

Shoe would "be a decided favorite with the public." Poe wrote in the *Southern Literary Messenger:* "We feel little afraid of hazarding our critical reputation when we assert that [*Horse-Shoe Robinson*] will place Mr. Kennedy at once in the very first rank of American novelists." For once even North and South could agree, and both the *New England Magazine* and the *Southern Literary Journal* thought the novel the equal of, if not superior to, Cooper's works. The critic of the *Knickerbocker* thought it "an excellent novel, with a most uncouth name." And the *American Quarterly Review* used the appearance of the work to praise Kennedy's versatility: "The author of this work is as remarkable for the variety as for the extent of his talents. Before the appearance of *Swallow Barn* he was known as an able lawyer, an acute politician, and an accomplished speaker. Since, by the publication of *Swallow Barn* and *Horse-Shoe Robinson,* he has placed himself in the front rank of the literature of his country. He does everything with great apparent ease; at the bar, in a public assembly, or with the pen, he is equally at home." George S. Bryan, a congressman from Charleston who shared Kennedy's tastes in literature and politics, wrote: "The voice of fame is constantly sounding your name in my ears. The newspapers have taken possession of you and 'Kennedy' with Irving and Cooper round the period in which our national literary glory is celebrated." [8]

Henry C. Carey published a first edition of three thousand copies in June 1835, and a second edition of equal size was necessary by autumn. Kennedy's profits amounted to $1,700. The novel was dramatized by Clarence Dane and given twice in New York, in 1836 and 1841, and a second version by C. W. Tayleure was performed at the Holliday Street Theater in Baltimore in April 1856. Kennedy attended the opening and noted the play's reception in his journal: "A great crowd was there and greeted it with vehement applause. It is amazingly noisy; and full of battles —and amuses the gallery hugely." [9]

In the introduction to the revised edition of 1852, Kennedy detailed the events of his meeting with the original Horse-Shoe Robinson while in Pendleton District, South Carolina, in 1819.

He also disclosed that on its first appearance in 1835, the novel had been read to the old veteran, who vouched that "it is all true and right—in its right place—excepting about them women, which I disremember. That mought be true, too; but my memory is treacherous—I disremember." Kennedy was obviously delighted to be able to quote his hero's testimony, but it rather overstated the case for the novel's historical accuracy. In 1846 Kennedy had written to Rufus Griswold, who was then preparing his *Prose Writers of America:* "He [Robinson] communicated to me some interesting particulars of his participation in the war of the Revolution, which I have introduced almost verbatim from his own narrative into my work." Which particulars he did not specify. In a chronology of his life, however, undated but carried through 1822, Kennedy wrote for 1819: "That January and February in Pendleton . . . . Here I saw Horse-Shoe Robinson, spent a night with him at Colonel Trimmer's. He told me of his escape from Charleston and his capture of five Scotsmen in the Revolutionary War." Again, on February 7, 1830, he wrote in his journal: "Invited Warren R. Davis, M.C., to dine with me today. He is an old acquaintance made while I was in the Pendleton District in 1818 [sic]. I want to get the story of Horse-Shoe Robinson from him."

These facts suggest that Kennedy used the recollection of two incidents heard thirteen years before, narrated by an old campaigner reminiscing of forty years earlier still, as the nucleus for a costume romance. The two incidents mentioned are not an integral part of the plot and seem to have been introduced for their inherent interest. The factual content concerning Robinson probably went no further than the memory of the meeting, with perhaps the addition of hearsay evidence learned at some later date. The early sketches for the novel bear this out. A memorandum, "get a good name for Robinson's horse," reveals the anecdote concerning that animal, "Captain Peter Clinch," to be pure invention. Other hints such as "Horse-Shoe Robinson to be described as a man of great versatility" suggest that Kennedy was not bound by a slavish adherence to fact.[10]

By the time the novel appeared in 1835, the original Horse-Shoe Robinson had left South Carolina to make his home in

Alabama. The editor of the Tuscaloosa *Flag of the Union*, Alexander Beaufort Meek, discovered in 1837 that Robinson was living only twelve miles from Tuscaloosa. Early in 1838 he set out to interview the old soldier for the newspaper. Meek found Robinson "seated under his own vine and fig tree, with his children around him, and with the partner of his early toils and trials still continued to him, enjoying in peace and safety the rich rewards of that arduous struggle." The garrulous veteran related many anecdotes concerning his encounters with the "Tory Vagrants," several of which, Meek reported, "Kennedy had not recorded in his book." [11] Horse-Shoe told Meek that he was born in Virginia in 1759. He moved to South Carolina where, at the age of seventeen, he enlisted in the Continental Army. His Christian name, he explained, was not Galbraith, as it appeared in the novel, but James. Meek also understood Horse-Shoe to say that he had been promoted to the rank of captain, although the Revolutionary pension roll lists him as "private S. C. Continental Line . . . annual allowance $80." [12]

Meek was curious to know if Kennedy's novel accurately portrayed Robinson's adventures during the Revolutionary War. Horse-Shoe assured him that "there is a heap of truth in it, though the writer has mightily furnished it up." Horse-Shoe went on to say that "the names of Butler, Mildred Lindsay, Mary Musgrave, John Ramsay, Hugh Habershaw, 'Jim Curry' and almost all the other characters are real and not fictitious." This statement, however, is contradicted by early drafts of the novel which show frequent changes in the names. Also, John H. B. Latrobe recalled that "the names of many of the personages were changed." [13] In fact, the newspaper reports that drifted back were invariably based on hearsay. An example is the following article, which was copied from the Mobile *Examiner* and appeared in the Baltimore *American* on May 28, 1838.

> The Tuscaloosa papers announce the death of James Robinson known as "Horse-Shoe Robinson" and the hero of Kennedy's exciting novel of the same name. He was one of the most ardent of the humble heroes of the revolution, and his astonishing bravery in all sorts of perils, was the universal theme of those who knew him. A friend of our side had visited the vet-

eran, within two or three years back. He described the old man as cheerful and enthusiastic at the mention of the glorious deeds of the revolution, as when in youth he met the enemy arm to arm on the plains and swamps of South Carolina. He loved to recite the deeds of his early days, and his memory was a complete storehouse of the heroic gallantries of the partisan leaders of the south.

The old man, we believe, lived in South Carolina, at the time Kennedy was searching for his book. The latter of course frequently applied to Robinson for the events of his chequered life. Whether he refused to gratify the anxious novel maker we do not know. Certain it is, however, that he disliked Kennedy; and seemed to be very careless of being made the hero of a story, or that his hair breadth escapes should become the subject of wonder among the patrons of circulating libraries.

Robinson was a man of the firmest integrity and almost perfectly ignorant of the rudiments of the simplest education. He was highly esteemed by the better informed persons whom curiosity led to seek his acquaintance.

Professor Rhoda Coleman Ellison, who discovered the interview with A. B. Meek and who traced Horse-Shoe in the Revolutionary pension roll, has also established that his name was not Robinson but Robertson.[14] He lies buried at Romulus, Alabama. The inscription on his tombstone reads:

> Major James Robertson, a native of South Carolina, died April 26, 1838, aged 79 years, and was buried here. Well known as Horseshoe Robinson, he earned a just fame in the war for Independence, in which he was eminent in courage, patriotism and suffering. He lived fifty-six years with his worthy partner, useful and respected, and died in hopes of a blessed immortality. His children erect this monument as a tribute justly due a good husband, father, neighbor, patriot, and soldier.

Kennedy wrote *Horse-Shoe Robinson* to please the public; he wrote *Rob of the Bowl: A Legend of St. Inigoe's* to please himself. "I was aware," he told a friend, *Rob of the Bowl* "was not likely to be so popular as 'Horse-Shoe Robinson.' The tale is somewhat antiquated in date, required a somewhat antiquated phraseology, and a description of ancient manners—ancient, I mean, in our calendar. Still, I like it better than 'Horse-Shoe' first perhaps for the natural reason that it is the youngest born, and secondly, because it required more antiquarian labor in which by the way I take some pride." [15] The success of *Horse-Shoe Robinson* had encouraged him to begin a new novel at once. It would be "a tale partly grave and partly comic descriptive of the manners of the old society upon the Chesapeake, at a period before the establishment of the government when the people still retained the subordination and respect of the old system of things before the revolution." [16] His interest in colonial Maryland was stimulated by an excursion in May 1836 to the site of the state's first capital, St. Mary's City, at the southern tip of the Western Shore. There he traced with an antiquary's delight the scattered and almost obliterated remains of the ancient town. From the inhabitants he heard legendary accounts of the state buildings, and these he seems to have followed carefully in his narrative.[17]

Returning to his home in Baltimore, Kennedy resolved to continue his investigations among the provincial records at Annapolis. These archives were in a state of deplorable neglect, having been left to mildew and rot in damp cellars and unfrequented cocklofts. Kennedy was assisted by the state librarian, David Ridgely, who had been directed by the Maryland Assembly in 1835 to search the various buildings for documents connected with the history of the colony. Ridgely rummaged through forgotten closets and garrets and pried into the recesses of the chancery, the treasury office, and the council chamber. From moldy boxes he uncovered council journals bearing dates as early as 1666, only to see them crumble at the touch. Among the documents Kennedy found one, a journal of the council from 1677 until 1686, which ignited his imagination and determined the locale and period of *Rob of the Bowl*.

> The record was complete [Kennedy said], neatly written in the peculiar manuscript character of that age, so difficult for a modern reader to decipher. Its queer old-fashioned spelling suggested the idea that our ancestors considered both consonants and vowels too weak to stand alone, and that therefore they doubled them as often as they could; and there was such an actual identification of its antiquity in its exterior aspect as well as in its forms of speech, that, when I have sat poring over it alone at midnight in my study, as I have often done, I have turned my eye over my shoulder, expecting to see the apparition of Master

John Llewellin—who subscribes his name with a very energetic flourish as Clerk of the Council—standing beside me in grave-colored doublet and trunk-hose, with a starched ruff, a wide-awake hat drawn over his brow, and a short black feather falling among the locks of his dark hair towards his back.[18]

Kennedy removed these records from Annapolis to Baltimore to study while writing *Rob of the Bowl,* and over the years (a familiar episode in the chronicles of book-borrowing and lending) he neglected to return them. At his death in 1870, the volumes passed to his wife, Elizabeth, and at her death in 1889 to her sister, Martha Gray. Meanwhile, in 1883 the Maryland Historical Society published the first volume of the archives of the state. More volumes appeared, but a hiatus remained from 1677 until 1686 for which the editors naturally could not account. They strove to bridge the gap by printing copies of papers belonging to that time preserved in the English Public Record Office. At Martha Gray's death in 1895, the original council records were discovered in her library. The executors of Kennedy's estate presented the records to the Historical Society, and subsequently they appeared as volumes fifteen and seventeen of the *Archives of Maryland.*[19]

Kennedy insisted that *Rob of the Bowl* was an authentic account of life in colonial Maryland. "Upon this task," he told the anthologist Rufus Griswold, "I bestowed a great labor, designing to illustrate in it a more attractive portion of the early history of Maryland."[20] Ordinarily, such a claim by an early American historical novelist could be largely discounted. During the 1820's and 1830's authors frequently assured their readers that their novels were not mere fancy but the product of painstaking research into original documents. Such scholarly trappings were intended to give an aura of reality to a genre often woefully lacking that indispensable ingredient. And perhaps these authors hoped that by offering their wares as a means of inculcating patriotism, they would disarm critics who viewed the novel, like the stage, with suspicion.

Kennedy, however, was not employing a convention in his claim for the historical accuracy of *Rob of the Bowl.* Two decades after the novel's publication, he observed: "I fear the world will hardly credit me in saying it has as much history as it has invention." The draft of a preface, prepared for the revised edition of 1852 but inadvertently omitted, is more explicit:

> I think I may claim for my work, notwithstanding its air of romance, that it is as yet the only sketch which has given a picture of the events of that time. It might amuse the reader if I were to open to his inspection the large groundwork of actual history upon which this superstructure is built. . . . It is sufficient for me to say that the vexations to which Charles Lord Baltimore—a most worthy and exemplary gentleman, and a most conscientious and excellent governor—was exposed in the course of a long and difficult administration, are as faithfully developed in this romance as they could be in any history I might write, that the principal personages who surround him in that trial are, for the most part, real actors in the events in connection with which they are presented, and that the picture I have given of the time, manners, temper, and the purposes of those who figure in it, making due allowance for the necessary privilege of romance, is a faithful embodiment of which I am conscious no more lively or truthful representation can be given than through the medium of fiction. Indeed, I would say that in this dramatic form of exposition, when well accomplished, we have the highest and best instrumentality for painting the truth.[21]

The works of Kennedy's contemporaries occasionally reveal a wide acquaintance with the American past—Cooper's *Lionel Lincoln*, for example—but none of Kennedy's predecessors wrote with the scrupulous fidelity to the surviving documents that marks *Rob of the Bowl*. For this reason it is a landmark in the development of the American historical novel. Such research, unique in Kennedy's time, has become today an accepted part of the craftsmanship of the historical novelist.

From his study of the council records, Kennedy chose the autumn of 1681 for the setting of *Rob of the Bowl*. He pieced together from the fragmentary evidence the shadowy outline of a turbulent era in the history of the province. Council proceedings, commissions, warrants, and depositions disclosed the tale of an abortive rebellion of Protestant settlers in Charles County against the Catholic proprietary at St. Mary's City. Captain Josias Fendall was popularly believed to be the ringleader, and Kennedy found abundant evidence to substantiate the charge. The bare and unadorned chronicles were woven by Kennedy into his narrative and served as a framework to fashion out a costume romance.

Fendall, a Protestant, lived on his plantation west of St. Mary's in Charles County, at that time the Maryland frontier. In 1681 he was not unknown to Maryland history, having served as governor of the province from 1657 to 1660. He apparently fancied himself a New World Cromwell, for he did his best to stir up disaffection, and at the Restoration he was ordered banished and his goods confiscated. Later he was pardoned and his estate restored, but he was forbidden to hold public office in the province. This much of Fendall's biography Kennedy probably got from *An Historical View of the Government of Maryland*, which had been published in 1831 by his Baltimore friend and fellow attorney, John V. L. McMahon.[22] The council proceedings contained the rest of the story.

In 1678 the people of Charles County insisted on electing Fendall to the assembly, a post he appears to have busied himself to obtain, but the governor and council sent word he would not be seated. By the spring of 1679, Fendall could no longer keep silent in the face of what he considered his persecution by Lord Baltimore. The echoes of plot and counterplot in England reached Maryland, and rumors that King and Parliament were at war revived Fendall's ambitions. Word reached St. Mary's that he was telling everyone within earshot that he would rally thirty or forty men and send Lord Baltimore packing home to England. Ordered to appear before the council to answer to these "false malitious and scandalous reports," Fendall prudently took thought and hastened to "willfully abscond himself." [23]

In 1681, the year of *Rob of the Bowl*, Fendall turned up again, this time charging that the Catholics and the Indians were conspiring to wipe out the Protestants. The massacre of five men and a woman at St. Mary's was pointed to as evidence that Lord Baltimore's policy toward the Indians was inadequate. Informants hastened to tell Lord Baltimore that Fendall had denounced him as a traitor. Moreover, Fendall had told the people that they were fools to pay taxes to fill the proprietary's pockets. Fendall denied these charges in July 1681, but he was promptly put under guard at St. Mary's. As more reports reached Lord Baltimore, he tightened Fendall's guard and forbade anyone to talk with him except by special order. In November 1681 Fendall was found guilty and fined 40,000 pounds of tobacco. He was ordered imprisoned until the fine was paid and then banished.[24]

While Fendall was on trial, further excitement was generated by rumors that the Protestants on the frontier would try to rescue him. A raid on the jail was planned by George Godfrey, an officer in the troop of Captain Randolph Brandt of Charles County. Brandt, a Catholic, informed Lord Baltimore of the plot. Godfrey was tried and found guilty of attempting to overthrow the government and was condemned to death, a sentence later commuted to life imprisonment.[25]

Another resident of Charles County was Colonel John Coode, a choleric, hard-drinking disturber of the peace who was destined to figure prominently in the rebellion of 1689. The council journal contained colorful evidence of his carousing and his salty vocabulary. At the time of Fendall's trial, Coode was brought before the provincial court on charges of blasphemy but was acquitted. Kennedy linked Coode with Fendall and Godfrey and, to emphasize the religious rivalry, introduced the Reverend John Yeo, a clergyman of the Church of England. From McMahon's history Kennedy learned that Yeo had caused Lord Baltimore trouble in England by writing to the Archbishop of Canterbury that the province was "a Sodom of uncleanness, and a pest house of iniquity." [26]

Having cast the villains in his provincial drama, Kennedy found his heroes among the members of the government at St. Mary's. Lord Baltimore himself plays a prominent role in the narrative. Colonists who figure only as names in the records of the time are brought convincingly to life in the novel. One of these is Colonel George Talbot, nephew of the proprietary, governor in his absence, and notorious in Maryland annals for the murder of the collector of the port of St. Mary's, Christopher Rousby.

> His frame was tall, athletic, and graceful; his eye hawk-like, and his features prominent and handsome, at the same time indicative of quick temper and rash resolve. . . . This gentleman was a zealous Catholic, and an ardent personal friend of his

kinsman, the Proprietary, whose cause he advocated with that peremptory and, most unusually, impolitic determination which his imperious nature prompted, and which served to draw upon him the peculiar hatred of Fendall and Coode, and their partisans. He was thus, although a sincere, it may be imagined, an indiscreet adviser in state affairs, little qualified to subdue or allay that jealous spirit of proscription which, from the epoch of the Protectorate down to this date [1681], had been growing more intractable in the province.

William Digges, Nicholas Sewall, and Henry Darnall, members of the council and intimates of the proprietary, are briefly characterized. The names of Kennedy's Indians, Jackanapes and Tequassion, are authentic, as is "John Rye the miller at My Lords Mill."[27]

In addition to the chief incidents of Fendall's rebellion, minor events from the record acted as a catalyst on Kennedy's imagination. For example, in November 1681 one of the colonists, a tailor named Edward Abbot, was found guilty by the provincial court of uttering "divers false and mutinous and seditious speeches." Abbot found this a sobering experience and humbly begged for pardon, offering as an excuse that "your Petitioner at the time of the words spoken was soe much in drink, that your Petitioner did not remember any thing either what was done or spoken at the time." Lord Baltimore granted the request of that "poore distressed and sorrowfull penitent Petitioner." The incident so amused Kennedy that he enrolled Abbot as a corporal in George Godfrey's troop, made him a scapegoat in the collapse of the plot to release Fendall, and introduced the petition verbatim at the conclusion of the novel.[28]

Kennedy incorporated a second minor episode almost without change. On January 28, 1681, Launcelott Sakell, a traveler from Albany, arrived at St. Mary's in the company of Clause Debore, a "Dutch Doctor," and alarmed the citizens with a tale of northern Indians who were planning to come south on a raid. The travelers were eventually called before the proprietary to tell their story. Kennedy employed the threatened Indian attack to forward his plot and used the Dutch Doctor as the prototype for a fully developed comic characterization.[29]

Even apparently insignificant details from the council journals did not escape Kennedy. The governor, the records reveal, had trouble finding a dependable man to operate the ferry across the Patuxent River. Taking the hint, Kennedy had a character exclaim: "I doubt if I have any chance to get a cast over the ferry to-night. Simon, the boat keeper, is not often sober at this hour: and if he was, a crustier churl—the devil warm his pillow—doesn't live 'twixt this and the old world."

An exchange of letters between Sir Henry Chicheley, deputy governor of Virginia, and Lord Baltimore finds a place in the story. The dwellings of the time, "Cornwaley's Cross," "Notley Hall," "Rose Croft," and the proprietary's house at Mattapany are landmarks in the landscape of the novel.[30]

For his denouement Kennedy needed a single event to fuse the strands of history convincingly together and to bring into bold relief the religious antagonism inherent in Fendall's rebellion. Kennedy found the answer among the records in a "lycense for prize playing." A trial by combat was ideal for his purposes. He had a Catholic challenge a Protestant, assembled a partisan crowd in a savage mood, and used the incident as a diversionary movement for Godfrey in his attempt to release Fendall. Kennedy found the following document in the council journal:

Lycense for prize playing

Maryland SS   By the Councill

Lycense is hereby given to John Beare and Richard Land, to play a prize at the severall weapons belonging to the noble science (such as shall be agreed on by them) publickly at such place in or neere St. Maries City, as they shall for this day appoint, provided that noe fowle play be used nor any riott or disturbance, tending to the breach of his Lsps. peace be by them or any of their associates thereupon offered. Dated at the Councill Chamber at the City of St. Maries this second day of October 1685:

Signed p ordr [31]
J Llewellin Cl Consil

Kennedy altered the date and the names of the players, but otherwise the passage was incorporated into the novel with only minor changes:

Order of Council

License given to Stark Whittle and Sergeant Traverse to play a prize at the several weapons belonging to the Noble Science (such as shall be agreed on by them) publickly at such place in or near St. Marie's City, as they shall for this day appoint: provided that no foul play be used, nor any riott or disturbance tending to the breach of his Lordship's peace, be by them or any of their associates thereupon offered. Dated at his Lordship's mansion, in the City of St. Marie's, this 9th day of October, Anno Domini, 1681.

J. Llewellin, Clerk [32]

In addition to the documentary evidence Kennedy found in the archives, he drew on a fund of traditional lore and local history with which he had been familiar since childhood: bloodspots on the floor of a house in Denton, Maryland, that came and went with the tide; the common belief that buccaneers had once frequented the Chesapeake; and, finally, one Billy of the Bowl. "This worthy," Kennedy wrote in some early notes for the novel, "flourished during the Revolutionary War and was connected with some exploit of capturing a small tender which got aground somewhere along the bay shore. I shall turn him to some account by representing a personage under the same nickname who shall move about in his wooden trencher with short crutches." [33] With poetic license Kennedy rechristened him Rob of the Bowl and removed him a century in time to the days of the cavaliers.

The completed novel was the product of a rich background of reading, research, and folklore. While vacationing in Virginia in July 1838, Kennedy began to write. "I make good from ten to twelve pages of Rob every day," he wrote to Elizabeth, "and work very much to my satisfaction." Unlike his earlier works, which were painstakingly revised, *Rob of the Bowl* was, as John H. B. Latrobe remarked, "struck off at the heat." "My book wore the heart out of me," Kennedy told Philip Pendleton, "in a bloody labor of forty days and forty nights, during which I sweated as never did Jonah in the whale's belly." [34]

Yet *Rob of the Bowl* contains, as Kennedy observed, as much fiction as history. The novel employs all the time-tested ingredients of swashbuckling romance: a grotesque and gnarled cripple inhabiting a haunted chapel with a toothless crone; a bloodthirsty buccaneer at the head of a crew of cutthroat freebooters; the inevitable dashing hero, Albert Verheyden, with a "cloud upon his birth," in love with, and beloved by, a beautiful heroine, Blanche Warden; and droll and eccentric commoners cavorting in raucous tavern scenes.

Much of the action, other than the narrative of Fendall's rebellion, borders on melodrama. A pirate, Captain Richard Cocklescraft, while engaged in smuggling with Rob of the Bowl, falls in love with Blanche Warden, daughter of the collector of the port of St. Mary's. In carrying out a plot to abduct Blanche, Cocklescraft first fights a duel with Albert Verheyden, secretary to Lord Baltimore, then murders a fisherman in cold blood. Cocklescraft is betrayed by Rob, who has discovered that Albert is the son whom he had deserted years before. The pirate revenges himself by killing Rob and, in violation of the code of romance, escapes scot free. Albert and Blanche fall into each other's arms, and Rob's booty is bequeathed to Albert, who justifies the acceptance of the rather tainted profits of smuggling by "some most liberal appropriations to charitable uses."

Kennedy employed his knowledge of Elizabethan drama for the tavern scenes. Dame Dorothy Weasel, the termagant hostess of The Crow and Archer, is a New World Mistress Quickly, and Captain Dauntrees is, as John Latrobe observed, "a sort of melting together of Harry Percy and fat Jack."[35] Latrobe might have added that Kennedy's debt to Shakespeare extended to the novel's structure, for the alternation of scenes involving historical personages with scenes of low comedy derived from *Henry IV*. Kennedy also followed Shakespeare's lead in making the highjinks of his tavern loungers a deft parody of the more pretentious deliberations of their betters. In at least one scene in the novel, the debt was explicit:

> "A dark road, John! It is a long time, I trow, since there has been a dark road for your night rides, with that nose shining like a lighted link a half score paces around thee. It was somewhat deadened last September, I allow, when you had the marsh ague, and the doctor fed you for a week on gruel—but it has

waxed lately as bright as ever. I wish I could buckle it to my head-strap until tomorrow morning."

A burst of laughter, at this sally, which rang through the hall, testified the effect of the falconer's wit and brought the groom to his feet.

" 'Sblood, you grinning fools!" he ejaculated, "haven't you heard Derrick's joke a thousand times before, that you must toss up your scurvy ha-haws at it, as if it was new! He stole it—as the whole hundred knows—from the fat captain, old Dauntrees in the fort there; who would have got it back upon hue and cry, if it had been his own;—but the truth is, the Captain filched it from a play-book. . . ."

"It is a joke that burns fresh every night," replied Derrick; "a thing to make light of."

The allusion is, of course, to Falstaff's comic apostrophe to Bardolph's nose in part one of *Henry IV*. And as this passage illustrates, Kennedy dared to adopt the archaic speech of the great dramas. Although this fondness for the literary colloquial at times seemed bookish and too consciously studied, still his scene was laid in 1681 and he could plead historical justification for the practice.

Kennedy smoothly blended fact and fiction to create a distinctive work in what V. L. Parrington called "the vein of the cavalier romantic." [36] *Rob of the Bowl* has a skillfully wrought unity of tone, a tone wistful and musing, like an antiquary lingering over the past for its own sake without feeling the necessity to point a moral or adorn a tale. Kennedy chose to subdue the violence inherent in his materials and deliberately pitched the novel in a minor key, preferring the leisurely creation of a mood. The vale of old St. Mary's was created in the romantic, muted shades reminiscent of the paintings of the Hudson River School. In the past it was not the violence that attracted Kennedy but the evanescence, the fleeting sadness of a time long gone.

It was in the handling of tone, however, that Kennedy was least true to his materials. In turning to the American past, he had hoped to weave a web of imaginative construction from his sources which would be, as he said in the preface, at once "lively and truthful." The council journals he examined revealed numerous instances of talebearing and charges of intolerance, and in such an atmosphere, fantastic rumors found easy credence. Yet

Rob of the Bowl contains no hint of the tensions of a wilderness community, unnerved by Indian attacks and inflamed to bloody reprisals. Kennedy's romance is picturesque but sentimental. He diluted the clash and struggle of the period into melodrama, and what remains is a charming but idealized chapter of Maryland's colonial past.

Rob of the Bowl was not a popular success. Lea and Blanchard of Philadelphia printed an edition of 4,000 copies for which they agreed to pay Kennedy $1,850, but the novel sold slowly.[37] George S. Bryan, Kennedy's Charleston friend, noted the reason for public apathy: "I read it myself with great satisfaction. But I am not a *test* of the average of readers. . . . I do not think that the story is as direct, rapid and concentrated as the popular appetite demands." [38]

In 1861 Bryan re-read the novel and came to a different conclusion: "It is only now that I appreciate 'Rob.' It is in my esteem your work of greatest genius—the purest *creation*." [39] Later critics who have given the novel the careful reading it deserves tend to agree with Bryan's revised estimate. Parrington thought *Rob of the Bowl* Kennedy's "best work" and "one of the most finished and delightful of our earlier romances," and Alexander Cowie called it a "minor classic" of its kind.[40]

Rob of the Bowl was Kennedy's closest achievement to fusing history and fiction, and, in retrospect, it appears the end product of a form he had been gradually evolving. He wished to fuse the techniques of the historical romance with native materials to contribute toward a distinctly national literature. He delighted in the American past, relished the American character, and was optimistic about the American future. Yet the nationalism of his novels is pervasive without being blatant. Like Irving, Kennedy was anxious to conciliate England, and he never suffered from the anglophobia that infected such writers as James Kirke Paulding and John Neal. Rather his novels were a manifestation of a growing self-assurance and a harbinger of a true cultural nationalism.

Although solidly grounded in the English classics, Kennedy seems to have left behind the imitative qualities of *The Red Book* in favor of obeying his own highest instincts as a literary craftsman. On his travels to the West he jotted down in a notebook the extravagant colloquialisms he heard from the settlers, and contemporary reviewers testified that his transcript of frontier speech was accurate.[41] He did not disdain in his own prose the native flavor of such words as *calculate, venturesome,* and *comer,* and only the *New England Magazine* rebuked him for these "Americanisms." [42]

Historical romance as he defined and practiced it was not frivolous amusement but had the exalted destiny of creating a national mythology. "Our literature," Kennedy told Rufus Griswold in 1851, "in the lifetime of the present generation, has grown to a maturity which has given it a distinctive and honorable place in that aggregate which forms national character." [43] Kennedy took an inoffensive pride in the contribution his books made to this emerging national character.

But Kennedy's intention in his work remains a matter of conjecture, for among his scattered references to the art of writing, no clearly articulated theory emerges. He seldom read literary criticism and had a profound contempt for professional critics. "It is a critic's privilege to show his spleen," he once wrote, "and almost his nature to be personally offensive. I can make all allowance for his indulgence of a reasonable amount of ill-nature, and set it down to the constitution or professional irritability of his class." [44] It is only by his occasional comments to other writers or by his own practice that it is possible to infer his method and intention. In a letter to his younger brother, Philip, written to encourage him in a literary career, Kennedy voiced his own predilections.

> I object to your stopping, in the midst of a grave argument, and laying down your pen and then cutting a few somersets on the carpet and afterwards writing them down—as somersets can be written—in the hiatus which this freak produces. . . .
>
> I have another remark to make in regard to your style. It is too distressingly *intense*. What new caprice has taken hold of you? You formerly wrote in a fine, clear, transparent style that was particularly good—but recently, you have so bedeviled and bemystified and transcendentalized your style with such cracking of heart strings, and subjectivity of emotion and such permutation into metaphysical millstorms, and are in such evident

tortures from unnatural retention of great walloping words to deliver them, that I sometimes don't know you. Pray write like PPK and let Walter Savage Landor and DeQuincey go their own gate without you at their heels.[45]

"A fine, clear, transparent style" would serve as an accurate description of Kennedy's own prose. In some of his later propagandist writing he could rouse himself to a fever pitch of intensity, but in belles lettres his style was graceful rather than powerful, transparent rather than memorable. With much contemporary writing he was plainly out of sympathy. In 1854 he wrote to George S. Bryan:

> We have so much *intensification* of late, such gushing emotions in such excruciating words, such a distillation of wonderful quintessences in such incomprehensible alembics of thought, and such a rattle and roar of poetical locomotives, that the man who will recall the art back to the domain of common sense, and restore the human heart to its old place in the human economy, and render it, once more an honest and intelligible viscus, will be, I think, entitled to a general vote of thanks, and, if he gets his desserts, be made Vice-President, at least, in the Republic of letters.[46]

The field that Kennedy marked out for himself and which was exactly suited to his talents, urbane and witty studies of manners and character, was a narrow one, yet his achievement within these self-imposed limits was of the first order. At its best, his prose was unrivaled for sustained beauty even by the man with whom he was so often compared, Washington Irving. Kennedy liked to philosophize in an ironic vein which never soured into cynicism, yet he lacked profundity and seldom plumbed the depths of the situations he developed. His novels, as James Russell Lowell remarked, "attempt no solution of the problem of the Infinite." [47] Kennedy moved skillfully over the surface of the limited ground he surveyed. He had a strain of picaresque realism, although it was not as vigorous as Simms's, and when he attempted the pathetic, as in the story of Abe and his slave mother in *Swallow Barn*, he bordered dangerously on bathos. While his sympathies were broad and he loved to picture himself as an amused and reflective observer of the human comedy, the philosophic content of his work was slight. The homely wisdom and mother wit of Horse-Shoe, while oracularly delivered, were, after all, only maxims rephrased in the jargon of the frontier.

Kennedy remained loyal to the conservative party in literature as in politics. His art, like his life, bore the hallmarks of gentle breeding—taste, restraint, sensitivity. He chose for the standard of his personal life the gentlemanly ideal, and his literary life partook of the same quality. James Russell Lowell, when he was editing the *Atlantic Monthly*, once acknowledged the receipt of an article from Kennedy with the words: "Forgive me for making you the victim of a confidence, but (apart from all the considerations of intrinsic merit) it is so seldom that the editor of an American Magazine has the luck to meet with a contributor who writes altogether like a gentleman, that such an event gives him a particular pleasure. There is so much cleverness and so little *style!*" [48]

Kennedy would have considered this the highest praise. Yet his devotion to the gentlemanly ideal should not be mistaken for that combination of timidity and conformity which came in time to be labeled contemptuously the Genteel Tradition. Kennedy's style was thoroughly masculine, modeled on the vigorous, racy idiom of the Elizabethans but tempered by the grace and fluency of the Augustans. His *Swallow Barn* inaugurated a tradition in American literature and is a classic of its kind, and none of his novels is without the qualities of charm and narrative interest. At a period when much of American fiction was vitiated by crudity and sentimentality, Kennedy enriched it with a finer sensitivity and taste than most of his contemporaries could command.

CHAPTER VII

"A Man of All Work"

THE FACT that John Kennedy had, after a fashion, found his place in the literary world did not mean that he had abandoned the world of politics. During the years following his marriage to Elizabeth Gray in 1829, years devoted to writing and to practicing law, he had continued to be a close observer of national affairs. Politics, after all, was what really mattered. Law he practiced diligently and successfully, but he was discovering that familiarity did not make it more agreeable. Of his profession he remarked with unusual cynicism: "I cannot say I have much respect for the law.... Our lawyers for the most part make the laws, and lawyers have no respect for justice. Our laws are policies—they minister to human passion and interest."¹ Writing he enjoyed, but compared with politics it was a graceful accomplishment, an "idle trade." Kennedy praised Henry Clay as "the man of *action*—eminent for his wisdom in that—and not the man of the pen— By the by, the best sort of man, after all, for posterity."² Politics had its distasteful side, truckling to the electorate and hobnobbing with connivers and contrivers, but it was the responsibility of a gentleman to take the lead in public affairs.

In order to trace Kennedy's continuing interest in politics, it is necessary to turn back to October 1829, the same month he began to write *Swallow Barn*. October 5, election day in Baltimore, was unusually quiet. There was none of the frenzy which marked the contest for the Presidency a year earlier when the city had cast triumphantly for Andrew Jackson. Then the country survived one of its periodic political upheavals, the Virginia Dynasty and the Secretarial Succession were routed, and Old Hickory was firmly ensconced in the White House. The new administration had been in office since March, and Kennedy was content. He found it eminently sound and conservative. So he rose early on October 5, 1829, to go to the polling place to vote the Jackson ticket. Suffering with a cold, he spent the remainder of the day indoors at the new home to which he had brought his bride of eight months. His spirits rose toward evening as the returns of the election made it clear that the Jackson ticket had carried Baltimore by large majorities. The day had been tranquil and unhurried, given up to reading and meditation, the kind of day John Kennedy thoroughly enjoyed. To a man inclined toward introspection, a man with a sense of the significance of his own actions, the day seemed an appropriate one on which to begin a journal. "I am this day," Kennedy noted with satisfaction, "eight months married, and one week in my own house in Charles Street, which I have just finished."

It was a moment of profound complacency, a moment to linger over and to savor. John Kennedy's life was falling into a predictable routine which would never stale. A man's life, he believed, should possess the order and symmetry of a Greek temple. This first entry in a journal which would run eventually to thirty-five volumes established a pattern; the coolly objective chronicle written with effortless fluency, the pen seldom pausing to revise or delete, the handwriting crisp and scrupulously legible, suggesting a temperament both systematic and deliberate. To Poe, who presumed to know much of such matters, Kennedy's handwriting was marked by "clearness, boldness, and precision" and betokened a "love of the elegant without effeminacy." [3]

If John Kennedy, therefore, in beginning his journal that autumn of 1829, sensed that his life had at last reached a point of equilibrium, he could find ample assurance in the drift of political events. The Jackson victory, he believed, augured well for the business community. The General was a wealthy Tennessee cotton planter who was believed friendly to creditor rather than to debtor interests. Some years earlier he had written a letter committing himself to a "judicious" tariff,[4] an ambiguous phrase which Kennedy interpreted as meaning a tariff for protection and not merely for revenue. Jackson's military career had identified him in the popular mind with expansionist and nationalist doctrines and to this image Kennedy warmly responded. And Kennedy had a personal cause for rejoicing. In his race for a seat in Congress in 1826, he had declared himself a Jackson man. Perhaps now the administration would recall him from political exile and assuage the stinging memory of that overwhelming defeat. His confidence in Jackson was so complete that he grew impatient with the opposition: "I wish the anti-Jackson party would meet and formally dissolve. It would save us a great deal of trouble and release us from the tyranny of the mob which under the late excitements and the undue importance which has been given to popular opinion has grown haughty and insolent." [5]

Kennedy's enthusiasm for Jackson failed to survive the Maysville Veto in the spring of 1830. This pronouncement ("the most absurd paper I have read") [6] struck at government financing of internal improvements by refusing to underwrite a turnpike within the borders of Kentucky. Maryland had profited from government-financed projects like the National Road, which stretched from Cumberland on the shores of the Potomac to Wheeling on the Ohio, and Kennedy had found espousing internal improvements a steppingstone to popularity ever since his first term in the Maryland House of Delegates. By backing the Potomac Canal Company in 1823, he had staked his personal popularity on what he considered to be the long-term welfare of Baltimore. He had lost the gamble then, and he had waited six years for the times to prove him right. Now the Maysville Veto effectively smashed his hopes for public works subsidized by the national government.

Kennedy was disappointed by Jackson's stand on internal improvements, but he considered the President's handling of the tariff a betrayal. Here was another issue closely connected with Kennedy's own career. His entrance into politics had coincided with a strong movement for protection. It was a policy on which, for once, Maryland's manufacturers and farmers could unite. Land prices and agricultural markets dropped sharply after the inflationary years from 1815 to 1818. Simultaneously the foreign market for grain which had flourished during the Napoleonic Wars was lost after 1815. Farmers were clamoring for a home market, and manufacturers, caught in the crash of 1819, were demanding protection from foreign competition. It was natural to turn to the government for a panacea, and the idea of protection obtained a strong hold on the popular mind. The men Kennedy represented in court and met at the Monday Club were ardent protectionists. This devotion to high tariff, however, was not merely a reflection of his devotion to self. Kennedy was irresistibly attracted to the idea of an industrial America, a self-sufficient nation drawing sustenance from commerce and manufacturing.

Kennedy's services in the cause of protection enhanced his reputation in Baltimore as "one of the most powerful champions of a prominent school of Political Economy." [7] He was invited to assist in preparing the official pronouncements of the Friends of Domestic Industry in New York and he organized the Maryland branch of the society in 1832. That year he was often in Washington listening to the tariff debates in Congress and engaging industriously "in that magnificent and unprofitable work of reforming the wild absurdities and anti-tariff obliquities of that stiff-necked and unconscionable generation, the nullifiers." It was exhilarating to meet and advise with Henry Clay and Daniel Webster and, as he boasted to Elizabeth, "to instruct the great men what to say." [8]

On the tariff Kennedy was, according to one observer, "perhaps the most zealous of his contemporaries." [9] In the troubled winter of 1833 when South Carolina passed its nullification proclamation abrogating the tariffs of 1828 and 1832 within its borders, and Jackson replied by asking Congress for authority to enforce the revenue laws by a call to arms, Kennedy was a hotspur in the cause. To Elizabeth he confided, "I consider civil war inevitable." He joined the alarmed manufacturers who rushed to Washington to head off the designs of the free-traders. The business community had not realized at home the danger the protective system was in, and so they grudgingly accepted the tariff of 1833 which secured them the benefits of protection for nine years. Kennedy privately denounced this compromise measure and believed the government should have enforced the laws at the point of the bayonet. He was vexed at the denouement of the affair and readily placed the blame on "the old dotard Jackson." [10]

As Jackson independently shaped the course of his administration and attracted a loyal and militant following, Kennedy saw in the direction of events a scheme "to create distinctions between the lower and higher orders of the people. The struggle at present is to give influence and power to the mob at the sacrifice of the peace and sanity and the most valuable principles of the Constitution." The villain of the piece was, of course, Andrew Jackson. "The old fool," Kennedy burst out; "I believe he is losing his wits from infirmity of body or passion." [11]

When President Jackson declared war on the United States Bank, Kennedy turned from criticism to open opposition. The actual break dated from a December morning in 1833. Calling at the Union Bank of Baltimore, which he had served as counsel for thirteen years, Kennedy was stopped by the president, Thomas Ellicott, a towering, angular man dressed in the somber black of a Quaker. Strangers saw implacable force of character in Ellicott's deep-sunk, cinderous eyes and heavy, determined jaw, and it was general knowledge among Baltimoreans that his iron will dominated the board of directors of the Union Bank. Ellicott was a close friend of Andrew Jackson's Secretary of the Treasury, the Baltimore lawyer Roger Brooke Taney. Earlier in the year when Taney, in carrying out the strategy of his Chief in the attack on the United States Bank, had withdrawn the deposits from that institution and placed them in various "pet banks," Ellicott's Union Bank was promptly selected. Since Taney was a director of the Union Bank, he was instantly charged with favoritism, and thinking men guessed that Ellicott's involvement in the pet bank scheme was greater than he might wish to acknowledge.[12]

It was concerning the matter of the deposits that Ellicott

wished to speak with John Kennedy. Now that the government's largess was bestowed on the Union Bank, Ellicott cautioned Kennedy that the officers could no longer afford the luxury of criticizing the administration at Washington. This hint touched Kennedy on an exposed nerve. Heatedly he attacked what he considered the folly of Secretary Taney in removing the deposits from the United States Bank, and, his voice rising with indignation, he assailed Jackson as a usurper acting in open violation of the Constitution. Ellicott replied pointedly that the government would scarcely extend its patronage to an institution whose officers openly criticized its measures. This argument was not calculated to persuade Kennedy. He countered with a brisk denunciation of Jackson, Taney, and the whole "flimsy affair" of the removal of the deposits. Jackson's conduct, he thought, deserved impeachment.

The following day the two men met again, and Ellicott, still smarting under Kennedy's remarks, dispensed with subtleties. The deposits, he explained, were worth twenty to thirty thousand dollars a year to the Union Bank and for Kennedy to complain of the pet bank system was to quarrel with his bread and butter. This frontal assault only rekindled Kennedy's anger. The politics of the bank's officers, he scoffed, were "neutralized." [13] For Kennedy the disillusionment with Andrew Jackson and all his works was complete.

Kennedy withdrew from the Union Bank and watched helplessly as Ellicott continued on his course. Ellicott's bungling of the bank's business ultimately lost him Taney's confidence and led to a breach between the two friends. Ellicott became involved in speculations with another Baltimore institution, the Bank of Maryland, which collapsed in March 1834, throwing the city into an uproar. Kennedy would later use this incident as the basis for his satire of Jacksonian democracy, *Quodlibet*. But that was still six years in the future. In the meantime he found it an excellent premise for political action.

On April 23, 1834, at a mass meeting in Baltimore's Monument Square, Kennedy told a crowd of ten thousand people that "the great and glorious Whig principles that worked out the Revolution and gave political liberty and independence to this land are again awake," and called on Maryland to form a State Whig Society. The lines of conflict were drawn. The following evening the Whig party of Baltimore was launched in violence and bloodshed as young men of both parties formed military organizations and rioted in the streets.[14]

The Jackson party struck back. "John P. Kennedy," wrote the editor of the Baltimore *Republican*, "was formerly a flaming Jackson man, and few men in Baltimore, perhaps, wrote more, spoke more, did more in favor of Jackson, or were more warm or violent in the cause than this same John P. Kennedy. He was closely allied to a merchant favorable to Jackson. Having subsequently married the daughter of a rich manufacturer . . . Kennedy became a great advocate of the American System." The Jacksonian merchant was Colonel Thomas Tenant, the father of Kennedy's first wife. Since Edward Gray was a violent anti-Jacksonite, the reader sensitive to innuendo caught the implication that Kennedy was as venal in marriage as in politics. It is not unusual for politicians to talk in such fashion, but this example of the yellow press of the 1830's explains Kennedy's outbursts at the "vile repositories of falsehood, venom, immorality and vulgar thought, the newspapers." [15]

The birth of the Whig party in Baltimore in the spring of 1834 formed a part of a larger movement, North and South, rising in opposition to the Jackson party, or as it was beginning to call itself, the Democracy. The new party was a union of disparate elements temporarily fused by their fiery hatred of Andrew Jackson. The President inspired the name of the opposition. The name *Whig* evoked stirring memories of resistance to tyrants in revolutionary days, and the leaders of the new party promptly identified "King Andrew the First" with George III. "The Whig Party," Kennedy said, "fought the Battle of Freedom in the Revolution: it has never faltered in its duty since." [16] The English Whigs were traditionally the symbol of parliamentary authority as opposed to the prerogative of the crown, and henceforth their American counterparts were dedicated to the maintenance of legislative authority over executive usurpation.

Although founded in dissent and sustained by discord, the Whigs soon evolved a positive philosophy and a specific platform. In John Kennedy's mind there was no question as to the part to be played by the new party. Attracted more to political theory than to grass roots manipulation and wirepulling, he formulated a practical, neatly dovetailed program which satisfied his passion for order. He believed the Whigs should be the party of property, the political spokesman for the business community, the guardian and representative of economic stability. The basis of this program—a central banking system, a protective tariff, a system of internal improvements—was the equivalent of the subsidization of industry by the government. Kennedy subscribed to a fourth measure, the distribution of the proceeds from the sale of the public lands. Maryland, in company with other seaboard states, had undertaken at its own expense a vast network of public works. If the revenue from the sale of the public lands was distributed among the states, it would relieve the crushing load of debt on Maryland. The West, so the argument went, would benefit by the works; it should bear its share of the cost. The distribution, as it was called, was a measure intimately bound up with Kennedy's political fortunes. As an early advocate of internal improvements, he was deeply concerned with the state's need for funds. If Maryland was forced to resort to direct taxation to meet its obligations, the outcry might end his career.

In evolving an economic philosophy consonant with the realities of the Baltimore mercantile world, John Kennedy fell heir to the tradition of Alexander Hamilton, whose *Report on Manufactures* in 1791 first evoked the vision of an industrial America. Kennedy, however, in looking for intellectual sustenance, turned not to the memory of that imperious statesman but to the prospect of the American future as illumined by the glittering rhetoric of Henry Clay. Kennedy became a zealous advocate of Clay's shrewdly named American System, and in its defense was, according to one rival, "more royal than the King." [17]

Few men could resist the personal magnetism of Henry Clay. Even those who distrusted the politician loved the man. His conversation vivid with anecdotes and spiced with profanity, his voice drawling and melodious, Clay was the prince of companions. Eighteen years older than Kennedy, Clay was a national figure, a war hawk in Congress and a peace commissioner at Ghent, when Kennedy was an impressionable youngster serving with the United Volunteers at Bladensburg and North Point. This early hero worship was tarnished by the presidential election of 1824 with its outcry of "corrupt bargain," a cry Kennedy was ready to believe. By 1830 Kennedy would have voted for Clay for President rather than an anti-tariff candidate, but it would be "a choice of evils. My objections to him are too deep to allow me to become his advocate." [18]

But Kennedy had not counted on the magnetism of Clay's personality. The men first met in February 1832, and Kennedy immediately fell under the spell of Clay's charm. He described the interview to Elizabeth: "I was introduced yesterday to Clay . . . . He immediately asked me if my father were still alive? Said he lived in Va &c &c—showing how singularly attentive he is to personal history of individuals. He invited me also to dine with him." In October 1833 Kennedy was invited to New York to deliver the keynote address at a convention of manufacturers. Clay arrived in New York on a triumphal tour, and, in the excitement which his reception occasioned, Kennedy was caught up in the celebrity's entourage. Clay sat on the rostrum at the Chatham Street Chapel the evening Kennedy delivered his speech, and as the loud and indiscriminate applause thundered up from the audience in appreciation of hearing its own views on the American System elegantly expressed, Kennedy was not unaware that the enthusiasm was in part owing to the presence of the distinguished and attentive Kentuckian. At a late supper Clay in a witty and ingratiating speech toasted "the Orator of the Evening." Who could resist this siren song? Kennedy's discipleship had begun.[19]

As a founder of the new party in Baltimore, Kennedy awaited impatiently the rewards of yeoman service in the cause of Whiggery. In the autumn of 1837 the party brought him out for the congressional race on a ticket with Charles Sterett Ridgely, scion of a notable Maryland family. The Jackson ticket was equally distinguished. Benjamin Chew Howard, son of the revolutionary hero, John Eager Howard, had already served three terms in the

House of Representatives. Howard entered politics the same year as Kennedy, 1820, and rose rapidly from city councilman to the Maryland Senate and, ultimately, to Congress. Howard's running mate was Isaac McKim, the acute and thin-visaged son of a Baltimore shipowner who had made a fortune in trade.

Presumably the issue of the campaign was the conduct of the country's finances by Jackson's heir, Martin Van Buren, who had come to the Presidency in March 1837. Nevertheless, the Jackson press in Baltimore virtually ignored both the issues and Ridgely in concentrating its fire on Kennedy. The charges of the congressional campaign a decade earlier were exhumed. By voting for the Potomac Canal Company, Kennedy had "betrayed the interests of Baltimore." His application for and subsequent refusal of the diplomatic mission to Chile in 1823 were used to make him appear a timeserver and an ingrate. He had spoken condescendingly of Baltimore as "not a reading community." It was rumored darkly that he was "an avowed infidel," and, what appears to have been something worse, he was a novelist. The editor of the *Republican* wrote: "Will the friends of Mr. Kennedy be so good as to give us a list of the *Novelists* and point, out of the thousands, to those who have been *statesmen*. Perhaps Mr. Kennedy may be the exception. He has been a man of all *parties.* He may be a man of all work." And again: "He is a very good writer of works of fiction; but as to matters of fact, and political economy, his head is as empty as a barrel with both ends out." To Jacksonites he was "the Apostate from your ranks" and "a fit tool of the Bank Aristocracy." Although the race was closer than some observers had expected, Kennedy and Ridgely lost by about two hundred votes out of twelve thousand cast.[20]

Fate, however, played into Kennedy's hands. In April of the following year, 1838, Isaac McKim died, and in the off-year election, Kennedy made a second canvass and won. The victory was generally interpreted as a personal triumph. He won the nomination unanimously, polled the largest Whig vote in the city's history, and ended a nine-year Democratic reign in Baltimore. Kennedy was jubilant. To his uncle, Philip Pendleton, he wrote: "It has been an interval of hard labour, intense excitement, bewildering success and frantic rejoicing. Did you ever know a more glorious triumph? . . . I wish you could get one glimpse of Henry Clay's face as it was yesterday when he came down to my room and dined with me." [21]

Kennedy hurried off to Washington to take his seat in the House of Representatives. Since the session was drawing to a close, Elizabeth remained with her parents and sister in Baltimore. She waited nervously for news of his debut and wrote timorous advice. A letter written at this time, one of a half-dozen to her husband which have been preserved among his papers, reveals her concern for his reputation. But like many women of her generation, she was puzzled by niceties of style.

> I am *very very* anxious dear John about your first speech, so much is expected of you that you ought to be *doubly* careful how you commit yourself. It would be bad indeed if you disappointed the expectations of your friends and I cannot help fearing you are not sufficiently prepared yet, do not be urged by the persuasions of *any one* to attempt a speech without careful preparation, and I cannot help thinking that for this session you ought not to speak[.] Papa says so much is expected from you in Phila. numerous persons were talking to him about you and he says their expectations are so much raised that it will be difficult for you to fulfil them. It is a great disadvantage, I should suppose for any man to enter congress under such circumstances but it must certainly be more incumbent on him to endeavor by *study* and *careful* preparation to justify the hopes that are entertained for him. . . . You know how proud I am of you and how anxious I am for your reputation far more than you are yourself.[22]

This counsel of caution he ignored. He had waited too long for his chance. Baltimore was a ringside seat from which to follow the progress of affairs at Washington. For over two decades he had watched from the galleries the deliberations of the great menagerie (the phrase is his own), and he had mingled with the lawmakers at Gadsby's Hotel. He had moved on the fringes of official Washington, an amused and fascinated observer. At last he was admitted to the inner circle.

Kennedy arrived at Washington the last day of April 1838 in wretched health from the strain of two campaigns within a year. He was suffering from an annoying inflammation of the skin which broke out across his forehead and cheeks, causing him acute pain and embarrassment. His lips were raw and badly inflamed, and his tongue was blistered and swollen. "The foul fiend has got hold of me," he wrote his uncle Philip. "My lips . . . [are] sore with a peeling soreness, like an onion, every day stripping a coat, and sometimes many coats in one day like the grave digger in Hamlet." [23] A Baltimore physician pronounced the disease a form of eczema and prescribed a salve which only succeeded in aggravating the condition. Kennedy's own diagnosis of the malady as more likely the result of anxiety than diet was borne out by his quick resurgence to health under the stimulus of Washington society.

Indeed, the gods appeared to be smiling auspiciously. He had last won an election in 1823. Fifteen years ago! Yet he was still young, forty-three years old, and already he could boast popular success as a lawyer, author, and now—congressman. And the latest victory was the sweetest. Kennedy liked to quote the patrician ideal that the office must seek the gentleman, the gentleman never seeks the office. But he too fiercely enjoyed the competition not to relish the victory. He exuded confidence. A correspondent for the *New York Times* described him as "a striking personage—of fine stature, vigorously though neatly formed, and remarkably careful in his dress and carriage. His head is a large one, with full phrenological development over an expansive forehead, which a sparce and rather uncontrollable suit of hair renders broadly visible. There is in his face a fine combination of features (more expressive perhaps than handsome)." [24]

On June 22, 1838, Kennedy rose to deliver his maiden speech in the House. It was ostensibly an attack on the independent treasury bill which the Democrats had proposed to fill the gap left by the expiration of the charter of the United States Bank. This bill was based on the idea of keeping the public money in the post offices, custom houses, and mints of the country until it was paid out. The Democratic fear of inflation, added to Jackson's war on the National Bank, had brought the party chieftains to a "hard money" policy. They would separate the government from all direct dealings with banking and establish a sound currency of gold and silver through legislation. Kennedy rehearsed the arguments for a renewal of the Bank's charter, but the speech was more notable for its frank espousal of the northern economic program and its vigorous defense of manufacturing—"the smoking forges of the West . . . the swift shuttles of the East." Kennedy made no effort to conciliate the South, but attacked South Carolina for its particularism and singled out Virginia for special rebuke: "Let Virginia give up her dialectics, renounce her spirit of dissertation, and debate, and betake herself to commerce and manufactures." Altogether the speech was an onslaught on Jackson's fiscal policy and a plea for the government "to confide in the integrity, the habits of business, the intelligence and interests of a board of merchant directors, rather than incur the hazard of the selfish and obsequious spirit, the alien temper and unskillfulness of a mere political functionary." [25]

Kennedy found addressing the House a disconcerting experience. He described the scene to his friend and neighbor, Josias Pennington:

> The Hall has a most unnatural vagueness in it for every sense; you hear nothing distinctly; you see nothing accurately. There is a great tomb-like, ill-timed, disconcerting reverberation over your own words from the vault above you; a most diabolical buzzing from sundry corners as if fifty dead kings were mocking you. The speaker, in your eyes, is a little man in a distant perspective, enveloped in drapery; you are perfectly sure he does not hear you; and his great eyes, which for politeness' sake he fixes upon you, glow like one of Fuseli's spectres from out of the damask curtains. Then, in the house itself, there is no sympathy; no nod of approbation to say—"I understand you," except from two or three civil Whig friends, who from respect to the cause and one of its advocates, sit by near at hand, either to be mortified at your proclamations of corruption or to laugh at your occasional attempt at a joke; every Locofoco has left the House except one—a grinning, malignant sentinel, to take notes to answer you. He sits close by, with a snaky eye fixed upon you and a livid face,—livid with hatred; and every now and then laughs scornfully, seizes his pencil, ducks down and writes like the devil for thirty seconds, and rises up again with the most infernal smile, as much as to say, "I have got you." [26]

Back in Baltimore after the close of the session, Kennedy was busy writing out the speech for pamphlet publication, "remasticating the stale food of a digested and forgotten speech." It was, he told Philip Pendleton, "the most supereminently flat bore of an occupation that ever man was condemned to. 'I wish I may be teetotally exflunctified' if I ever write down another dribblet of my brain that is dropped in any public place again. Who reads the cursed thing after it is done? *Done!*—that is a good word for it—yea *overdone* would have suited still better . . . done forsooth! there will not be a rare slice in the whole mass." [27] Having seen the speech through the press, he hurried off to Virginia to accept the congratulations of the Pendleton clan and to spend the summer writing *Rob of the Bowl*.

When Congress convened in December 1838, he made one major speech, a review of Jacksonism from its inception. Couched at a level of invective that matched the temper of the times and relieved a decade of pent-up irritation and despair, the speech was a slashing, partisan diatribe pointed toward the next congressional campaign. On the basis of his triumph a year earlier, Kennedy was, as usual, in buoyant spirits and sure of re-election. Yet there were murky shadows in the local election picture. The Democrats, having failed to gauge accurately the extent of Kennedy's personal popularity, were busily marshaling the organizational strength which had dominated Baltimore politics for a decade. Elizabeth was apprehensive. Across the bottom of one of her husband's exultant letters, she scribbled a postscript: "Don't mind what John says I have heard from the best authority that it is very doubtful. I think he will be beaten." And so he was. More than fifteen thousand votes were cast, an increase of about four thousand over the congressional election two years before, and Kennedy ran approximately four hundred votes behind his Democratic opponent.[28]

Defeat left him weary and dejected. It was exasperating to be beaten just as he was tasting the first delights of Washington society, and doubly so when the margin of defeat was greater than it had been in 1837. Now his personal victory of 1838 could be interpreted by the Democrats as a political fluke, a sin of commission for which a righteous electorate had atoned by ousting at the first opportunity this aristocratic minion of the money power. Moreover, his exclusion from office came just at the moment when the Whig party seemed on the verge of a national triumph. He was beaten on the eve of the presidential year, and he found himself denied a share in that exuberant political romp, the Whig Log Cabin and Hard Cider campaign of 1840.

In December 1839 at Harrisburg the Whig National Convention, a coalition rather than an organized political party, nominated sixty-seven-year-old General William Henry Harrison for the Presidency. Kennedy observed that "although we in Maryland very ardently wished to see Mr. Clay put in nomination, yet the better opinion being for Harrison we cannot but be content." [29] Clay's adherents found this shift in allegiance quite easy to make. The General's availability was unmatched. Although early in the century he had been a territorial governor and later had served several terms in both houses of Congress, he had been long enough out of public life to dissociate himself from all contemporary issues and, best of all, he had no enemies. He had defeated the Indians at Tippecanoe in 1811 and now, like a Cincinnatus, lived in semi-retirement on an Ohio farm. It is from such materials that myths are made.

For the second place on the ticket, the Whigs named John Tyler of Virginia. Tyler had served his state with distinction as representative in Congress, governor, and senator and at the age of fifty-one was known as a southern gentleman of tact and suavity. His career had been marked by a rigid opposition to centralized power. He had opposed the United States Bank, and in the tariff crisis of 1833 when Congress had passed the Force Bill giving Andrew Jackson power to employ the military to enforce the revenue laws, John Tyler had voted in a minority of one. Such a stand took courage, yet even his friends suspected that there was not a little vanity in this idolatrous devotion to consistency. His place on the ticket placated the South and put the Whigs on every side of every significant question of the day.

It was left to Kennedy's most vitriolic critic, the Baltimore *Republican*, to furnish unwittingly a battle cry for the campaign. The paper's Washington correspondent had observed sarcastically that the old General might easily be persuaded to withdraw if he had a pension of two thousand dollars a year, a barrel of cider, and a log cabin. Exactly right! the Whigs shouted gleefully. The Whigs were indeed the bulwark of hard cider and log cabins in America and would defend them to the death against the champagne and palaces of Martin Van Buren and the Democrats. Tip and Ty had found their rallying point. The Hurrah of 1840 was under way.

With no immediate stake in the outcome of the presidential contest, Kennedy retired to the seclusion of his library at Mount Vernon Place to contemplate the wheel of political fortune which had so perversely swung from prosperity to adversity. He found solace in imagining himself an aloof spectator of events, a philosophic observer of the strife for place and power. He turned over in his mind again and again the insidious shift in the temper of Baltimore politics. Kennedy recalled the idols of his youth. When he entered public life in the 1820's, the haughty and overbearing William Pinkney was United States senator from Maryland. Pinkney did not suffer fools gladly and disdained to curry favor with the voters, yet the public willingly honored his unmistakable talents. So had it been with the other great figures of Kennedy's youth: William Wirt, Samuel Smith, Robert Goodloe Harper. To attempt to take a liberty with such men was unthinkable. They had composed an aristocracy of talent and virtue, and Kennedy mourned its passing: "Society had a more aristocratic air than now, not because the educated and wealthy assumed more, but because the community itself had a better appreciation of personal worth, and voluntarily gave it the healthful privilege of taking the lead in the direction of manners and in the conducting of public affairs." [30]

During the months following Kennedy's defeat for re-election, he was preoccupied with the reasons for the change. The growth of a city is a natural process and creates no surprise to those who grow with it. But pausing to look back, Kennedy could trace the effects of uncontrolled expansion. The population, twenty-one thousand in 1800, had reached sixty thousand in 1820 and by 1840 had passed the hundred thousand mark. Industrial growth magnified problems of urban life which were new and beyond immediate solution. The problems of low wages, the rising number of unemployed workers, inadequate housing for the poor, and the influx of paupers seeking the benefits of charitable institutions increased rapidly after the crash of 1837. Class distinctions were manifested in bizarre ways. When fancy dress balls became the rage in Baltimore, a mob formed about the entrance of the ballroom to stare and shout impertinent remarks. They took vengeance by advertising their own fancy rag ball to mimic the elite, and to judge from Kennedy's irritation, the satire was effective.

The vice and crime resulting from congested urban conditions occasionally erupted into open violence. In August 1835 the city had been terrorized for five days by a frenzied mob. Incited by alleged swindles connected with the collapse of the Bank of Maryland, vandals prowled Baltimore streets, cowed the municipal authorities, and furiously sacked the homes of the bank's officers. Rioting and bullying were common at elections in "Mobtown," as Baltimore was called by its detractors. For such people, Kennedy observed, "the excitements of political association are a pleasure and a pastime." Each member "of the great property-owning class" had the franchise, but so too did "the profoundly ignorant, the vicious and dissolute, the frequenters of tippling houses, the idle, the unthrifty, the fraudulent debtors, the decayed and brokendown workmen, the outlawed and cast off members of society under bar for incorrigible faults." [31] This substratum of society Kennedy feared might become a morass into which all American politics would sink.

Alarmed at the drift of these speculations and finding himself momentarily on the political shelf, Kennedy had leisure to take up his pen in defense of his political principles. "I have thought," he noted in his journal, "it might tend somewhat to the advancement of our cause if I were to write some essays directed to the examination of the present condition of parties and the development of their principles and pretensions. I shall attempt it." [32] So at the age of forty-five, he fused his vocations of politician and author to write his satire of Jacksonian democracy, *Quodlibet*, which V. L. Parrington called "the most vivacious criticism of Jacksonianism in our political annals [and] one of our few distinguished political satires." [33]

Kennedy thought first of writing "a grave dissertation or Estimate of the Character, Principles and Manners of the United States." Accordingly he set about this plan but grew bored after filling a dozen pages of his notebook with random political comments. He began again, this time writing some satiric sketches of familiar political types. A thread of narrative began to emerge as he revised, and in subsequent drafts he evolved the history of the Borough of Quodlibet. He had hit on a subject which, of all others, most absorbed his interest. He was writing of people he knew intimately and understood thoroughly. Writing rapidly and facilely, in six months he had the book in the hands of his publishers, Lea and Blanchard of Philadelphia.

The account of the rise of the Borough of Quodlibet is told by Solomon Secondthoughts—nicknamed "Sober" by the local wits —a prosy and precise bachelor whose name alluded to Martin Van Buren's famous remark that "the sober, second thought of the people is never wrong." Solomon is the borough's schoolmaster, preening himself on petty triumphs and a Boswell to every party hack. Years of classroom drill have made his mind sluggish and his wit ponderous. Kennedy endowed him with a style that is a tour de force of sustained drollery. It is self-conscious and pedantic, studded with puns and starched with contrived metaphors, and completely in character with the absurd narrator. Solomon's pen can swell an obscure spring to comic significance:

> The fine, copious, old spring—where there has been many a barbecue in my time—was pouring out its crystal treasures, as some poet says, with prodigal bounty, and transferring them, as the Secretary does the deposits, by large draughts, from the living rock to the running Rumblebottom—in fact, taking them out of one bank, and distributing them between others. Not far from this spring, adumbrated by overarching boughs—the reader will excuse this poetical orgasm—for fifteen years and upwards have I been visiting this fountain, sacred to Pan, (we used to have fish frys here,) and have grown poetical at the sight thereof —it is my infirmity.

Quodlibet is a rundown and shabby village which awakens suddenly to a gimcrack prosperity after the removal of the deposits by President Jackson in the fall of 1833. Time, in Quodlibet, is thus dated from "The Removal . . . [the] great epoch in our annals—our Hegira—the A. U. C. of all Quodlibetarians." The acme of Democratic finance is the Patriotic Copperplate Bank of Quodlibet which begins business with "about six bales of pinkish silk paper, and a very superior cylinder press." The skyrocket rise of the bank is owing to its involvement in local Democratic politics. The bank presidency is bestowed upon Middleton Flam, Quodlibet's representative in Congress and the man responsible for getting Secretary of the Treasury Taney to place federal deposits in the bank. The guiding spirit of the bank is a pettifogger named Theodore Fog. Fog is joined in the scheme by Nicodemus Handy, an early example in American fiction of a familiar figure in American politics—the off-stage manipulator content with personal anonymity and intent on the reality of power.

The bank ("an exact miniature copy of the Tomb of Osymandias") is supplied with ready cash through the liberality of Fog, "the remains of a trust fund in his hands belonging to a family of orphans in the neighborhood of Tumbledown, who had not yet had occasion to know from their attorney, the said Theodore Fog himself, of their success in a cause relating to this fund which had been gained some months before." Fog is cunningly forced out of power by Handy, the bank cashier. The vagaries of Democratic finance are played out to the end; the Copperplate Bank collapses, and Handy absconds to Europe, leaving Fog to redound the blame on the Whigs.

In squabbling over the spoils of the bank, the Democratic party splits into True Grits, New Lights ("milk-and-water, flesh-and-fowl, half-hawk-half-buzzard-Middling Democrats"), and Mandarin ("kid glove") Democrats. Each faction has its spellbinder, and the various schools of stump oratory are burlesqued in a series of skillful parodies. Nicodemus Handy, a member of the elegant Mandarin faction, speaks "after the manner of a table of contents (a habit which he has acquired since he has grown rich)": "Sensible of the great honor—endeavor to discharge with fidelity—obvious incapacity—but exceedingly flattered by the testimony of your regard . . . ."

Handy's clichés contrast strikingly with the originality of Theodore Fog, a True Grit, who describes the mind of Secretary Taney as "endued with a radiating faculty sufficiently intent to light up the bottom of a bog, impart a vitreous translucency to the home of the frog, and illuminate the abode of the bat with a luster more brilliant than that which glittered through the boudoirs of the palace of Aladdin."

The great tradition of bombast and buncombe is represented by Middleton Flam, a New Light. Flam is the aristocratic son of a Federalist father. He is the lord of Quality Hall on Poplar Flats, but when leveling becomes the fashion, he finds it expedient to denominate the estate *E*quality Hall on Pop*u*lar Flats. When a heckler at a rally charges him with building Equality Hall "for show," that statesman is not unprepared with an answer.

"Show, sir! Of course, it was put there for show. What else could it be put for? What is any portico put up for? It faces toward the road, sir—it was designed to face toward the road. When I built that portico, I wished the people, sir, to see it; the best I have shall always be shown to the people. I trust, sir, that my respect for the people shall never so far abate, as to induce me to neglect *them*. My house, sir, intrinsically is that of an humble citizen; there are a dozen equal to it in this county; but that part of it which is intended to gratify the people is unsurpassed here or anywhere else. I have laid out, sir, a small fortune on that portico to gratify the people: all that I have comes from them—all that I ever expect to be, I hope to derive from them: who has so good a right as they to require me to put my best foot foremost, when they are the spectators? On the same principle, sir, when I appear in public, I dress in the most expensive attire, I drive the best horses, and procure the finest coach. My turnout is altogether elaborate, studiously particular—simply because I hold the people in too much esteem, to shab them off with anything of a secondary quality, while Providence has blessed me with the means of providing them the best. That, sir, is what I call a keystone principle in the arch of Democratic government: that is the sentiment, and that alone, which is to give perpetuity to this—"

"Fair fabric of freedom," said Theodore Fog, who was among the auditory and perceived that Mr. Flam hesitated for a word to convey his idea.

"Thank you, my friend," courteously replied Mr. Flam, "I am indebted to you for the word—fair fabric of freedom."

"A Man of All Work"

Although politically inspired, *Quodlibet* is not narrowly political in its orientation but is in the broadest sense a penetrating criticism of Jacksonian America. Kennedy intended the Borough of Quodlibet as a microcosm, "an abstract or miniature portrait of this nation." More concerned with doctrinaires than with doctrines, he was satirizing a new breed of men, impudent, grossly ignorant, and wanting in political morality. His was the contempt of an intelligent, respectable conservative for "mushroom banks" and their "swarms of scrub aristocrats in the shape of presidents, cashiers, directors, and clerks." He saw in their subterfuge a scheme to entrench a political faction by arraying class against class. Symbol of the age was Middleton Flam's Equality Hall, with its spacious "grecian Temple porch with niches for statues," which, on closer examination, proved to be a white pine portico disguising a rickety clapboard cottage.

> The grounds were embellished with sundry structures apparently at great cost . . . which, when examined would be found to be, for the most part, painted imitation of a very cheap kind. Thus there was to be seen from the portico, peering above a thicket on the Grasshopper Run, an old castle with ivy-crowned battlements, greatly enriching the view: at the end of the long walk in the garden, a magnificent obelisk rose forty feet above a bed of asparagus; the entrance to the stable-yard was through the Gothic archway of an old chapel, exceeding pleasant to behold; and the ice pond was guarded by a palisade composed of muskets, lances, swords, shields, and cannon, flanked at each end by a pile of drums and colors. All these several embellishments a nice observation would determine to be executed in oil paintings, upon wooden screens sawed into the requisite figures.

Kennedy scorned the pretension of these years which manifested itself in a classical revival in architecture, filling the forests with Greek and Roman temples. The borough's name itself satirized the accompanying rage to ransack antiquity for place names suitable to the grandeur of the unfinished republic. It was a world Kennedy found vulgar and tawdry, yet he kept his temper, and his raillery was never reduced to peevishness or partisan spite.

Quodlibet is full of scenes minutely observed and sharply rendered, vivid with the devotion to detail of a limner's portrait.

Yet the book, for all its wit, exudes the musty flavor of ancient jests. The cutting edge of some of its humor has been blunted by buried allusions and battles fought and forgotten; but like all good satire, many of its best thrusts are universal in their application. Kennedy was writing in the classic tradition of English satire, and his debt, particularly to Swift and Sterne, is on every page. Yet *Quodlibet* is also in the native grain. During the 1830's the most effective criticisms of Democratic policy had taken the characteristic forms of indigenous American humor. From the West had come Davy Crockett, "half-horse, half-alligator, a little touched with snapping turtle." Crockett exemplified the tall tale and bombastic talk that were hallmarks of American humor, and the Whigs had exploited him as an example of their common touch. Kennedy's ear was tuned to the racy, idiomatic diction, the incongruous but peculiarly apt adjectives, and the homely metaphors drawn from common speech. His best scenes amusingly rendered this American vernacular.

When *Quodlibet* appeared anonymously in September 1840, several newspapers attributed it, singularly enough, to John Quincy Adams. The Baltimore press immediately ascribed it to Kennedy, and, as he noted in his journal, "sundry points in the Book, familiar to our people in Baltimore, have so confirmed that impression here, that it is put down as a thing which it is but affectation for me to repudiate." [34] Quodlibet was, in fact, Baltimore thinly disguised. The borough had grown at an astonishing rate, "the increase being altogether without an example in the history of civilization." Similarly, Baltimoreans loved to boast that "among all the cities whether of America or of the old world, in modern or ancient times, there is no record of any one, which has sprung up so quickly to as high degree of importance as Baltimore." [35] Rumblebottom Creek ran through Quodlibet to the Basin as did Baltimore's Jones Falls. On the outskirts of Quodlibet the nabobs built homes on Copperplate Ridge "in all manner of Greek, Roman, and Tuscan fashions" as did their Baltimore counterparts on the hills and rainwashed ravines near the Washington Monument. One such Baltimorean was Benjamin Chew Howard, son of an opulent Federalist and successful candidate for Congress against Kennedy in the campaign of 1837. In Middleton Flam, representative from Quodlibet, Kennedy's readers detected rather more than a passing resemblance to Howard.

For local readers the story of the Patriotic Copperplate Bank of Quodlibet bore a marked resemblance to the history of Thomas Ellicott's Union Bank of Baltimore, which Secretary of the Treasury Taney had designated as a "pet bank" when he removed the deposits from the Bank of the United States. Kennedy had naturally followed the fortunes of the Union Bank since he had served as its counsel until his break with Ellicott in 1833, and he had watched Ellicott's subsequent involvement in speculations with the Bank of Maryland lead to the collapse of that institution in March 1834. In the history of Quodlibet's Copperplate Bank, Kennedy blended parts of the histories of the two Baltimore banks, and in Nicodemus Handy, cashier of the Copperplate Bank, he intended a gibe at Thomas Ellicott.

And the parallel with Baltimore explains the one vicious caricature in the book, Eliphalet Fox, editor of the *Quodlibet Whole Hog*. "His temper was sour and peevish . . . though seemingly meek, even to a degree of asininity, in his demeanor." His paper was a "cross-grained, querulous, tart and vinegarish little folio [which] like all poison-concocting animals, grew venomous as it grew older." In 1840 it is Eliphalet Fox's *Whole Hog* which suggests that William Henry Harrison be given a log cabin, a pension, and a jug of hard cider. Here Kennedy ripped the disguise away. It was the Baltimore *Republican* which originated this notorious remark, and Fox was evidently intended as a lampoon of the *Republican* editor, James H. Cox. In his three campaigns for Congress Kennedy had sustained bitter personal attacks from the *Republican*. And now he had his revenge.

In this case, as in others, the temptation to pinpoint his targets was irresistible. Kennedy occasionally turned pamphleteer and introduced excerpts from the contemporary record—a circular from Taney, a Jackson letter, a clipping from the *Globe*, an excerpt from a speech in Congress. He tended to confuse information with inspiration and *Quodlibet* suffered in proportion.

Quodlibet was the least popular of all Kennedy's works, the edition of 1840 numbering only 1,500 copies. The author suggested a new edition in 1843 but his publishers, Lea and Blanchard, reminded him that " 'Quodlibet,' for all its wit, humor, excellent sarcasm and really well timed issue, was not a 'good book' for the publisher." [36] It did not reappear until 1860. At that time Kennedy had some misgivings about reprinting it and blunted the more stinging barbs. He realized the ephemeral nature of some of the satire and in a new preface commented, a little sadly, upon "the grotesque retribution which history inflicts upon distempered parties after a few decades of oblivion . . . which engrossments, with all their concomitant gravities and glorifications, twenty years have shriveled into the dimensions of a pleasant farce—a little stage imbroglio of comic conceits and fussy nothings."

Although *Quodlibet* was not widely read, it generated enthusiasm among a few discerning contemporaries. William Gilmore Simms, although as fervent a Democrat as ever lived, appreciated the book's merits. "Quodlibet," he wrote, "was a trenchant Whig satire, over which that party, renowned for its sense of the proprieties, may have chuckled decorously, but which, we suspect, they did not justice to in any more earnest manner—for which, we apprehend, they did not pay!" [37]

The Baltimore lawyer and occasional litterateur, John H. B. Latrobe, thought *Quodlibet* "the ablest work that has yet proceeded from Mr. Kennedy's pen. We would not be understood to endorse Quodlibet in a political sense; but as a literary production, a keen satire, in a word, a 'Pickwickian sense,' it has our strong recommendation. The estimate that was at once put upon it when it appeared, the great names to which it was attributed, showed the opinion entertained of it by the public, and we do not know a similar work in America that is to be compared to it." [38]

The most enthusiastic praise came from another Democrat, the arch-romantic novelist John Esten Cooke, who shared Kennedy's interest, but not his views, in politics.

> That this work—'The Annals of Quodlibet'—should have been regarded as a mere political squib, and not as a masterpiece of humor, worthy to rank with the finest books of that description

in the language, I confess astonishes me. The book does not exhibit the delicate humor of Irving, but it is from beginning to end the richest comedy. The characterization is extremely minute, vivid and striking . . . the humor is so rich and abounding that, as the reader advances page by page, he feels an ever-increasing charm. Permit me this apparently extravagant commendation of 'Quodlibet.' It is a work in which Mr. Kennedy allowed his humor to revel, and exhibit, in the freest manner, its richness and strength.[39]

And the author himself looked on his handiwork and rejoiced. "I shall take an opportunity," he wrote Philip Pendleton, "to send you a new work which I know will greatly delight you—Quodlibet. You will find it a veritable history of the war, and afford you a good laugh. When you have read it, send it to my mother for her perusal. She is politician enough to relish the battering of the enemy." [40]

Having thus performed the duty to the Whig cause expected of a "literary character," John Kennedy turned back to the Log Cabin and Hard Cider campaign, now generating an excitement that carried all before it.

CHAPTER VIII

A Whig in Harness

THE NATIONAL CONVENTION of Whig Young Men assembled in Baltimore the first week of May 1840 to set in motion the campaign for Harrison and Tyler. The city was used to political carnivals, but not even the most hardened veteran of the hustings could recall such a spectacular grass roots uprising. In the wards Tippecanoe Clubs were busily circulating Harrison almanacs, Harrison badges and buttons, Harrison pocket handkerchiefs, buckeye canes, and, when enthusiasm lagged, barrels of hard cider. Men from every state in the Union flocked daily into the city to be in time for the opening of the convention at Washington Hall on May 2. As a member of the committee on organization, John Kennedy was caught up in the vortex of this campaign maelstrom.

A giant procession on May 4 climaxed the hilarity. The newspapers estimated the throng at one hundred thousand people, a crowd equal to the population of Baltimore. Streets and shops were decorated with flags and bunting, portraits of Harrison, and signs proclaiming the most famous of all American political war cries, "Tippecanoe and Tyler, Too." Spectators clung perilously to roof gables and leaned from balconies and windows, shouting, cheering, and waving flags as the parade of dignitaries and state delegations threaded its way slowly through the crowd, past sidewalks "wedged by a solid mass of men," toward the Canton Race

A Whig in Harness

Course. In the procession was a huge canvas ball ten or twelve feet in diameter which had been rolled all the way from Ohio, symbolizing the political revolution rolling inexorably over the country. Log cabins abounded. Drawn by matched teams of horses or oxen, they were decorated with animal skins, buck horns, plows, and the tools of frontier husbandry. The latch string of each hung conspicuously out, and in back was the inevitable barrel of hard cider.

At the race course the delegates passed under a triumphal arch flanked on one side by a full-scale log cabin and on the other by a miniature Fort Meigs bristling with guns. As the guns fired and a band struck up, the politicians mounted two platforms, one for the committee of arrangements and one for the invited guests. All the Whig stalwarts were on hand: the beloved Henry Clay, his disappointment over losing the nomination carefully masked; and Daniel Webster, lacking Clay's personal warmth, but awe-inspiring, his eyes smoldering beneath a massive brow and his voice tremulous and thundering. The Whig lieutenants took turns exhorting the faithful for Change and Liberty until late in the evening. The orators were still going strong the next day in Monument Square when, towards nightfall, the convention finally adjourned. Words failed the correspondent of *Niles' Register:* "All that pen could write, all that the mouth of men could speak, all that the imagination can conceive of beauty, grandeur, and sublimity, would fall short, far short, of the reality." [1]

At the very moment that Whig spellbinders were addressing the multitude at Monument Square, across town at the Musical Hall the Democrats, evidently undaunted by this rowdy show of strength, were nominating Martin Van Buren for a second term.

Through it all John Kennedy was in conspicuous attendance on the great. Each night there was a sumptuous dinner, and after the cloth was drawn, Kennedy, playing tactfully the role of Baltimore host, offered witty toasts, welcomed the party sachems, and introduced them in graceful and flattering speeches. It was a part he coveted, and he performed it with skill. His leadership among Baltimore Whigs was now assured, and it was confirmed several weeks later when he was named a Harrison elector for President.[2] As the Log Cabin and Hard Cider campaign rollicked along, Kennedy was stumping everywhere in Maryland—Denton, Bladensburg, Hagerstown, Frederick, Annapolis—and often in Pennsylvania, Delaware, and Virginia. At barbecues and clambakes he sweated in the parching sun of a Maryland summer while the hard cider flowed and the crowds, flushed and jubilant, roared for Tip and Ty. After nightfall the frolic continued in the glare of crackling bonfires and the flickering light of torches. Elizabeth and the Grays hurried north to Saratoga Springs to escape the Baltimore summer, but Kennedy stayed on in the sizzling heat to direct the attack on the fast-fading Democrats. The hullabaloo rose to a crescendo as the states, one by one, went to the polls, and when the returns of this raucous contest were in, the Whigs had swept the country. In the electoral college Harrison had 234 votes, Van Buren 60.

Kennedy was exultant. "These fellows," he exclaimed, "are walloped, flabbergasted, and teetotally exflunctified." [3] And victory, he discovered, brought power. As Whig leader in Baltimore, he was "the medium of communication between the citizens of Baltimore and the Government in relation to nearly every appointment." Two months before the inauguration Daniel Webster came over from Washington to dine with Kennedy at Mount Vernon Place, and that evening they closeted themselves in the library to begin carving the patronage melon. In February Webster, now generally known to be Harrison's choice for Secretary of State, over a Washington dinner table broached a new plan. He intended to create the post of undersecretary, and he wished Kennedy to take it. Kennedy agonized over the decision. He was flattered by this show of Webster's confidence, and the idea of an appointive post appealed to him. He had, however, an understanding with the Whig organization in Baltimore to run for Congress. Consequently, he declined. He was anxious, he explained, "to make some little reputation in the representation of the city." [4]

When General Harrison arrived at Baltimore on his way to Washington, Kennedy was a member of the welcoming committee. He was curious to meet this man whom he had so wholeheartedly supported yet had never seen. Astute, caustic John Quincy Adams had confided to his diary the opinion, and the fear, of many Whigs: "[Harrison] is not the choice of three-fourths of those who have elected him. His present popularity is all artificial. There is little confidence in his talents or his firmness." [5] It was unlike Kennedy to be as pessimistic as this, but he compared uneasily the parallel between General Harrison's manner of coming to power and General Jackson's, and so he was relieved to find Old Tippecanoe "uncommonly vigorous, frank, in exceeding good taste." [6] Kennedy entered the city with Harrison, who was greeted by a cheering throng, but the old gentleman, worn out with crowds and courtesy, was too weary to speak.

In Baltimore, observers guessed that the Whig surge of 1840 would carry the congressional ticket in May 1841. Kennedy had received the nomination almost by default in the late 1830's when the Democrats held the city, but now that nomination seemed tantamount to election, the papers named a new aspirant almost daily. Kennedy and Daniel Webster huddled again after Harrison's inauguration and agreed to postpone all local patronage questions until after the Baltimore elections in May. This was shrewd strategy, for it gave Kennedy a strong bargaining position, but the delay threw the local politicos into an uproar, and the cry went up for Kennedy's scalp. In April the convention met and, after airing some grudges, nominated Kennedy on a ticket with Alexander Randall, a son-in-law of William Wirt. The Democrats put in the field, in Kennedy's opinion, "a very sorry shoemaker [and] an old Federalist." [7] Kennedy's letter accepting the nomination outlined his program. He favored a well-ordered national banking power; he believed the compromise tariff of 1833 was satisfactory for protection; and he would elevate the credit of the states, sadly damaged since the panic of 1837, by distributing the proceeds from the sales of the public lands.[8] The campaign was short and intensive, and "after a fatiguing time spent in transversing the district, and the usual amount of vulgar vituperation from that type of Locofocoism in the Republican," Kennedy won narrowly, his margin less than eighty votes out of more than fifteen thousand cast.[9]

The storm signals were flying when Kennedy left for Washington. The quarreling factions of the Whig party in Baltimore were only a sideshow compared to the drama unfolding on the national stage. On April 4, 1841, one month after the day of his inauguration, William Henry Harrison died, and there succeeded to the office of Chief Executive John Tyler, a man, John Quincy Adams observed, "never thought of for it by anybody." [10] The Whigs speculated darkly on this Virginian they had so casually brought to power. Kennedy was apprehensive: "A great deal of talk of the succession of the V. President Mr. Tyler. . . . He is reported an abstractionist of the worst school of Virginia—against a Bank, protective duties, internal improvements, distribution of the proceeds of the lands, in fact against everything useful. . . . Undoubtedly his true course is to respond to the sentiment of the nation evinced in Harrison's election and carry out the Whig measures without reference to his personal opinions. As a man of honor he should do this." [11]

The extra session of Congress which had been called by Harrison at the insistence of Henry Clay convened on May 31, 1841. Anticipating a short session and not wishing to subject his wife to a summer in Washington, Kennedy left Elizabeth in Baltimore in the care of her parents. From the first his reports were discouraging. "We are squabbling today about committees, in which we disclose quite as much unreasonable dissension as on all other matters of the session. Whether we shall break in two for good, or keep together is still a problem of some interest to those who hope the Whigs will retain their power. I hope all will end well, although I am afraid of it." [12] As the humid and stifling heat of July closed over Washington, tempers flared easily at the political infighting which accompanied a major realignment of power. The House of Representatives slogged along in disputes and stalled in delaying tactics. In the gossip of boarding houses or the informal caucusing of a congressional mess, one heard it said that the success of the session, and perhaps the fate of the Whig party, hinged on two men—President John Tyler and Senator Henry Clay.

Years of disappointment over his great ambition had sobered the easy nonchalance of Henry Clay. No one grasped more clearly than he the bitter irony that the party which, a year earlier, had refused him the honor of highest office now looked

A Whig in Harness

anxiously to him for leadership in the crisis. Incurably autocratic, he returned from Kentucky determined to drive Tyler before him. Kennedy thought Clay "the Wellington of the times, authoritative, sagacious, and trusty in every strait." [13] Clay was ready with a program. He immediately introduced a resolution into the Senate which proved to be the American System as of old. Its chief points included the repeal of the Independent Treasury, the incorporation of a national bank, provision for an adequate revenue by the imposition of new duties, distribution of the proceeds of the public lands, and the passage of appropriation bills.[14]

The Whigs who were assembled in Washington turned now to look more closely at John Tyler, the titular leader of their party. Tall and gaunt with a classic profile, he was a man of broad culture, famed for the simplicity and cordiality of his manner. His opinions were no secret. He was a strict constructionist of the strictest sect of Virginia, and only hatred of Andrew Jackson had brought him into the Whig camp. His admirers described him as strong-willed, self-sufficient, and unswerving; his opponents called him dogmatic, vain, and obstinate. He was a proud man, one not likely to be browbeaten by threats or persuaded by appeals to self-interest.

When Congress convened, Clay was in control. In both houses his adherents held the key posts—Kennedy was chairman of the Commerce Committee—and the first step in Clay's program, a bill repealing the Independent Treasury, was rapidly pushed through and signed by Tyler. The rest of the program began to go piecemeal through Congress. The distribution, although hobbled by a southern-inspired amendment that yolked it to the tariff, cutting off distribution whenever import duties rose above twenty per cent, was passed. Kennedy worked himself into a collapse helping to whip this measure through the House and had to retreat to the Gray's home at Ellicotts Mills for several days to recover his strength.

Clay's aggressive tactics had begun to antagonize all but his most devoted friends as one by one the foundation stones of his American System were laid. Only the national bank, the cornerstone of the entire edifice, remained. This was a measure dear to

Whig hearts. Andrew Jackson had slain the Monster in the war of the 1830's, which produced the Whig party. The pro-bank wing of the Whigs had kept their faith through the long years of Democratic rule, and now deliverance was at hand. Nevertheless not all Whigs were enthusiastic about reviving the bank. The savage denunciation by the radicals of the Democratic party, the Locofocos, made many Whigs wary of stirring up old charges of aristocracy and class domination. Tyler had repeatedly expressed his belief that no bank was constitutional which did not provide for the specific consent of each state to the operation of the bank within its own jurisdiction. He made it clear that in his personal opinion a bank created "to operate *per se* over the Union" was unconstitutional. Clay knew this, but he would not yield. "Clay stands like a column," wrote Kennedy, "more glorious than in his most vigorous day. There is in him neither change nor shadow of turning: not only firm and stable, but conspicuously, eminently *right*. He lives or dies on the integrity of his twelve years' course. He is *exactly* where he was in 1829—and consistent with all that he has uttered during the interval." [15] Clay whipped his forces into line, bullied the opposition into submission, and rammed the Bank Bill through Congress. Washington waited to see what Tyler would do. Flying rumors had him reconsidering, wavering, then dissembling, and finally, writing the veto message. It came in mid-August. Kennedy joined the Whig caterwaul: "All our dreams, all our thoughts, and all our noise in veto." [16]

Kennedy watched the growing breach between the Whigs in Congress and Tyler with mixed exasperation and despair. On the bank question he abandoned ultraism as impracticable and began to plump for compromise. "I have turned moderator," he told Elizabeth, "from being a perfect hot blood in the affair. It is all a conspiracy of the Locos to obtain power, and we but favor their design by taking a stubborn position. In this conviction I have concluded that our duty is to take *any* bank, or *shadow of a bank* which Tyler will agree to." [17] A second bank bill was passed and sent to Tyler early in September 1841. It was the product of numerous conferences between Tyler, the cabinet, and members of the House, and it was generally understood that it had the sanction of the President. Tyler hotly denied that he favored it, although the Whigs carefully circulated the impression that he did. "Well, let him veto that *if he dare*," Kennedy wrote Elizabeth; "it is everywhere understood to be his own bill, and he will not have the effrontery to deny that in public." [18] The author of *Swallow Barn*, the delineator of the dogmatic and inflexible Frank Meriwether, might have been expected to understand Virginians better. Like Clay and the Whig conservatives generally, Kennedy grossly underestimated Tyler's fixed and fearless determination to make himself President in fact. His answer was a swift and stinging veto of the bill.

The veto set off a crisis in the cabinet which Tyler had inherited from Harrison and with which he had found himself increasingly at odds. Tyler returned the bank bill with his veto message Thursday, September 9, 1841, and on Saturday all cabinet members except one resigned. Webster stayed on to complete negotiations with Great Britain in the pending settlement of the northeastern boundary question and, the disconsolate Whigs repeated in stage whispers, to satisfy a venal love of office.

Personal ambition had obscured the issue. Clay's refractory mood suggests that his chief incentive was consolidating his leadership in the party and frustrating Tyler's claims. Clay would be sixty-seven in 1844; it would probably be his last opportunity to grasp the elusive scepter of the highest office. On the other hand, Tyler's path of duty seemed to his critics to parallel rather closely the path to the succession. He was suffering from delusions of presidential grandeur. Tyler himself pleaded constitutional scruples for vetoing the bank bills. He was provoked, however, by Clay's arrogance and the sniping of the Whig press. Although testimony in the controversy is conflicting, it tends to exonerate Tyler of duplicity. That he put conviction above party expediency is to his credit, yet he appears to have been ensnared by the hobgoblin of a foolish consistency. Having accepted the nomination from a party whose very reason for being was hatred of executive usurpation, he might have salved his conscience and respected the popular will as revealed in Congress by letting the bill become a law without his signature. He chose to fight, but he refused to tell Congress precisely what detailed legislation he thought should be enacted. He would veto, but he would not lead.

Whether or not guided by consistency, Tyler appeared to men like Kennedy to be a chameleon politician, a dealer in equivocations. A statement which appeared to mean one thing proved to mean another. Tyler failed in his relations with his advisers to give the appearance of consistency and seemed, consequently, a petty, if not a cunning, man. Moreover, the Whigs were enraged when Tyler, like a latter-day Jackson, surrounded himself with a kitchen cabinet. This and not the bank vetoes presumably led to the breakup of the cabinet on Saturday, September 11, 1841. On Monday, September 13, about sixty Whig congressmen met and adopted the "Whig Manifesto" which coolly read Tyler out of the party. It was written "with a few hints from Clay" [19] by John Kennedy.

Attendance at this caucus was the test of party orthodoxy, for the Manifesto narrated the official Whig version of the history of the extra session. After crowing over the measures successfully passed by the Whig majorities in Congress, it rehearsed the congressional case against Tyler, finding him guilty of ignoring his advisers and of scheming to form a new party with himself at its head. In writing the Manifesto, Kennedy kept his personal feelings carefully in check, for privately he considered the affair "a history of baseness, falsehood, privation, and hypocrisy on the part of Tyler quite unexampled in history." The tone of chill moderation was carefully calculated to close Whig ranks by recalling the party to a lofty patriotism. The Manifesto counseled the Whigs to treat Tyler with all the respect due his high station and to support him in all that was right, opposing what was wrong, but it utterly repudiated all responsibility for the measures of his administration.[20]

As the Democrats were quick to point out, the contrast between the wrangling of the session and the pretensions of the Manifesto was ludicrous. They deflated bombast with ridicule.

> The general design of the "Manifesto" is to portray the sufferings of a daring and chivalric band of free booters, who, under the meek and pious mask of patriotism, had "maintained

with unexampled devotion" a "contest of nearly twelve years duration . . . ."

In this brief outline we feel that we have not done justice to Mr. Kennedy's talents. To be fully and properly appreciated, the romance must be carefully read. We commend it to the readers of fiction with this single remark, that if we had not been aware that Mr. Kennedy never leaves the flowery paths of the imagination to gather materials in the field of real life, we should have suspected that the "Manifesto" was intended as a satire upon a small band of politicians who have been recently "exfluncted." [21]

Tyler sent Kennedy a message that he had better confine himself hereafter to romance and not indulge his taste for political manifestoes. Robert Tyler, who served as his father's secretary and who once dedicated a book of poems to Kennedy, snubbed him when the men passed in the street, and when Kennedy called at the White House, the President refused to see him. Kennedy fumed, kept silent publicly, and poured out his wrath in private: "In my opinion no whig, I might add no *gentleman* of either party, would take office with Mr. Tyler without disgrace. He is convicted of treachery and falsehood." [22]

As the author of the Whig Manifesto, Kennedy considered it his duty to write a history of the Twenty-Seventh Congress, developing in detail the entire chain of events leading to the Whig break with Tyler. By the time Congress adjourned *sine die* on March 3, 1843, the separation between Tyler and the Whigs had ripened into the deadliest hostility. Kennedy used the interval between sessions to write *The Defense of the Whigs*.

The Defense essayed nothing less than a history of the two dominant parties back to their roots in British political institutions. It neatly schematized American political history into two antagonistic tendencies: the Court party or Tories, the friends of executive power, the present-day Democracy; and the Country party or Whigs, the friends of legislative power, the present American Whigs. Kennedy saw these two political tendencies as existing prior to the Revolution and as continuous from that time. Neither had undergone a substantial sea change by being conveyed to the New World. The Tories, according to Kennedy, were reborn as Federalists after independence was secured and sank into insignificance during the Era of Good Feelings only to reappear in 1829 as adherents of Jacksonism. The Whigs of the Revolution fought the battle with Federalism under the banner of the Republicans and, in the mid-thirties, emerged again as Whigs to oppose Jacksonism. It was an ingenious version, or inversion, of party history which made Clay, a champion of the Hamiltonian economic system, the heir of Jeffersonianism, and Jackson, the destroyer of the bank, a neo-Federalist. That Kennedy argued from these premises proves only that the traditional party names were bankrupt of meaning as descriptions of political realities. Actually he was employing a device already hallowed in the annals of American party warfare—using the name *Federalist* as a bludgeon to pommel the opposition.

Kennedy was searching for a counterattack to the familiar Democratic charge that the Whigs were a moneyed aristocracy. Kennedy was particularly vulnerable. His association with bankers and manufacturers and his affluent mode of living laid him open to charges of affectation and snobbery. The Baltimore *Republican* played this theme with every conceivable variation. To a Kennedy letter on the tariff, a correspondent answered: "Now we will bet a pound of tobacco to a coon skin that the very moment Mr. Potomac Kennedy was writing this epistle (so full of *pretended* love for home mechanics) that his aristocratic person was clad with the products of foreigners, and his dwelling ornamented with articles of the same character." And again: "[Kennedy] is, and always was, aristocratical in his feelings toward his fellow citizens . . . before the election he is very polite when he meets you, and after the election he is as cold and reserved as possible." [23] To this charge Kennedy replied that the warfare was not between economic classes, between the House of Have and the House of Want, but between the elected representatives of the people and a tyrant. American life was not threatened by a greedy propertied class but by a leeching bureaucratic class, the obsequious hirelings of an untrammeled Chief Executive. Alexander Hamilton, the philosopher of federalism, wished the President chosen for life, and the Federalists tradi-

A Whig in Harness

tionally feared a popularly elected legislature. Jackson, "King Andrew the First," had used his power with what the Whigs considered royal disdain, employing the veto more than all his predecessors combined. *Ergo,* Jackson was a Federalist.

Having got Jackson into the Federal camp, Kennedy had next to trace the Whigs to the old Republican school. All things considered, it was a simpler matter. Although the Republican party which Jefferson led to power in 1800 remained in theory agrarian and opposed to federal centralization, Jefferson was forced during his two terms as President toward a latitudinarian reading of the Constitution. The Louisiana Purchase was made without specific constitutional warrant. The embargo of 1807 had required an extremely elastic reading of the regulation of commerce clause. And the National Road was justified only by the subterfuge of obtaining the consent of the states through which it passed. Jefferson's successor, James Madison, had found it impossible to stem the tide of centralization. It occurred to Kennedy that the great issues of the Whig Program had been codified during the second administration of Madison (1813–1817). It was a point in history when the extremes of federalism had been tempered with an infusion of democracy. The tariff, the national bank, government aid to internal improvements, and a plan for paying off the public debt were begun when Madison, in his second term, had swung toward economic nationalism. In short, from Kennedy's point of view, "it settled the policy of the government."

This view of history was particularly appealing to Kennedy. It was during Madison's second term that Kennedy had fought at Bladensburg and North Point, which in these later years seemed to him a time of "sunshiny holiday attraction." [24] It was the government of Madison and Marshall for which he had taken up arms, not that of Jackson and Taney. And it was during the political calm of the following years that Kennedy had won his first, overwhelming political victories, wielding a magic over the Baltimore populace that he had somehow never recaptured. Those days crystallized in his mind as a fixed point, an apex toward which American political thought had been gradually evolving, and from which the country since that time had been falling insidiously away.

When Kennedy turned from the lineage of parties to a review of John Tyler's defection, *The Defense* abandoned history for invective. Kennedy's patience with Tyler ("preeminently *the most contemptible creature in the Nation*" [25]) was exhausted. Back in September 1841 when Kennedy had spent the weekend in his chambers writing the Whig Manifesto, he had included a personal attack upon Tyler which had been deleted from the final draft. Now he rummaged through his papers, found the discarded paragraphs, refurbished them, and included them in *The Defense*.

> His few partisans in the nation are clamorous in demanding Justice to John Tyler. Justice, assuredly, he will obtain from the pen of History.
>
> It will describe him as vain glorious, weak and accessible to any extravagance of flattery; of a jealousy quickly provoked by the ascendancy of superior minds, and nervously sensitive against the suspicion of being under their influence. . . . Variable and infirm of purpose, he will be exhibited as ever halting between opposite opinions. Anxious to impress the world with a reputation for inflexibility, he will be shown to be, in fact, without a judgment of his own . . . .

And so on for several pages. Kennedy's Baltimore friends of similar political persuasion read this rebuke with grim satisfaction and declared *The Defense* "the best thing he ever wrote, and as captivating a perusal as a romance." [26] Kennedy sent a copy to Henry Clay, and that aging combatant hastened to write a letter of "warm commendation" [27] to Kennedy, now the prose laureate of Whiggery. Clay usually ignored political writing, but if he turned over the pages of *The Defense*, he must have read with a wintry smile the description of himself as "a private tiller of the soil; unostentatious citizen; with no official power."

The Defense of the Whigs made almost no impression when it appeared in February 1844. Through the influence of Horace Greeley, a lusty partisan of the Whig economic platform, it was brought out by Harper and Brothers in New York in a cheaply bound, pamphlet edition. Kennedy blamed the publisher for the failure.

> I did not tell you [he wrote to Elizabeth from Saratoga] how scurvily I have been treated by the Harpers. Upon inquiry, as I passed through New York, how many copies do you think

they have issued of the Defense of the Whigs? Four thousand two hundred! They have never advertised it, neglected all supplies, and, in fact, by their indifference virtually suppressed it. . . . I have asked the Harpers to give it back to me and let me print an edition myself. They promise me an answer as I pass through New York. If I had published it by any obscure bookseller in the Country I could not have fared worse. I will remember this of Messrs. H. They are so much occupied by other things and care so little about politics, that they have put me under the table.[28]

There were other reasons for the failure of *The Defense*. Horace Greeley suggested one: "I am a little afraid that the growing disaffection between Tyler and the Locos with the natural desire of our friends at Washington not to quarrel with anyone who wishes to be at peace with them, will circumscribe the usefulness and circulation of this work." [29] More important, Kennedy spoke for the northern economic program and his pamphlet was embarrassingly specific for leaders anxious to cultivate a national following. Southern planters who had preferred northern Whig conservatives to northern Democratic radicals as the lesser of two evils, now were growing uneasy over the threat a strong central government and an industrial North held to their peculiar institution. The South would remain in the Whig fold only as long as the economic issues were satisfactorily vague. And finally, the style of Kennedy's *Defense* doomed it to obscurity. In an age when every man in public life was at the mercy of a scurrilous press, even Kennedy's onslaught on Tyler seemed tame. The irony was too finely drawn. Had Kennedy devoted his talents to what the great party leaders were unwilling or unable to do, a systematic definition of Whiggery, the historian of American political ideas would be greatly in his debt. But he could not decide whether he wished to write Whig propaganda or a serious critique of political realities. In comparison with the documents brought out by the opposition such as Calhoun's *Exposition* (1828) of state rights and nullification, *The Defense* sinks to the level of a campaign pamphlet.

The Tyler feud conclusively put at an end any lingering sentimental attachment Kennedy might still have felt for the South. Tyler, in Kennedy's eyes, shared the Virginian traits of Frank

Meriwether, master of Swallow Barn, but where Meriwether's provincialism was softened into a lovable eccentricity by Kennedy's sense of the ludicrous, his partisan hatred distorted Tyler into a bigot whose devotion to state rights amounted to treason to country. Kennedy's sense of humor had deserted him; he was suffering from the obsession that he condemned in Tyler's attitude toward Clay—monomania. "The common sentiment of the nation is rising against Virginia politicians, and I think we have now the last of that class in the administration of affairs for the next twenty years. *Nullification* and *abstraction* will sink into bywords of ridicule and with them their whole school of professors." [30] So wrote Kennedy to his wife in 1841 at the height of the controversy, and twenty years later, his prediction so tragically in error, he insisted that the first cause of civil war was John Tyler.

The noise of the Bank War did not, as might be expected, drown out entirely the business of the session. Quietly but steadily, Kennedy worked at a number of pet projects. Like John Quincy Adams, who may have influenced him in this, Kennedy believed the resources of the national government should be employed in the public interest, interpreting this interest in the broadest possible terms. Amid the routine labors of the House of Representatives, the fact-finding chores of his Commerce Committee, and the interminable correspondence with his Baltimore constituents, Kennedy pressed for a naval academy, which was formally opened in 1845, and for subsidized exploring expeditions. He served also on the committee headed by Adams concerned with the disposition of James Smithson's bequest, a fund of over five hundred thousand dollars, which was eventually used to found the institute which bears the donor's name.

It was Kennedy's reputation as a friend to men of science which led the inventor of the telegraph, Samuel F. B. Morse, to seek him out, and Kennedy's sponsorship of that invention through the House of Representatives is an attractive episode in his congressional career. Morse had won distinction as a portraitist and had served as professor of painting and sculpture in the University of the City of New York. In the early 1830's he had dabbled in nativist politics in New York City but had abandoned it to concentrate on the telegraph. Kennedy first heard of the telegraph while serving in Congress in 1838. In the autumn of that year the House Commerce Committee invited Morse to display his instrument in its rooms in the Capitol. In February of the following year, he exhibited it before President Van Buren and his cabinet. Although interest was intense, a bill introduced into the House never reached a second reading. In the wake of the financial collapse of 1837, wary representatives did not want to be caught voting for what many of them feared might prove to be a practical joke.

In 1842 Morse was again in Washington seeking financial aid. He must have been an optimistic man to expect, in the depths of an economic depression, to win patronage from an indifferent Congress engrossed in a feud with Tyler. This time Morse strung wires between the rooms of the House Commerce Committee and those of the Senate Committee on Naval Affairs. Messages were sent back and forth to convince the legislators, and again enthusiasm revived. One Whig member of the Commerce Committee, Caruthers of Tennessee, only admitted that he was satisfied that the invention was practicable when Morse sent the message, "Tyler deserves to be hanged." [31] Kennedy's Commerce Committee reported in favor of the new invention in December 1842, proposing that $30,000 be appropriated for testing the device under the direction of Morse and the general superintendence of the postmaster-general.[32]

On Monday, February 20, 1843, Kennedy tried to get the telegraph bill before the House of Representatives but cries of "No! No!" shouted him down.[33] On the afternoon of the following day he asked Millard Fillmore to give him the floor to move the telegraph bill. Fillmore agreed only upon Kennedy's promise that if debate arose, he would not persist in the motion. Kennedy first moved that the Secretary of the Treasury rather than the postmaster-general oversee the telegraph expenditure. This amendment was carried.

Next Cave Johnson, a Democrat from Tennessee, arose. He had been a gadfly of Kennedy's throughout the session, perversely opposing even minor matters of routine business which Kennedy introduced. Johnson wished to suggest that since Congress was to encourage science, it should encourage the science of mesmerism in Washington. Houston of Alabama interrupted to propose that since the government was to sponsor magnetism and mesmerism, Millerism, the religious sect awaiting the second coming of Christ in 1843, should be included in the bill. Edward Stanly of North Carolina said he had no objection to including mesmerism provided the gentleman from Tennessee, Cave Johnson, was the subject of the experiment. At this, the House burst into laughter. Johnson replied that he had no objection provided Stanly was the operator. "Great Laughter" noted the reporter for the *Congressional Globe*.

A representative arose to demand that the chair rule the amendment out of order as not in good faith and therefore injurious to the character of the House. The Speaker answered that he could not judge the motives of members in introducing amendments. "It would require," he added, "a scientific analysis to determine how far the magnetism of mesmerism was analogous to that to be employed in telegraphs." ("Laughter.") Twenty-two members of that august assembly next voted in favor of the amendment to include mesmerism and Millerism. The amendment being defeated, the House voted to report the telegraph bill from the Committee of the Whole to the House.[34]

Four days later, February 25, 1843, Kennedy moved the bill for the third reading. The yeas and nays being called for, the bill passed the House 89 to 83, with seventy representatives not voting. Subsequently, the Senate passed the bill and Tyler signed it into law. Morse immediately set about constructing his historic line between Washington and Baltimore. In the House Kennedy continued to defend the telegraph. Two years later, in February 1845, he told the House that Morse had written to him to say that the $30,000 was gone and more was needed.[35] On the last day of the session, March 3, 1845, Congress provided $8,000 for the continued operation of the line constructed between Washington and Baltimore but refused to appropriate funds for its extension.

Three decades later, Morse paid tribute to Kennedy's role in the history of the telegraph.

Men of character, men of foresight, men of erudition, in ordinary affairs, were unable to forecast the future of the telegraph: motions disparaging to the invention were made, such as to appropriate part of the sum for a telegraph to the moon. The majority of Congress did not consent in this attempt to defeat the measure by ridicule; and the bill was passed by the close vote of eighty-nine to eighty-three. A change of three votes, however, would have consigned it to oblivion. That this was not its fate is mainly due to the perseverance and foresight of the distinguished member from Maryland, Hon. J. P. Kennedy, co-operating with those from New York, New Jersey, and Ohio.[36]

Among Kennedy's journals and letters, there is not a word to denote his connection with the telegraph in any way.

Kennedy was less successful in his efforts to advance the cause of international copyright. Interest in this subject flared up periodically. In 1836 a memorial of fifty-six British authors asking for copyright protection in the United States had been ignored by Congress. The question was revived in 1842 chiefly through the publicity given the issue by Charles Dickens during his visit to America in that year. Dickens was in Washington in March 1842, dined with Kennedy, and tried to kindle interest in the subject. Henry Clay in particular sympathized with the predicament of the authors denied royalties on their works pirated by American publishers and fought resolutely for a copyright law. On January 6, 1842, he asked and obtained leave to bring in a bill which was promptly bottled up in the Committee on the Judiciary. The Senate was lukewarm, and Clay believed, wisely, that no report was better than an adverse report. The friends of the measure now looked toward the House of Representatives for relief, and on March 14, 1842, a petition signed by Washington Irving and twenty-five others was presented by Edward Stanly of North Carolina and referred to a select committee of which Kennedy was named chairman.

The magazinist and man-about-New York, Nathaniel Parker Willis, came down to lobby for the cause and enlisted the services of Adams and Webster. Kennedy drafted a bill, but Willis thought it too detailed and liable to "embarrass the muddy wits of some of our geese of the Capitol and cause too much discussion." [37] The committee did not report for want of time, and later Kennedy had it revived but nothing was done. Many publishers were naturally opposed, but there were also political reasons. In the wake of the panic of 1837, the default of state governments and corporations on debts owed to British creditors revived Anglo-American differences. The Democrats had for years made political capital of twisting the lion's tail, and the Whigs, traditionally friendly toward England, were unwilling to expose themselves to fresh charges of excessive affection for an ancient foe.

For Kennedy these years at Washington were the realization of a lifelong dream. He would have preferred the Senate, a tantalizing ambition destined to elude him, yet he was too sensible to allow his longing for greater things to taint the satisfaction of immediate achievements. The life was hectic, often "fruitless, inane, absurd," [38] but it was also exhilarating. His letters make this clear. Asked by John H. B. Latrobe to deliver the dedicatory address at Baltimore's Greenmount Cemetery, Kennedy replied:

House of Reps, June 12, 1838

My Dear Latrobe—
How can you ask me to contract such engagements at such a time? Write for the Cemetery quotha! Dost want to put me in it? I'faith not a line does man, woman or child get from me, at nearest, before October. Here is a fellow boring me to get an autograph, devil take him. I shall write to him declining. Yours in the midst of Clerk Franklin reading a long bill.
J.P.K.

It was quite in keeping with Kennedy's character that, eventually, he made the dedicatory address.

Life at Washington never failed to buoy up his flagging spirits. Returning to the capital after devoting the summer of 1838 to writing *Rob of the Bowl*, he told Elizabeth: "I am thriving past all expectations. I believe my principal ailment was nervous prostration from too much labour with my pen, for since I have quitted that implement I have risen like a balloon." [39]

Letters to and from Elizabeth, however, were a poor substitute for the domestic circle at his home on Monument Square. He was unwilling to shuttle between Washington and Baltimore, so in December 1841 he and Elizabeth and her sister, Martha, engaged chambers in Third Street with the representative from Boston, Robert C. Winthrop, and his wife. Winthrop, a descendant of the Puritan governor John Winthrop, was a man of cultivated tastes and scholarly interests and in 1841, at the age of thirty-two, was considered one of the most promising politicians in America. His manners were formal and precise, characterized by what his son and biographer called "a certain native *hauteur*." He liked to say that he was born a conservative, and while he shared the gentlemanly ideal of the duty of public service, he was distressed by the atmosphere of self-seeking and misrepresentation at Washington, and he had no talent in a scramble for office. Such a man would naturally find much in common with Kennedy, and the friendship formed at Washington ended only with Kennedy's death. Winthrop's son thought Kennedy "the most genial of companions and most entertaining of correspondents" and believed he was the closest of all his father's friends.[40] The two men invited the urbane, conscientious Millard Fillmore, representative from Buffalo, and his wife to occupy the adjoining rooms, "though they are not," Winthrop feared, "exactly the right persons." [41]

Kennedy and Winthrop frequently entertained at intimate, carefully select dinners. A Southerner was seldom included. Among the guests was Francis Granger, congressman from New York and postmaster-general under Harrison, who had earned the hostility of slaveholders by joining John Quincy Adams in opposing southern restrictions on the right of petition. Adams himself frequently dined at Third Street. The former President had become fond of the freshman congressman from Baltimore, who was twenty-eight years his junior, and it appears that their friendship reached as great a degree of intimacy as was possible with that independent and solitary Yankee. Adams respected Kennedy's talents and praised his speeches in the House as "masterly," "powerful," "able and elaborate," and "spirited and ingenious." Kennedy was secretly proud of this friendship, but he was frequently baffled by the behavior of "this most inscrutable old man." [42] Since the old Puritan liked to think of himself as a literary gentleman, their talk was more often of books and authors than of politics, for Adams did not share Kennedy's dogged loyalty to party. Kennedy tried to get Adams to head a list for a Clay dinner in 1842, telling him that "the Clay flag was to be raised, and fire away at Tyler." Adams excused himself as being too old for public dinners, and said tartly that he would "ask for an exposition of their principles." [43]

In 1843 when Adams was planning a trip to Buffalo, his wife, Louisa, an admirer of Kennedy, wrote to invite him to accompany them: "Unaccustomed to use the language of flattery; I can only assure you in sincerity; that the ready wit, blythe conversation, and kind manners of such a friend as yourself, would alone give zest to a journey likely to be so full of incident; and admirably calculated in all probability to furnish pleasant reminiscences to the delineator of Rob of the Bowl the Hero of Times Past." [44] Kennedy, confined to his home with his face and hands broken out in a scaly, inflamed rash, had to refuse. He remained in the library, glum with disappointment, as the journey, widely reported in the press, turned into a triumphal march.[45]

Among the lay leaders of Whiggery, Abbott Lawrence, the Boston cotton magnate, dined occasionally at Third Street. Lawrence was a power in Boston politics and typified the great merchants who were beginning to replace the bankers as leading patrons of the Whig party. The witty and polished Charles Augustus Davis, once a friend of Nicholas Biddle and director of the New York branch of the United States Bank, and now in the commission business in Wall Street, came down from New York. Davis enjoyed a life of affluence, and his home was a favorite resort of the Knickerbocker authors. He shared Kennedy's literary tastes and in the mid-thirties had written the sprightly satires of Jacksonism, *The Letters of Jack Downing, Major.* Another New Yorker, Philip Hone, was a friend of these congressional years. Like Davis, Hone sought out men of letters and made them welcome at his board. He liked and admired Kennedy and thought *Horse-Shoe Robinson* "the best American story I have read." [46] From the army, pompous General Winfield Scott, out of politics but longing to be in, was occasionally included.

All together they formed an intelligent, vigorous, masculine society. If they spoke patronizingly, as did Philip Hone, of the "vulgar and uneducated masses," [47] it was because they viewed realistically a stratum of society which, alike in Boston, New York, Philadelphia, and Baltimore, was brutalized and criminal. Moreover, the tactics of their opponents in pitting class against class made them self-conscious of their elevation in American society. Successful in the world of affairs, they liked to believe that every man was self-made, making himself either eminent and respectable or wretched and debauched. Most believed, as did Kennedy, in the stewardship of wealth: "He who has but one talent accounts for that one. He who has ten has a larger stewardship and larger accountability." [48]

Amid the harebrained idealisms and utopian schemes that marked the decade of the 1840's, this Whig circle viewed its world steadily and whole. The leaders of the common man had grasped the reins of government from the rich and well-born, but they fought back as a stubborn and effective minority using the economic weapons at their command. Many felt alien in bumptious and leveling mid-century America and looked wistfully toward England for a stable and meaningful tradition. Englishmen of whiggish sympathies in Washington were certain to find a warm reception at Third Street. Lord Morpeth, who shared Kennedy's enthusiasm for both politics and literature, was a frequent guest during his visit to the capital in 1842. He was, Kennedy observed, "certainly amused with the Country." Lord Ashburton cultivated the acquaintance of Kennedy and Winthrop during the negotiation of the northeastern boundary question in the summer of 1842. Lord Ashburton's successor, Sir Richard Pakenham, became close friends with Kennedy, the two men touring Canada together in the summer of 1847.

If the culture of these American Whigs now seems stale and derivative, in their time they instilled into public life a wholesome tone which was a valuable if not a vitalizing force. In Washington men of promise were destroyed by drunkenness; gambling was widely tolerated and, in the case of some colorful politicos, covertly admired. The floor of Congress was not exempt from scenes of violence, and debate often sank to the level of common quarreling. In this atmosphere Kennedy and Winthrop and their circle required respectability as a qualification for office, not only to consolidate respect for the Whig party, but to retain the function of government within the ranks of gentlemen.

The most eloquent testimonial to the Whig circle at Washington of which Kennedy and Winthrop were the center came from the French minister, Adolph Bacourt, a captious and vituperative critic of all things American. Traveling through Baltimore he had found the city "as gloomy as a tomb," the Washington Monument an "organ pipe," and the Roman Catholic Cathedral in bad taste, wholly "abominable." At Washington his official duties proved a tedious and repulsive exile, with one exception: "I have been to see Mrs. Kennedy and Mrs. Winthrop. Their husbands are members of the House of Representatives, and on the Committee of Commerce, in which I am interested. They are the two most distinguished men amongst this strange American people." [49]

CHAPTER IX

"New Men, New Measures, New Country"

AT THE CLOSE of the Twenty-Seventh Congress, March 3, 1843, John Kennedy was back in Baltimore and ailing. Some months earlier, in October 1842, he had seriously injured his hip in a fall from a horse, and in his anxiety to return to Congress he had not allowed it sufficient time to heal. Confined to his bed, he began to suffer acute dyspepsia. By the autumn of 1843 his face and chest were covered with a severe rash. He fretted over the effect his appearance would have on the coming campaign. The fall elections were postponed, however, for the Maryland legislature, half Whig and half Democrat, had been unable to agree on a new district law. In January 1844 the new legislature, now controlled by the Whigs, promptly districted the state, strengthening Kennedy's bailiwick by a gerrymander. He was nevertheless sufficiently alarmed by a squabble in local party ranks to appeal to Robert C. Winthrop for help, but in vain. It was an imposition. "You know not what you ask," replied this Boston exquisite. "I would do almost anything to secure your election, but a Caucus Speech is a thing my gorge rises at." [1] Kennedy's illness left him *hors de combat*, so his lieutenants stumped the wards while he sat in his library writing a series of letters to the press, "an odd but a most effective mode of electioneering—to sit at the desk and fulminate pen wise." [2] His fears proved groundless, for he won the election handily in a statewide sweep that carried all six Whig candidates for Congress.³

Kennedy took almost no part in the session. The Democrats controlled the House, Kennedy was named to no committee, and "so had nothing to do but look on and laugh with Mr. Adams." In 1844 elections and interest centered on the presidential contest. On May 1 the Whig National Convention meeting in Baltimore unanimously nominated Henry Clay for the Presidency. His friends rallied round, for it seemed at last that Harry of the West was to have his turn. Of the opposition, Kennedy remarked with unconscious irony: "What a ticket, Polk and Dallas! If we can't beat them we shall deserve our fate." In midsummer Kennedy set off for Sharon Springs in the lovely Cherry Valley region of New York on a trip that was part pleasure and part politics. He journeyed by way of Boston, visiting Robert C. Winthrop and delivering several Clay speeches en route. Philip Hone of New York joined Kennedy at Sharon Springs, and the two friends determined on drinking the medicinal waters which Hone said were "nauseous in taste, and emitting a smell a hundred yards before you come to the spring more offensive than the foulest drain in New York." But Hone and Kennedy were determined on taking the cure, and while drinking the first glass each gaily held the other's nose.⁴

During the autumn of 1844 Kennedy's morale continued high, for he found the "elections are coming on well, although the contest between Clay and Polk is closer than we supposed it would be." ⁵ Before the month was out, the disaster came. In New York the Liberty party, an organization dedicated to extirpating slavery by direct political action, appeared on the scene. In a three-way race its candidate polled over fifteen thousand votes while Clay ran over five thousand behind Polk. The loss of the Empire State was decisive, and James Knox Polk with a plurality of the total vote cast became President of the United States. Conservatives were dismayed and alarmed. "Old Harry," Kennedy told a Baltimore merchant, "is magnanimous and dignified in his last words and falls like a hero. Strange times are ahead. The old thirteen and their principles are out of fashion, and we are starting upon a new era, with new men, new measures, new country." ⁶ From the ashes of Clay's defeat three issues were destined to rise, phoenix-like, auguring ill for Kennedy's political future and for his country's—nativism, Texas, and, most portentous for evil, slavery. Had Kennedy the gift of prophecy, he would have seen no reason for optimism as, on October 25, 1844, he entered upon his fiftieth year.

After the disappointment of Clay's defeat in 1844, Kennedy published a letter in the New York *Tribune* [7] that was destined to have far-reaching consequences on his political future.

> It is fundamental in this government that the true People of America shall speak truly in their elections; that their voice shall not be suppressed by fraud or violence; and that neither shall it be out weighed by voices *un*American—I mean by that, that no man shall vote in our elections who has not a heart to feel with American people, and a mind so acclimated as to understand, at least, the difference between American and Foreign interests. To compass this great end, we must have a modification of the Laws of Naturalization—such modifications as shall lengthen the term of probation, exact greater care in the introduction to citizenship, and strengthen the securities against fraud. We say with all our heart—all hospitality to the stranger, full privilege of holding lands, full protection to property, full encouragement to his labor, but no privilege to interfere in the Government or Legislation of the nation until he has lived long enough in the country to understand its interests, to resist the cajolery of the demagogues who would make him through his ignorance, the instrument of his basest designs. . . .

Thus the genie of nativism, so recklessly evoked, would before long prove impossible to control.

Nativism was a highly volatile element for Kennedy to introduce into the local political scene. In Baltimore, as elsewhere, anti-immigrant feeling was inseparable from anti-Catholicism. The Irish in Baltimore were predominantly Roman Catholic, and the political rivalry frequently had religious overtones. Intolerance flared up suddenly in August 1839. An insane nun escaped from the Carmelite convent in Baltimore and ran through the streets hysterically begging for protection. For two days angry mobs milled about the nunnery, and order was maintained only by calling out volunteer corps and auxiliary police.

Although unsympathetic toward Roman Catholicism, Kennedy counted many friends among Baltimore Catholics and scrupulously avoided partisanship. Unwittingly he was drawn into a sectarian controversy. In 1845 he published a biographical sketch of George Calvert, first Lord Baltimore,[8] originally delivered as the second annual address of the Maryland Historical Society, an organization Kennedy served as vice-president for many years. The pamphlet was a graceful tribute to the Lord Proprietary, but in the course of the exposition Kennedy suggested that the scheme for colonizing Maryland had been motivated by the desire for wealth and family reputation as well as for a haven for a persecuted minority. Today this sounds obvious enough, but at the time the history of the colonial fathers ran to uncritical eulogy. The Baltimore *Catholic Magazine*, in a caustic review, rebuked Kennedy's defective historical sense, his irreverence for tradition, and his bad manners. Kennedy replied in good humor, defending history against the charge that it be panegyric and defending himself against the charge that he had debunked Lord Baltimore. He won a clear victory in the pamphlet war, but the notoriety given to the skirmish, coupled with his recently proclaimed nativist views, undoubtedly left a residue of suspicion in the minds of his opponents, particularly those who did not read his heavily documented and closely reasoned *Reply*.[9]

Kennedy's nativism was in part his pride in his own Pendleton ancestry, in part his awareness of the influence immigration was having on American institutions. His nativism was still another manifestation of the intense nationalism which permeated every aspect of his life and thought. His earliest essays, "The Swiss Traveller," were staunchly chauvinistic. *Horse-Shoe Robinson* celebrated the epic struggle for independence. Kennedy pointed out in his *Defense of the Whigs* that the party name evoked memories of the revolutionary struggle, and in so doing he appealed to old American stock. This nationalist cast of his mind was amusingly revealed in an encounter while on a journey through upstate New York. He recorded it in some notes prepared for an essay on "National American Chivalry" which he never completed. The anecdote is so rich in its revelation of the essential man that it deserves quotation in full.

I was riding in the train from Niagara towards Albany. We stopped at Rochester twenty minutes to take tea. There was a delicate, quiet little woman in the car who was travelling without anyone to take care of her. She occupied a seat near mine and went, with the rest of the crowd, to the hotel. I was back in my place some minutes before the time was out, and in this interval two tall, bony, begrimed and rough looking fellows came in and appropriated to themselves the seat of the little woman. I ventured to say, in a civil way to them, that they had the seat of a lady who had gone to tea. The car by this time was filling up so rapidly that she would have found it difficult to get another seat without disturbing an occupant. The answer I got was in a gruff voice. "We paid our dollar for Auburn and it is as good as any lady's." I thought I would clear my proposition of all irrelative matter, and state the argument to them in another shape. So I said, "It isn't the question of what you have paid for *a* seat, but your right to buy *this* seat which has been already sold to a lady, who will be here in a moment to ask for it." "We have got as much right to it," said the principal speaker, "as any woman in the State, and I would like to see who is going to put us out of it." This nettled me, and I was about to get up and call the conductor to settle the point; but I resolved to let off a shot, so I replied. "I have no doubt that you two *together* would prove too much for the lady if it should come to a boxing match; so I will advise her to give it up. Some of her own countrymen here will give her a seat. She couldn't expect *you* to do that." "How do you know I am not an American myself?" cried out the first speaker very angrily, and standing up with his fist doubled. "Everybody in the car knows that," said I. "An American is never uncivil to a woman."

Just as I said this I saw the lady bustling along towards her seat and half a dozen or more of the male passengers rising to offer their places and advising her not to trust herself into the neighborhood of the two Scotchmen who were waiting to fight her. She accepted one of these offers amidst a laugh that was echoed through the car and the belligerent usurpers of her seat finding that there was a considerable native force around her in very good humor to see me through the affair sat down and muttered their malice in low tones for some time and at last discreetly but sullenly became silent; thus saving me from a crisis in which I should have been obliged to choose between a heroic defense and an inglorious retreat.[10]

Besides nativism, a second inflammable issue was thrust upon the political scene during the 1840's—Texas. Although President

Tyler insisted on meddling with it, seeing in the issue a springboard to re-election, seasoned politicians wished valiantly to declare a moratorium on the question. Agitation was certain to reopen the slavery question and fan anew the flames of sectional animosity. Nevertheless Tyler worked busily. His first efforts to bring Texas into the Union had been stymied by opposition from the Senate and the Secretary of State he had inherited from Harrison, Daniel Webster. Forces were in motion, however, which were riveting the attention of America on the Southwest. Editors and politicians who made a career of Anglophobia rumored darkly that Great Britain's interest in Texas was stealthily being secured while the United States dozed. The South declared Texas essential to maintaining the "sacred balance" between free and slave states. Martial fever against Mexico flared up with every unattested tale of a border raid. Sensing the rise of expansionist fervor, Tyler was emboldened to make his bid. Webster's successor in the cabinet, Abel P. Upshur, made a formal offer of adoption, and Texas, although inclined to be coy, eventually sent a representative to Washington to arrange for a treaty. After Upshur was killed in an explosion aboard the warship *Princeton*, Tyler picked John C. Calhoun, a violent expansionist, to complete negotiations, and on April 12, 1844, the treaty of annexation was signed.

Kennedy listened with disgust to such news of these machinations as was freely gossiped about Washington. Back home in Baltimore, the Democrats passed resolutions at a public meeting favoring the annexation of Texas. Kennedy answered with an open letter to the press.[11] The entire business, he explained, was a plot of "our Polonious President," a mischievous and Machiavellian scheme "by which this second-hand hero of the Vetoes has hoped to win that most impossible of honors, a vote from some State in favor of another term." The United States, Kennedy argued, had enough territory to engage its attention for at least fifty years, and Maryland, drained of population by the opening of new states, had much to fear from the acquisition of new territory. A traveler through Maryland could readily see good soil untilled, mines unexplored, and farms abandoned. "What is Texas?" Kennedy asked. The border of this sprawling territory was so indefinite that it was uncertain what the United States was annexing. Kennedy found it peculiar that the party of strict construction, whose founder had agonized over purchasing Louisiana, now had no scruples whatsoever about admitting a foreign nation. "The opinions of Jefferson, however, are of small authority in his own school when they stand in the way of a party purpose." And finally he flung in the teeth of the South the charge that Texas was but a pawn in a larger game to form eventually a confederacy based on the "essential blessing" of slavery. John Quincy Adams told Kennedy the letter was "the best which the subject has called out," and it was picked up and puffed by northern papers, especially as it was "the product of a Southern man." [12]

Politically it boomeranged. The Democrats in Baltimore held a mass meeting in Monument Square and adopted resolutions of censure. Just as in Jackson's time, Kennedy had failed to assess accurately the importance of a popular movement. The expansionist fever was rampant and could not be checked by those who wished to conserve and consolidate. Young America was demanding that Texas be acquired to fulfill the young nation's manifest destiny. Kennedy, no longer the hotblooded private of Bladensburg and North Point, underestimated the strength of this emotion. And his stand against the annexation of Texas deepened the impression, already widespread in slave-owning Maryland, that Kennedy was not "safe" on slavery.

In 1830 Kennedy owned a slave, but the Negro, proving "a liar, thief, and rascal," was sent to Virginia to be sold. At the time Kennedy declared, "I will never own another slave, and should not have taken this fellow if he had not been given to me by my father. My intention was to send him to school and let him free when he became of age." [13] Another old Negro couple, retainers of Kennedy's mother, were given their freedom after her death, much against their will, but they proved incapable of earning a living and Kennedy ended by supporting them out of his own pocket. His personal attitude toward individual slaves seems to have been characteristically southern: an easy familiarity mixed with what Henry Adams called the southern "habit of command."

An incident during his trip to Sharon Springs with Philip Hone in 1844, described in a letter to Elizabeth, illustrates this facet of his character. "I am getting very tired of this place as it is deserted by its inmates. You know I am a great enemy to solitude. I could not yesterday get up a game of billiards with *any* white man and so took Charley, the marker, a colored gentleman of the first circles, who has charge of the billiard room and an adjoining barber shop. One or two Georgians who are here remarked to me that that condescension on my part was quite familiar to them. Necessity however knows no law, and solitude reconciles us to strange playmates." [14]

Kennedy prided himself on the consistency of his public position on slavery, but in private his opinions were undergoing change. He was growing concerned about the moral implications of the institution and impatient with southern agitation to reopen the slave trade. When Kennedy spoke of the southern "chivalry," it sounded more and more like stately profanity. He seldom spent his summers among the planters at White Sulphur or Berkeley Springs in western Virginia but went north by rail to Saratoga. At Congress Hall he met pretty belles and their charming mothers from New York and Boston and young men from Harvard or Yale whose philandering was financed by fathers in Wall Street or State Street. And when the fathers themselves arrived, there was no maundering about state rights or blathering about the glories of a slave empire, but hardheaded discussion of Erie bonds, bank stocks, and the tariff. Kennedy dreaded "this horrible dream of abolition," but before the decade of the 1840's was out he was writing, "I cannot reconcile myself to the opinion that one man can ever obtain a lawful title to the possession and ownership of another." But he quickly modified this with the reservation of the man who lived among slaves: "Manifestly emancipation would be a greater evil than the continuance of slavery." [15]

Politically he took the familiar conservative position that slavery was primarily a local problem and that Congress had no authority to interfere with the institution in the slaveholding states. The agitation of the question at Washington he believed to be the demagoguery of men hoping to gain popularity at home.

"New Men, New Measures, New Country"

While in Congress he uniformly voted for the "gag rule," which automatically laid upon the table any petition relating to slavery. The Wilmot Proviso, which would outlaw slavery in any territory acquired from Mexico, Kennedy believed a *"mere contrivance"* to stir up controversy. He told Winthrop,

> I am myself opposed to the Wilmot Proviso and should *affect to lament* even your qualified views on that subject. I think it great nonsense to talk about restricting slavery *in space*. I hope to see it restricted in *numbers* and *influence*, and that I believe is best promoted by allowing every Southern man to emigrate and take his slaves with him to the d---l if he chooses. The more the merrier and the farther the better. The notion of packing them up "to knot and gender" in Mississippi, etc. seems to me to be as absurd as to say that Negro slaves not be taken to Liberia. If they *will* have Mexico, the only indemnity in it which I can see is to fill it with the negroes of Maryland, Virginia and Kentucky. I think they will ultimately rise into a better condition there than they will ever do with us.[16]

Kennedy's refusal to take a decided pro-slavery position cost him his greatest ambition, a seat in the United States Senate. When a seat became vacant after the mid-thirties, his name would be brought before the Maryland legislature only to be howled down by the pro-slavery forces. The suspense was more tantalizing than outright repudiation. But like his idol, Henry Clay, Kennedy discovered that his experience and his identification with specific issues hindered his election. He lacked availability. He was not spared the final mortification of seeing his youngest brother, Anthony, an amiable, shallow man devoid alike of talent and experience, presented the senatorship in 1856 by the Know-Nothings, a wretched coalition, purportedly nativist, which emerged for a single season from the wreckage of the Whig party in Maryland.

Three issues then, nativism, Texas, and slavery, loomed on the horizon in the spring of 1845 as Kennedy surveyed the local situation. He was indifferent to another term in the House of Representatives. In June 1844 he told Elizabeth, "I am *so* tired, as the children say, of this Congress, that I am determined I will never try the House of Reps, or Rips, again."[17] In April 1845 he suffered a severe attack of typhoid fever, which left him enervated and depressed, and the following month he told Winthrop he would definitely not seek the nomination. His health was poor, he wanted leisure for writing, and he would have to fight "a good deal of discontent, at least apathy" to regain his seat. There was, however, some hope of success. The wards in Baltimore had been "equalized," and Kennedy's bailiwick was now considered a Whig stronghold.[18]

With the Baltimore Whigs in a state of unrest and indecision, Kennedy abruptly left the city with Elizabeth and the Grays for Sharon Springs determined to forget politics for the summer months. The trip was memorable for a delightful visit with James Fenimore Cooper at Otsego Hall, the novelist's castellated home at Cooperstown some twenty miles from Sharon Springs. Cooper and his wife and daughters guided the Kennedys to "The Vision," the mountain top described in *The Pioneers,* and Cooper impetuously insisted on pushing on to "The Prospect," a higher point on the mountain, in the face of a threatening storm. The group was caught in a cloudburst at the peak and returned to the Hall drenched and bedraggled. The Kennedys donned clothes from the Coopers' wardrobe, "a species of masquerade," while their own things were drying. Everyone was in the merriest of moods. Cooper "told all manner of stories and brought out all his pleasantries. . . . [He] gave some very intimate particulars of his experience in mesmerism, to which he had recently become a convert." He invited the Kennedys into his library to see his autographs, pictures, and memorabilia. The adventure, or misadventure, at The Prospect had done more to establish intimacy between the two families than a dozen formal meetings in society could have achieved.[19]

Kennedy returned from Sharon Springs to find that he was the unanimous choice for Congress of the Whig convention. "I was obliged to accept," he noted in his journal, "because it was made a present of by my friends, and because I have resolved never to ask such a favor and never to decline such a duty when I am called upon." [20] From the first it was hopeless. A nativist ticket was in the field, and the statements of editors of both parties showed it to be a Whig splinter movement. Since Kennedy had won the nomination unopposed, and since his nativist proclivities were well known, a separate nativist movement could only be interpreted as dissatisfaction with his course in Congress, particularly on Texas and the slavery issue. The Natives drew off eleven hundred votes, and Kennedy ran nine hundred behind the victorious Democrats.[21]

"But this is our fate," he lamented to Winthrop; "a gallant and spirited company of the best men of the land, continually sacrificed to every whim of the foolish, and to every design of the wicked. The principle of a genuine love of country, unmixed with the hopes and promises of personal reward, is too *spiritual* for a party." [22] Kennedy was undoubtedly sincere, but he was deaf to the overtones of self-pity in this outcry. His position on the great issues of the day was sound and statesmanlike, arrived at by close study of the issues, yet there is little evidence that he appreciated or remotely understood the discontent even in Maryland. He was a humane and generous man, and his sympathies went out to individual cases of poverty and oppression. But the great liberal democratic movement he underestimated and distrusted. He later came to question the value of universal suffrage and thought it necessary to "lessen the frequency and limit the objects of popular elections." [23] The age of the common man found him intent on retaining power in the hands of the uncommon few. The political career of such a man in Jacksonian America was necessarily brief, and Kennedy's was fast drawing to a close.

Although Kennedy rationalized his defeat by fancying it would give him uninterrupted leisure for writing, in the autumn of the next year, 1846, the Baltimore Whigs determined to bring him out for the Maryland House of Delegates. His first reaction was to decline, but the party managers argued that his name would carry the election for the entire ticket, and a victory would strengthen him for the congressional race in October 1847. Kennedy also felt an obligation to run connected with his long and ardent support of internal improvements in Maryland. The rage for public works at government expense, which had begun during the early 1820's when he was serving in the House of Delegates, had reached a stage bordering on mania by 1836. That year the Maryland legislature appropriated eight million dollars for an astonishing system of internal improvements, floating a bond issue to finance the project. Simultaneously the state was projecting or constructing a railroad to Annapolis, a railroad from Baltimore to the Susquehanna, a railroad to the Eastern Shore, a railroad from Baltimore to the Ohio, and a magnificent canal from tidewater on the Potomac to the Ohio River.

The legislature had made the appropriations when money in Europe was abundant and American securities were in demand. Then came the panic of 1837, and the folly of Maryland's undertaking became painfully apparent. By 1840 the public debt of the state was $15,000,000, bearing an annual interest of $600,000. With bonds selling at a discount of thirty-five per cent and the state unable to borrow, the treasury found itself without funds to meet the interest payments falling due in October 1841. From that time until January 1848, Maryland paid no interest on its public debt.

To finance the internal improvements, Kennedy had joined with eastern Whigs in battling for the distribution of the proceeds from the sale of the public lands. When this failed, the years following the suspension witnessed various experiments to evolve a system of equitable taxation and adequate machinery for collection. By the mid-forties the times were ripe for resumption of payments. Business was on the rise throughout the country. The legislature had curtailed expenses and strengthened the collection of taxes. Maryland's financial agents abroad, the Barings of London, were of course vitally interested in seeing the state resume payments on the debt and agreed to contribute three to four thousand dollars to secure the election to the legislature of Whig candidates who were known to be in favor of paying the debt. Kennedy canvassed the city for a week and won the election by fifty-nine votes. Two more Whigs won by narrower margins.[24]

The Whigs at Annapolis unanimously named Kennedy Speaker of the House of Delegates. It had been twenty-five years since he had been, in his own words, "the gay boy" of the legislature, and now he found himself being introduced to young representatives whose fathers had served with him in the 1820's. "I have got my boys in the House in excellent order," he reported to Elizabeth. "They think me a prime disciplinarian, and I begin to make quite a figure in the Speaker line." He found much to approve in his own handling of the various questions. "I find I am almost the only one looked to in the important questions. The impression I have made is very good and my control and authority increases." He took advantage of his position to push through a long-cherished measure to preserve the moldering documents of colonial times stored helter-skelter in the state buildings at Annapolis which he had turned up in 1836 while engaged in research for *Rob of the Bowl*. In the face of opposition from representatives who charged a steal and a sellout to Baltimore "thieves," he had the papers transferred to the Maryland Historical Society, which had been organized three years earlier. The great question of the session, the resumption, was firmly handled and the Maryland Resumption Law was passed March 8, 1847. Payment of the interest on the public debt was resumed January 1, 1848.[25]

After the close of the session, Kennedy remained in Baltimore until June and then left on a tour of Canada with the British minister at Washington, Sir Richard Pakenham. It was a vagabond journey, the two friends lingering when they were diverted and hastening on when they were bored. At New York Kennedy renewed his acquaintance with the cosmopolitan Nathaniel Parker Willis and the actor Charles Kean before pushing north. In Canada he found little to praise and much to blame. There was "a considerable amount of Snobbism," "a spirit of imitation of the mother country, and the desire to be *unlike the Yankee.*" The Canadians kept third-rate inns and remained obstinately unmoved by the palpable superiority of their southern neighbor. The chief characteristics of Ontario he thought were "filth, sluggishness, and total ignorance of the go ahead principle." He was further irked to find *Horse-Shoe Robinson* for sale at Toronto in a pirated and badly garbled version. Back in Boston on familiar ground and among familiar faces, his spirits revived. Robert C. Winthrop introduced him to Henry W. Longfellow, who had just brought out his narrative poem, *Evangeline*, and to William H. Prescott, who had just received news of the London success of his *History of the Conquest of Peru*. Kennedy talked Whig politics with Daniel Webster and Edward Everett, then returned to Baltimore in mid-July, having spent forty-five days and $311.23.[26]

If Kennedy believed that service in the House of Delegates would mean victory in the congressional campaign of 1847, he was doomed to disappointment. The Whigs again presented him with the nomination, but the issues of the American System were stale. In 1846 Democratic majorities in Congress passed the Walker Tariff, a measure essentially for revenue rather than protection, and revived the Independent Treasury. In each case the principle for which Kennedy stood had been defeated, and now he attempted to force discussion on a bored electorate. And he turned, unluckily as it proved, to the burning issue of the moment, the war with Mexico.

In March 1845 Texas came into the Union by joint resolution of Congress, and Mexico promptly broke off diplomatic relations insisting, among other grievances, that the Nueces River, and not the more southerly Rio Grande, marked the lower border of Texas. In January 1846 General Zachary Taylor was ordered to advance from the Nueces to the Rio Grande. By April American and Mexican armies were face to face on opposite banks of the Rio Grande, and when Taylor refused an ultimatum to withdraw his troops beyond the Nueces, the Mexicans attacked. Polk promptly sent in a war message stating that Mexico had shed American blood on American soil, and the House of Representatives declared war. The House next authorized a call for volunteers and a ten-million-dollar appropriation, but sixty-seven Whigs voted against this measure, foreshadowing opposition to the administration that increased as the war progressed. Kennedy insisted on injecting the issue into the Baltimore campaign. He wrote a series of six letters to the press, denouncing President Polk as unworthy of the confidence of the country and charging that the war was brought on by an unconstitutional use of the executive power. Arguments were in vain, for in time of war a man differs with the administration at his peril. If one believed the Democratic orators in Monument Square, the Whigs as a party were rather worse than the Mexicans.

The result was inevitable. "We were beaten here by pure

fraud," Kennedy explained to Winthrop, "if any fraud can be pure. A thousand votes bought and brought in." Fraud had played a part, but that was not the whole story. Kennedy's reverence for consistency had required him to oppose the war issue, and it had beaten him.[27] But the Whigs learned fast, and in 1848 they nominated General Zachary Taylor on a platform reciting his military character and reputation. Kennedy approved of Old Rough and Ready and campaigned for him. But defeat had dampened his enthusiasm. He had run for elective office in Baltimore twelve times during a political career spanning twenty-seven years; five times he had lost. He would not run again. "I mean," he wrote in his journal, "to systematize my time and study, and give a close attention hereafter to the cultivation of a literary reputation."[28]

CHAPTER X

The Literary Life

IN RESOLVING to resume his literary career following his defeat in the congressional contest of 1847, John Kennedy was conforming to a familiar pattern. From beginning to end the first love of his life was politics. As long as he could play a role in the drama of public life, he used his pen only insofar as it advanced his political fortunes or those of his party. His four novels were written during the periodic calms which occur as inexorably under the American political system as do the party battles. He found time to write innumerable letters to newspapers on political topics, but he contributed nothing to the literary journals despite their constant pleas for help. Thomas W. White of the *Southern Literary Messenger* failed to persuade Kennedy to write for the magazine, as did its later editors, Edgar Allan Poe and John R. Thompson. William Gilmore Simms, after taking control of the *Southern Quarterly Review*, tirelessly dunned Kennedy for contributions, but in vain. Kennedy was repelled by the personal abuse and petty caballing of much of the literary criticism of his time. Writing for the reviews was, as he himself might have said, *infra dignitatum;* privately he called it "pewter mug" circulation. When he did hint to Simms that he might be readying an article, it concerned "a little scruple on the score of some ultraisms in Southern politics," [1] which would have been anathema to the extremist *Southern Quarterly*.

The Literary Life

Politics moreover was indisputably man's work, while the literary life, in the eyes of many Americans, was suspect, an effeminate business at best. A writer in the *New York Mirror*, for example, remarked in 1836 that "the profession of literature stands apart from the money-making business of life, and is viewed not without a sentiment of distrust, if not of ridicule and aversion." A Baltimore newspaper editor, in the course of a tribute to Kennedy's work in politics, showed surprise that a literary man should have either the taste or capacity for public affairs. The political circles in which Kennedy moved quite cheerfully ignored his writings on other than political topics; that is, the Whigs ignored them, for the Democrats considered the reputation of being a romancer a sin of commission and solid grounds for disqualifying him from office. Kennedy once wryly observed that by writing a novel he had "committed a crime which the Locos consider my deepest sin." [2]

It irked Kennedy that there were few men who would believe "that the successful use of the goose quill does not unman a man." A robust, masculine American, Kennedy, like Hawthorne, wearily cursed the mob of scribbling women and heartily despised the lunatic fringe the arts attracted. He had, he said, "no desire to look 'literary.'" To Elizabeth he wrote: "I think the tribe, *author*, is not altogether the best of the Twelve of Israel. There is a little touch of Signor de Begnis in most of them—bravura and voluntary, with a stretching out of the neck for applause. These soldiers of the quill, I fear, do not often leave me greatly prepossessed with my comradeship." [3] This suspicion of "literary men" was revealed in a letter to Elizabeth written from Philadelphia in 1832 retailing some gossip concerning Nathaniel Parker Willis.

> N. P. Willis after playing the fool and rake all over Europe, and spending his master's money and getting his bills dishonored, crept back in disgrace to England, without a penny, intending, I presume to become a hack writer, and fell ill . . . and then got better and wrote some verses, and attracted the sympathy of a lady who sent him sweetmeats, and cordials, whereupon taking heart and growing well, he wooed and won her, and lo! it turns out that she was a widow with—I am almost afraid to

say it—fifty thousand pounds sterling per annum, somewhat oldish to be sure.

There's poetical justice for you! [4]

In the dedication to *Horse-Shoe Robinson* Kennedy praised Washington Irving for "convinc[ing] our wise ones at home that a man may sometimes write a volume without losing his character." Irving, more certain of his calling, was amused by Kennedy's defensive posture. "I know," Irving told Elizabeth Kennedy, "he takes pride in showing the world that a literary man can be a man of business; but in my humble opinion a literary man on a low motive is worse than a beggar on horseback—and will bring up at the same end of the journey in half the time." [5]

Kennedy's choice of subject for his next book was in part motivated by his desire to show that a man might with honor combine success in public life with distinction in literature. His friend and patron William Wirt had been just such a man. He had loomed uncommonly large in the narrow world of Kennedy's youth. During the years that Kennedy and Cruse were writing *The Red Book*, Wirt was generally conceded to be the most distinguished man of letters in the Union. His *Letters of the British Spy*, first published in 1803 when Wirt was thirty-one, had by 1832 reached a tenth edition. To that edition Peter Hoffman Cruse contributed a biographical sketch, and the same year Kennedy dedicated *Swallow Barn* to Wirt. Wirt brought out another collection of essays, *The Rainbow* (1804), and with some half-dozen friends contributed to *The Old Bachelor* (1814), but neither of these achieved the popularity of *The British Spy*. His last book, *Sketches of the Life and Character of Patrick Henry* (1817), capped his literary career and by 1859 had reached a fifteenth edition. It was ironic, V. L. Parrington observed, that this son of a Swiss emigrant tavernkeeper should come to be accepted by old-school Virginia gentlemen as the literary representative of the Old Dominion.[6]

Wirt had a modest opinion of his writings, and after 1817 he turned his attention exclusively to the law. He served as attorney-general under Monroe and Adams, and after the death of William Pinkney in 1822, Wirt held undisputed sway as the first lawyer of Baltimore if not of the nation. He was an orator in the grand manner. A purple passage from his speech at Aaron Burr's trial for treason was for decades a favorite declamation piece for schoolboys. A tall, portly man of majestic bearing, Wirt's austere presence was lightened by his genial wit and his gifts as a raconteur. He was at once canny and honest, ambitious and ingenuous. In every society he made himself liked. He seemed to his countrymen the very model of a republican statesman. He liked Kennedy and had secured for him in 1823 the appointment as secretary of legation in Chile. At Wirt's death in 1834, the Baltimore bar called on Kennedy to deliver the commemorative address.[7]

In determining to write a biography of Wirt, Kennedy thought it the duty he owed the memory of "a very intimate and kind friend." He may also have felt that a biography would add substance to his own literary reputation. He had before him the example of Washington Irving, whose life of Columbus, published in three volumes in 1828, had been well received. The fact that Irving and John Quincy Adams had already declined to write a life of Wirt might have served as a warning that the materials were not propitious. Kennedy nevertheless undertook the biography in 1843 at the request of Mrs. Wirt, estimating that "some few hours' labor a day ought to enable me to get this work before the public in the course of the year."[8] But politics interfered, he had difficulty digesting a plan, and the necessary background reading and research required more time than he had anticipated. He set about the task in earnest in the autumn of 1847, and it occupied him for the better part of the next two years.

The work did not go easily. Many of the extant letters proved to be prosy tracts, "didactic essays merely, somewhat florid and over-sentimental." Moreover, Wirt's life was singularly devoid of dramatic incident, for such triumphs as he tasted were the ephemeral victories of the law courts. Even his reputation as an advocate rested unsubstantially on the sketchy reports of cases which but dimly shadowed forth the reasons for his greatness. Before the bar he was genial and persuasive, but he was neither a judicial statesman like John Marshall nor a legal theorist like James Kent.

Kennedy's research was meticulous and thorough. He traveled

to Richmond to interview surviving friends, searched files of magazines for reviews of Wirt's writings, and wrote dozens of letters to track down dates and details.[9] As the pieces began to fit into place and as friends came forward to offer their aid, he gained interest, and the pile of Wirt's papers on his library table no longer seemed a reproach. He took liberties with the original letters, improving a phrase written in haste and occasionally bowdlerizing a racy expression. "I was obliged," he told a friend, "to peruse the letters with a free hand and in some cases to rewrite papers which being thrown off in haste required this service. I did this however sparingly and conscientiously as I am certain Wirt would have done for himself, if opportunity or necessity for revision had occurred to him." [10]

Although Kennedy avoided eulogy, he subscribed to the school of biography, *de mortuis nil nisi bonum:* "I hold it to be the biographer's duty to turn the virtues of an illustrious man to the best account, by giving them a prominence which shall conciliate all regard. The faults of a good man are but transient blemishes, which quickly fade from view. His virtues are unchangeable, ever present and imperishable. He who has to speak of both should observe the proportions indicated by this truth." The evils that men do will not, evidently, live after them; at least, those of Wirt would not be immortalized by his biographer. It is difficult now to see how Wirt's daughter could find fault, as she did find fault,[11] with Kennedy's impeccable portrait of her father. Kennedy wished his subject to be held up as a model for Young America and dedicated the book to the young men "who seek for guidance to an honorable fame." Consequently, what was raffish in Wirt's character—his youthful drinking which had made his name a stock allusion among temperance orators, and his love of a practical joke—was muted or ignored.

Considering the fact that Kennedy had undertaken a biography related to a period of American history as yet largely unwritten, his *Life of Wirt* is an exceedingly able performance. In comparison with what had been done previously in the field, it can claim to be one of the first important American biographies. Kennedy had chosen a subject for which he was ideally suited. His own life had been endued with a spirit and enlarged by an experience equal to that of Wirt. The similarity between the external incidents of their lives is particularly striking. Both were natives of Maryland, were in a large part self-educated by desultory reading, followed the law as a profession, and turned ultimately to literature as a diversion. Both had had a share in the political history of their country. Both had attempted a biography, Wirt his life of Henry, and Kennedy his life of Wirt, and each had become successively excited, bored, and exasperated by the experience. Wirt complained that the discipline of checking and cross-checking facts which biography demanded was "like attempting to run, tied up in a bag." Kennedy likewise found the task he had set himself "a great drag." [12] In the distaste for legal studies, the early diffidence and inclination toward solitude, the youthful provincial dislike of New England, and the early horror of public speaking, Kennedy discovered his own predilections in the life of William Wirt. The biography was also shot through with its author's politics. Kennedy could not resist a hit at his old enemy, John Tyler, and Wirt was endowed with a fully evolved Whig philosophy that might have startled that excellent gentleman (within the limits of good breeding) could he have known in what cause he was being summoned to testify.

The Life of Wirt was a commemorative biography, ponderous as such lives often are, imposing and stately, deferent to those still living and weighty with moralizing. The change in fashions in biography has exaggerated its defects. It seems now ill-proportioned and padded with letters that are either trivial or without sufficient annotation. For the modern reader the greatest disappointment is Kennedy's failure to breathe life into his hero. The author who had drawn the memorable frontier scout Horse-Shoe Robinson and the Virginia country gentleman Frank Meriwether somehow failed to strike fire in this portrait of his distinguished friend. Yet such was the cultural climate of the time that this, Kennedy's dullest book, most effectually advanced his contemporary fame.

"Everybody talks to me about my book," he wrote Elizabeth from Boston, "and persuades me that it is very popular." [13] The success of the biography (it was reprinted within a month and ultimately went through six editions) astonished both author and publisher, and even the *United States Magazine and Democratic Review* called it "one of the most interesting books ever published in this country, . . . one which should be in the hands of every young man."[14]

The biography, however, was caught in the crossfire of sectional reviewers. William Gilmore Simms, in the *Southern Quarterly*, complained that Kennedy too readily conceded that Massachusetts, and not Virginia, deserved the honor of leading the colonies into independence. On the other hand, the *North American* was generally favorable but found the "excessive laudation" of "the first families of Virginia" repellent to its New England proclivities. Kennedy strove to please. At the suggestion of Philip Hone, he deleted a letter from the second edition in which Wirt had spoken disparagingly of New England, even though it had been especially introduced to contrast with a later, more favorable, opinion formed after he had made his first trip to the North.[15]

John Reuben Thompson, editor of the *Southern Literary Messenger*, had difficulty finding a reviewer. He hoped to get James E. Heath, author of a novel of Virginia, *Edge Hill*, and first auditor of the state, to review the biography, confident that his Whig leanings would assure the book a sympathetic hearing. But Heath refused because he found himself about to be proscribed by the Democratic majority in the Virginia legislature and dared not take the risk. The editor of the Richmond *Times* also declined, so Thompson despaired and asked Kennedy to find a reviewer in Baltimore. Kennedy refused. When a review finally appeared in April 1850, it eschewed politics.[16]

Kennedy's attempts to conciliate both North and South earned him nothing. Too unorthodox for the *Messenger*, he was sufficiently identified with the South to find his books the victim of a conspiracy of silence among the northern reviewers. "What in the d - - - l," he burst out to Blanchard and Lea, "is the reason those Yankees will not say a good word for anything out of Yankeedom?" In desperation he wrote to the New York journalist Park Benjamin, once a resident of Baltimore, asking him to review the *Life of Wirt* in a northern journal. But this seems to

The Literary Life

have been an isolated instance, for the manufacture of stage thunder for his works was a form of self-assertion which he found repugnant. But if it was humiliating to beg for recognition of his book in the North, it was galling to find it ignored in the South, for even this biography of a distinguished Southerner sold better in the North than in the South or West.[17]

In his journal, December 14, 1849, Kennedy analyzed the profits from the first edition.

To the author after two years hard work	$568.50
To the mechanics who got up the book with 5 months hard work	1650.00
To the book sellers for one month very light work	1962.00
Total proceeds of a popular work which sells an edition of 1000 in one month, after deducting 71 copies given away [47 to editors and 24 to Kennedy] & the remaining 929 selling at 4.50	$4180.50

"It is," Kennedy remarked dryly, "an edifying exhibition of bookmaking."

After the appearance of the *Life of Wirt*, Kennedy's curiosity was aroused to know the total profit he had realized from his books. He spent a spring day in 1851 going over letters and contracts with his publishers, all of which he had carefully preserved. He summarized the results in his journal.[18]

Swallow Barn	1 edition of 2,000	$782.69
Horse-Shoe Robinson	1 edition of 3,000	1200.00
	1 edition of 3,000	500.00
Rob of the Bowl	1 edition of 4,000	1850.00
Quodlibet	1 edition of 1,500	100.00
Defense of the Whigs	1 edition of 4,000	nothing
Life of Wirt	1 edition of 1,000	284.25
	1 edition of 3,000	750.00
	1 edition of 750	225.00
	Total receipts to this date	$5691.94

Kennedy's bookkeeping of course may not have been accurate. One's personal accounts seldom are. Yet the total is a revealing commentary on authorship in America during the 1830's and 1840's. The small profits realized from his books do not mean that he was the dupe of knavish publishers or the passive victim of the copyright laws. He disliked the market place; "I have such an aversion," he once wrote, "to all affairs that are connected with the management and care of money, which I think is founded on good grounds." Yet in a joust with a northern publisher, he was eager to show that a southern writer could be as shrewd and relentless as a Yankee trader. Eager to keep his books in print, he tried repeatedly to interest Blanchard and Lea in bringing out a uniform edition of his works together with a volume of miscellanies, but the firm was cool toward the proposal.[19]

In the 1840's George P. Putnam of New York established his publishing firm and began reissuing the works of established American authors. He contracted with Washington Irving in 1848 for a collected edition, and with Cooper the following year. In 1850 Putnam agreed to bring out *Swallow Barn* in a revised and illustrated edition, offering Kennedy a royalty of twelve and one-half per cent, the same, Kennedy noted proudly, as Cooper and Irving received.[20]

Kennedy did not relish the thought of revising. "I doubt the policy of laboring on old books. Why not let them go as they are?" He told Putnam that he had made a "somewhat extensive revisal" [21] of the text, then, in a new preface, referred to "the few differences which may be found between this and the first edition." A major change was the deletion of a forty-five-page essay on the character of the intrepid soldier of fortune, John Smith. This was a painful excision, for it had been worked with care from Samuel Purchas's *Hakluytus Posthumus* and Smith's own history of Virginia. Dropping it from *Swallow Barn* was an improvement, for the sketch, admirable in itself, had only a tenuous relationship to the structure of the work as a whole. John Latrobe recalled that the chapter "was necessary to give the respectability of size to the production" [22] for Kennedy had exhausted his supply of anecdotes. The implied criticism was just, but the statement was only partly true, for the essay on Smith was one of the first chapters written. The minor changes in phrasing were invariably improvements, and Kennedy's own comment concerning them is accurate: "Some quaintness of the vocabulary has been got rid of—some dialogue has been stript of its redundancy—some few thoughts have been added—and others retrenched." A signal improvement was the striking out of some archaisms, the result of his familiarity with the Elizabethans and a whim which cropped out in his personal letters and even colored his speech, but which in the novel seemed an affectation. Another change of significance was a carefully revised and expanded chapter, "The Quarter," a discussion of the problem of Negro slavery.

With the angry tempest stirred up by the crisis of 1850 in Washington still in mind, Kennedy gave careful thought to the attitudes toward slavery expressed in the novel. The arguments were essentially the same as in the first edition of 1832, but the chapter was carefully revised to make it more conciliatory in tone. Such a categorical statement as "a subject so indefensible as slavery" or such a damaging admission as "a black man cruelly whipped by order of his master" was softened or expunged. The phrase "New York and Virginia" was generalized to "North and South." Altogether the chapter, as expanded and revised, was a point-by-point refutation of abolitionist charges. Kennedy admitted as much to William Gilmore Simms. "The mawkish sentimentality which has been so busy of late in inventing sympathy for the pretended oppressions of the negroes, it strikes me, may under a new edition of Swallow Barn, which is rather a good, natural and I am sure true picture of the amiable and happy relation they hold to society—be opportune at this moment, and so far as it may be well received an antidote to this abolition mischief." Kennedy was somewhat piqued by the criticism of his brother, Philip Pendleton Kennedy, himself ambitious for literary distinction, that *Swallow Barn* was marred by the intrusive sermon on slavery which was quite without dramatic relevancy. The same point was made by Robert C. Winthrop, who, when urging Kennedy to read *Uncle Tom's Cabin* instead of condemning it outright as propaganda, reminded him that he had been guilty of a similar offense in *Swallow Barn*.[23]

Kennedy watched with alarm the influence of abolitionist criticism on the planter, goading him to extremes in his defense of slavery. But there were other, more basic, forces than Yankee criticism transforming the face of the South. Conscious of his role as social historian, and looking back from the vantage point of 1850, Kennedy observed that "time and what is called 'the progress' have made many innovations. . . . The Old Dominion is losing somewhat of the raciness of her peculiar, and—*speaking in reference to the locality described in this volume* [24]—insulated cast of manners. . . . An observer cannot fail to note that the manners of our country have been tending towards a uniformity which is visibly effacing all local differences."

Jay B. Hubbell, in his excellent introduction to a modern edition of *Swallow Barn*, found it curious that Kennedy should lament the decline of Virginia social life. Professor Hubbell attributed this to the transitional state of society in 1825, a vacuum created by the decline of the great planters ruined by the Revolution and not yet filled by a new generation coming to power. He concluded that in 1850 Kennedy chose to ignore this new aristocracy.[25] The locality described in *Swallow Barn* was, however, the Valley of Virginia. The sleepy hamlets of Martinsburg and Winchester of Kennedy's boyhood had no planter elite in 1850 but were rapidly becoming railroad terminals, and the traditional agriculture was giving way to mining and manufacturing. Although Kennedy had placed Swallow Barn on the James River, it was western Virginia that had furnished material in 1830. Consequently, it was the progress wrought in the vicinity of Martinsburg, not the Tidewater, that he had in mind when he began to revise in 1850. Kennedy's cousin, John Esten Cooke, in *Leather Stocking and Silk*, a novel obviously inspired by *Swallow Barn* but permeated by the romantic haze which would come to characterize the plantation tradition, was more explicit.[26]

> The antique character implied by the term *old* has passed away from Martinsburg . . . . It is now a busy, bustling town, which daily raises its two thousand heads and hushes its two thousand tongues to listen to the shrill steam whistle of the cars; but even this event, which in the old time would have furnished so much food for neighborly gossip, and street-corner harangues attracts attention but for a moment. The hurry, the bustle, the healthy activity which spring from trade, and announce prosperity, commence:—and Martinsburg, thus absorbed in her joyful present, scarcely ever gives a thought to her past.

The Literary Life

That past was as picturesque as the present is prosaic: not only the manners and personages, but the town itself.

The revised edition of *Swallow Barn* was well received. No American book, Putnam told Kennedy, reproduced after a lapse of time had done better. The sale was brisk, and Putnam was encouraged to bring out new editions of *Horse-Shoe Robinson* in 1852 and *Rob of the Bowl* in 1854.

With the republication of his novels in the 1850's, Kennedy's reputation as one of America's foremost contemporary writers was secure. His scrapbook, "Ego," [27] bulged with flattering and often fulsome notices of his books. He had been praised by the important literary men of his generation—Poe, Irving, Cooper, Paulding, Simms. With fame came influence in literary circles, and Kennedy found himself constantly applied to by authors anxious to make their mark. It is characteristic of his view of life that he responded to such petitions as a duty he owed to the country's cultural life. Moreover, he felt his own material prosperity gave promising writers a claim upon his kindness. Kennedy's role as a Baltimore Maecenas is the most attractive aspect of his varied career, and its prominence has partially obscured his own contribution to American literature. He offered counsel and more material help without ostentation and without hope of personal reward, and his encouragement of literature—a national literature in particular—was the habit of his mind. Typical of Kennedy's attitude is this reply to an aspiring author who found himself unable to repay a loan: "Pray think no more about it. A more prosperous day shall come, and then you will repay the debt to me, by giving the amount of it to any good and worthy man of letters who may fall in your way in a time of need. You cannot do me a greater favour than to apply this fund in that way, wherever your convenience and the necessities of a fellow craftsman in our idle trade may furnish you a proper opportunity." [28]

Kennedy discovered that his fame spurred several of the family circle in Virginia to emulation. He was looked to by those given to trifling in belles lettres as a useful intermediary between a landed gentleman and his publisher. One of these aspirants to distinction in letters was his younger brother, Philip. Philip wanted to write and turned naturally to his eldest brother for help, and John's services extended far beyond encouragement in a literary career. Philip was wayward and ungovernable from youth. He graduated from the law school of Henry St. George Tucker in Winchester, but he seems never to have practiced and by the 1840's was fast slipping into alcoholism. John urged him to write regularly for the reviews, criticized his manuscripts carefully, and exerted influence with Rufus Griswold in New York and Robert C. Winthrop in Boston to get Philip's writing into print. Philip published one book, *The Blackwater Chronicle*,[29] an amusing sketch of a trip with a group of friends into the Virginia wilderness. John was "delighted with it. It is so joyous and so fresh with the finest artistic tints of the landscape paper." [30] The book went through a number of printings in America and England and was long attributed to John Kennedy or David Strother, who did the illustrations.

Philip Kennedy was loyal to the Union, and in 1862 he was captured by Confederate troops and carried off from Martinsburg. Far gone in drink, he died soon after. He left a large collection of manuscripts, which John believed worthless and burned, with the exception of a memoir of Philip Pendleton Kennedy's kinsman, close friend, and hunting companion, Philip Pendleton Cooke.

Cooke was another of the Pendleton clan whose literary career owes a debt to John Kennedy. Cooke's mother, Maria Pendleton Cooke, was Nancy Kennedy's sister. Philip Cooke, who had grown up in Martinsburg, was another of the vast fraternity of American authors who entered literary history after an apprenticeship at law. He hoped to have leisure, he told Nathaniel Beverley Tucker, to "imitate my cousin J. P. Kennedy and become a novelist." [31] It would be easy, as easy for a complacent Virginia gentleman as bringing down a wild turkey with a single shot. As a writer Cooke possessed unmistakable talent, but his life was a continual struggle for freedom from financial troubles. It was a mortifying experience for a proud young Virginian to be dependent on his father. The elder Cooke, moreover, had the free and easy habit of endorsing his friends' notes, and after 1838 a series of obscure but relentless financial reverses plagued him with disastrous results. In 1839 Kennedy told Elizabeth that he believed the elder Cooke "as crazy as a Bedlamite," [32] for although his wife remained ignorant of his obligations, the sheriff had sold out his personal property, his land was mortgaged beyond redemption, and young Philip and his wife were to be thrown upon the mercy of her father. In 1846 Kennedy himself foreclosed a note on Cooke which his son Philip had endorsed.[33] About this time he interested himself in the young man's literary career, and he may have been prompted by a desire to smooth over a family dispute.

Kennedy's most important services for Cooke began in the late summer of 1845. During that time he frequently had been among the literati. In August he visited James Fenimore Cooper at Cooperstown, and in September he mingled with the Knickerbocker circle that frequented the home of Philip Hone in New York. There he met Rufus Griswold, who was preparing a revised edition of *The Poets and Poetry of America*. In the original volume Cooke's work was relegated to an appendix, and Kennedy hinted to Griswold that the young poet was writing and needed encouragement. Kennedy sent word to the Valley to have Cooke submit his poems to Griswold promptly. This Cooke did, and he was rewarded by seeing his work promoted from the appendix to the body of the next edition.[34]

The appearance of the poems inspired Cooke to set about getting a literary reputation in earnest, and he interpreted the help of cousin John in the first venture as a lien on future favors. Cooke not only longed for literary fame, but he wanted "a little 'Springs' and 'travel' money." He told Kennedy that he needed "3 or 400 dollars per annum for 'the usual trimmings,' and this sum, probably, you can tell me how to make with my pen. Books, unless they catch the public taste by a turn or by chance, I suppose do not bring money—besides publishers are hard to be got. . . . Please tell me something about these things, and (if you can *without trouble*), put me in the way of becoming an established author." [35]

It was not a particularly modest request, but Kennedy agreed to help. Cooke was impatient and wrote again in two weeks inquiring what, if anything, Kennedy was doing. He desired "seriously, at once," to publish and "urgently" wanted information and introductions to publishers. Kennedy wrote to Griswold, asking his advice and suggesting that Cooke be launched by Park Benjamin, who was trying to establish a publishing house in Baltimore, but Griswold answered, counseling New York. The doors were now open to Cooke, but his manuscript was not forthcoming. Perhaps he had needed money quickly and had got it from another source, but more likely he found it difficult to get down to writing. Plantation life was intellectually slack, keyed to the physical and the sensuous. Cooke complained to Poe that on a visit to the country "I saw more of guns and horses and dogs than of pens and paper. Amongst dinners, barbecues, snipe-shooting, riding parties, etc., I could not get my brain into humor for writing to you or to anybody." [36]

A year later, November 1846, Cooke had a sheaf of poems ready called the *Froissart Ballads*. He wrote to Kennedy and Griswold to remind them of their promise of a year before to help him to publish. Cooke was rather vain of the fact that he was "quite as ignorant as any country gentleman ever was of the *business* part of literature." This ignorance did not extend to the business of puffing the volume, for he was astute enough to cultivate Poe in the North to fill his sails and in the South the editor of the *Southern Literary Messenger*, Benjamin B. Minor ("well bred, courteous, and all that sort of thing"). When Kennedy, who had just completed a campaign for the House of Delegates, did not answer immediately, Cooke wrote again suggesting that "perhaps the interest which you seemed to take in my 'literatures' has cooled with my delays." [37] Kennedy had reason to be exasperated with Cooke's procrastination and his patronizing attitude, but Kennedy understood Virginia life, understood it far better than did Cooke and most of his contemporaries. He too had gone to Virginia on a holiday planning to write only to be caught up in the lax, indolent world where literary ambition was easily dulled by the diversions plantation life offered.[38]

Griswold suggested doling out the poems to *Graham's Magazine* a few verses each month, believing that this would be good advertising. Kennedy told Cooke of this plan and invited him down to Baltimore to talk over his literary future. In December

The Literary Life

1846 Kennedy delivered the manuscript to Griswold in Philadelphia to conclude the best bargain he could. In 1847 the *Froissart Ballads* appeared, published by Carey and Hart, and dedicated to Kennedy, "the literary head of the Pendleton clan." Kennedy's efforts did not cease with publication, for in April he wrote to Griswold, asking him to persuade a northern man—he suggested R. H. Dana—to review the volume.[39]

Cooke's debt to Kennedy went further than his influence and assistance with publishers. Cooke admitted to Griswold that "only Mr. Ky's urgent entreaty and remonstrance whipped me up to the labour."[40] Also, Cooke's efforts in fiction, in particular "The Two Country Houses," were indebted to Kennedy's use of rural settings in *Swallow Barn*. This influence extended to Cooke's younger brother, John Esten Cooke, whose *Leather Stocking and Silk* clearly evinces its relationship to *Swallow Barn*. John Esten Cooke later wrote that he believed Kennedy "one of the most intelligent men of his generation." He praised *Swallow Barn* "and especially 'Quodlibet,' which I do not believe has been excelled by Irving, Longstreet or any of our writers."[41]

Kennedy also encouraged David Hunter Strother, a close friend of Philip Cooke and Philip Kennedy and the son of a Berkeley Springs hosteler and companion of John's youth. Kennedy gave young Strother an occasional commission for a painting and allowed him to do the illustrations for the revised edition of *Swallow Barn*. These illustrations Kennedy thought particularly apt "not only from the artistic execution, but still more from the fact that they are generally portraits from real life. . . . They represent persons and scenes in Virginia with great fidelity."

Kennedy was pleased when Strother entered the Union Army in 1862 and promptly used his influence at Washington, when Strother applied for advancement, to have the young man, "a gentleman of the best fighting blood of our country," promoted from captain to lieutenant colonel. After the war Strother gained some reputation as a magazinist and illustrator under the pseudonym of "Porte Crayon."[42]

A passage in Kennedy's journal dated October 10, 1849, records his most famous instance of patronage.

On Tuesday last Edgar A. Poe died in town here at the hospital from the effects of a debauch. He had been to Richmond, was returning to New York, where he lived, and I understand, was soon to be married to a lady in Richmond of quite good fortune. He fell in with some companion here who seduced him to the bottle, which it was said he had renounced some time ago. The consequence was fever, delirium, and madness, and in a few days a termination of his sad career in the hospital. Poor Poe! he was an original and exquisite genius, poet, and one of the best prose writers in this country. His works are among the very best of their kind. His taste was replete with classical flavor, and he wrote in the spirit of an old Greek philosopher.

It is many years ago—I think perhaps as early as 1833 or 4 that I found him in Baltimore in a state of starvation. I gave him clothing, free access to my table and the use of a horse for exercise whenever he chose—in fact brought him up from the very verge of despair. I then got him employment with Mr. [Thomas W.] White in one department of the editorship of the Southern Literary Messenger at Richmond. His talents made that periodical quite brilliant whilst he was connected with it. But he was irregular, eccentric, and querulous, and soon gave up his plan for other employment of the same character in Philadelphia and New York. His destiny in these plans was as sad and fickle as in Richmond. He always remembered my kindness with gratitude as his many letters to me testify. He is gone. A bright but unsteady light has been awfully quenched.

Kennedy's memory was accurate, and his services have been generously acknowledged by Poe's biographers. The two men first met in Baltimore in the fall of 1833. Kennedy had just published *Swallow Barn*, while Poe was living in obscurity on Amity Street with his aunt, Maria Clemm. In June 1833 the Baltimore *Saturday Visitor* offered prizes for the best short story and poem submitted, the judges to be Kennedy, John H. B. Latrobe, and a local physician, James H. Miller. In October the three men met at Latrobe's house to sort through a pile of amateurish manuscripts. In the interval of filling wine glasses and lighting cigars, Latrobe came suddenly upon a manuscript, heretofore overlooked, written in painstaking Roman characters, and bearing the unmistakable stamp of genius. The prize of fifty dollars was promptly awarded to "MS Found in a Bottle," one of the *Tales of the Folio Club*. Kennedy noted at the time that "the whole exhibits a great deal of talent, and we advised him to publish it." [43]

The Literary Life

Kennedy supplemented this advice with practical help. He took it upon himself to find a publisher for the *Tales* and submitted them to Henry C. Carey, the publisher of *Swallow Barn*. Carey was able to sell one of the tales, and in December 1834 Kennedy told Poe of this transaction in a letter of consummate tact.

> I requested Carey immediately upon the receipt of your first letter to do something for you as speedily as he might find an opportunity, and to make some advance on your book. . . . He recommends, however, that I should allow him to sell some of the tales to the publishers of the annuals. My reply was that I thought you would not object to this if the right to publish the same tale was reserved for the volume. He has accordingly sold one of the tales to Miss Leslie for the *Souvenir*, at a dollar a page, I think with the reservation above mentioned—and has remitted me a draft of fifteen dollars which I will hand over to you as soon as you call upon me, which I hope you will do as soon as you can make it convenient. If the other tales can be sold in the same way, you will make more for the work than by an exclusive publication.[44]

Three months later, on March 15, 1835, Poe, in desperate straits, asked Kennedy's help in obtaining a teaching position in a Baltimore public school. Kennedy immediately replied with an invitation to dine at Mount Vernon Place, which elicited this pathetic reply: "Your kind invitation to dinner today has wounded me to the quick. I cannot come—and for reasons of the most humiliating nature [in] my personal appearance. You may conceive my deep mortification in making this disclosure to you—but it was necessary. If you will be my friend so far as to loan me $20, I will call on you tomorrow—otherwise it will be impossible, and I must submit to my fate." [45]

At this crisis in Poe's affairs, Kennedy urged him to apply to Thomas W. White of Richmond for an editorial position with the *Southern Literary Messenger*. Kennedy's influence obtained for Poe his position on the *Messenger*, and this intercession with White seems to have been a turning point in Poe's career, for all his efforts to find employment had proved fruitless up until that time. Poe was grateful for the favor and later told Kennedy that "without the timely kindness you once evinced towards me, I should not at this moment be among the living." [46]

In September 1835 Poe wrote to thank Kennedy for his kindly offices. But despite the improvement in his fortunes, Poe was "suffering under a depression of spirits." He asked Kennedy to write him immediately. "Convince me that it is worth one's while —that it is at all necessary to live, and you will prove yourself indeed my friend . . . you were my friend when no one else was." [47]

Kennedy answered at once.

> I am sorry to see you in such plight as your letter shows you in. It is strange that just at the time when every body is praising you and when Fortune has begun to smile upon your hitherto wretched circumstances you should be invaded by these villainous blue devils. It belongs, however, to your age and temper to be thus buffeted, but be assured it only wants a little resolution to master the adversary forever. Rise early, live generously, and make cheerful acquaintances and I have no doubt you will send these misgivings of the heart all to the devil. You will doubtless do well henceforth in literature and add to your comforts as well as to your reputation which, it gives me great pleasure to tell you, is every where rising in popular esteem.[48]

Poe waited until January 1836 to reply. He was now "in every respect, comfortable and happy," and he assured Kennedy that he would "never forget to whom all this happiness is in great degree to be attributed. I know that without your timely aid I should have sunk under my trials. . . . Contrast all this with those circumstances of absolute despair in which you found me, and you will see how great reason I have to be grateful to God—and to yourself." [49]

Kennedy was ready with advice, often very good advice. He did not respond, however, to Poe's requests to write for the magazines. In December 1840 and again in June 1841 Poe unsuccessfully appealed to Kennedy to send something for the projected *Penn Magazine*. In later years Kennedy also refused to advance Poe money. In October 1845 Poe wrote to say he was sole owner of *The Broadway Journal* but had exhausted his funds. Would Kennedy lend him fifty dollars for three months? Kennedy was in Virginia at the time, but when he returned to Baltimore he replied that "good wishes are pretty nearly all the capital I have

The Literary Life

for such speculations." But he closed his letter with a warm invitation to Poe to visit him in Baltimore.[50]

Poe complained, in a moment of pique, that "he has treated me somewhat cavalierly—professing to be a friend." Yet Kennedy was an early friend, a steadfast one, and among the few men who were loyal to Poe until the end. "Mr. Kennedy," Poe said, "has been at all times a true friend to me—he was the first true friend I ever had—I am indebted to him *for life itself*." [51]

Kennedy praised Poe to his contemporaries and believed him to be the finest writer America had produced. In 1867 George W. Fahnestock of Philadelphia, a philanthropist and gentleman of leisure whose dilettante enthusiasms included American literature, wrote to Kennedy asking him to verify a daguerreotype of Poe. Kennedy's reply reveals that twenty years after Poe's death, and only sixteen months before his own, his estimate of Poe remained the same.[52]

> I was very intimate with Poe, during the period of his residence in this city, and followed the story of his unhappy career with great interest after he left us. I have never known, nor read of anyone, whose life so curiously illustrated that two fold existence of the *spiritual* and the *carnal* disputing the control of the man, which has often been made the theme of fiction. His was debauched by the most grovelling appetites and exalted by the richest conception of genius. In his special department of thought, our country has produced no poet or prose writer superior to him—indeed, I think none equal to him. This photograph is very good, though it does not belong to his best days. You may see in it the sensualism which, in the later stages of his life, became conspicuous in his physiognomy. But still, the likeness is very true and perhaps the best now extant.

The surviving records do not suggest an intimate friendship between the two men; considering their diverse temperaments, it is hardly to be expected. Twelve letters from Poe to Kennedy still exist; there is not one that does not ask a favor. No incident of Kennedy's life portrays him more sympathetically, yet none is more characteristic of the man.

The literary life, the encouragement of an American literature through performance and patronage, brought its satisfactions, but it was not enough. After Kennedy's defeat for Congress in 1847, he had resolved to cultivate his literary reputation and to forget politics. "I am done with public elections," he declared in 1850. "I prefer my books. . . . My experience is abundant to convince me that nothing is more humiliating, nor more thankless than the sentiment engendered throughout the state by any man whose public service is sufficiently patriotic and useful to give him a little distinction. Envy, detraction and malice are sure to be his only reward." [53] Yet as he wrote, there were in motion forces which would recall him to the national stage. Politics was in his blood; when the call came, he could not refuse to answer.

CHAPTER XI

Cabinet Officer

WHILE JOHN KENNEDY in 1850 was writing his valedictory to politics, the country was teetering on the brink of civil war. At Washington extremists North and South were intent on forcing a crisis. John C. Calhoun, a dying man, exhorted the South to challenge once and for all the North or be forever humbled. He wanted an effective fugitive slave law, the positive protection of slavery in the territories, and a dual Presidency, with the South represented and empowered to veto legislation hostile to its interests. The North saw a chance to wrest control of the national government after generations of southern domination. It wanted legislation favorable to its commercial and industrial interests. Abolitionists were demanding that slavery be barred from the territories and that the slave trade be abolished in the District of Columbia. The nation moreover was afflicted with growing pains. The sprawling territories acquired from Mexico must be organized into states; California, its population swollen by the gold rush, was demanding admittance; and the Texas–New Mexico boundary had to be settled. The stage was set for one of the momentous, full-dress debates which have occurred periodically in congressional history. In the winter of 1850 the great triumvirate—Clay the conciliator, Calhoun the defender of state rights, and Webster the spokesman for northern industrialism—were called from the wings for the finale of their illustrious careers. Kennedy, with the entire nation, turned anxious eyes toward Washington.

At this juncture the tantalizing rumor of a chance for high office fanned the embers of Kennedy's ambition. In January 1850 the Whig legislature met at Annapolis to choose a senator, and Kennedy was mentioned prominently in the Baltimore press as likely to be chosen. February came, and still no decision was forthcoming. Henry Clay came over from Washington to spend several days as a house guest and assured Kennedy he was needed in the Senate. Kennedy began to hope, but the appointment went to another. Robert C. Winthrop wrote from Washington that gossip attributed Kennedy's proscription to a fear that he was "not altogether *safe* on the Slavery Question." This Winthrop did not consider a slander. "It will one day or other be the glory of us both, that we were not altogether *safe* on the Slavery Question." [1] Some months later Kennedy heard, not without a twinge of envy, of Winthrop's appointment to the Senate from Massachusetts.

Kennedy watched helplessly as Clay's panacea for the country's ills, a congeries of compromises called the Omnibus Bill, went down to defeat aided by Winthrop's vote. Harry of the West was at loggerheads with President Zachary Taylor, a situation which reminded veteran observers of his dispute with John Tyler eighteen years before. While in Washington to hear the debates, Kennedy was approached by Joseph Gales, editor of the *National Intelligencer*. Gales was alarmed over the threat of secession and offered Kennedy five thousand dollars a year to write an article a week for the paper in support of the Union. Kennedy reported the conversation to Elizabeth: "I told him I would write anything that might help such a cause, but that I would not undertake to do it as a contract for *twice the sum*—in fact that no money could buy my leisure from me. That if I wrote at all it should be for the sake of the cause and not for money. . . . He said there was no man in the United States with whom he would make such an engagement but myself." [2]

On March 2, 1850, a letter by Kennedy, "The Friends of the Union," signed "Maryland," appeared in the *Intelligencer*. It was a ringing call to Union sentiment. The talk of disunion he condemned as "the fancy of phrenzied minds heated to an unwholesome temperature by too much pondering over imaginary griefs." He enumerated the wonders of the new nation. "Fable cannot exaggerate the features which give to this era and generation a Titanic aspect, and render them the most remarkable in human annals . . . the Panama Railroad, the great overland track between the Atlantic and the Pacific, the marvels of California, the new Territories, the ocean steamers, the wonderful growth of cities, the telegraph, the iron-roads that, in the lines of a great multiplication table, are overlaying the States and welding and riveting them together by inseverable bonds." Threatening to subvert these achievements was, on the one hand, northern abolitionism "which began in the foul dreams of a few morbid doctrinaires" and, on the other, southern ultraism, which held sway with "men of the greatest influence in society" stung to fury by the vilification of the anti-slavery press. Between these two extremes stood "the great party of the Friends of the Union."

> These men *do not intend to see this Union dissolved.* They have grown up in the shadow of the Union, and know nothing and can conceive nothing outside of it. They will not endure much talking of disunion, nor weaving of political sophism, nor balancing of metaphysical scruples touching the integrity of this circle of States. They are practical; they are prosperous, and very busy in laying the foundations for still greater prosperity. They are proud of the glory of the country, its old associations of colonial history, its war of independence, its Constitution and Union, and they do not mean to see these obliterated by the quips and quillets of supersubtle logicians. . . . Ambitious men may plot, and passionate men may fume, and the micromegas of the villages may work up the loungers of a tavern-porch into a tempest of maudlin wrath for the nullification of Wilmot Provisos; but a mighty nation will not be jostled out of its career by such small flies upon the wheel as these.
> If I am to live to see a struggle to keep these [states] together, I shall be in the first and in the last array of those who shall still work and hope for the Union.

Five days after this article appeared, Daniel Webster rose in the Senate to deliver his Seventh of March speech. Kennedy read it in the *Intelligencer* the next day and pronounced it "a grand and majestic speech, full of wisdom." And in his speech Webster had paid Kennedy a subtle compliment he knew how to appreciate. "I perceive that he has read 'Maryland' in the *Intelligencer*," Kennedy noted in his journal. "That essay furnished him a good deal of material which he has used with excellent effect." [3]

Denied a share in the battle raging at Washington, Kennedy took what solace he could from an unexpected honor in Baltimore. In March the University of Maryland conferred upon him the degree of Doctor of Laws and elected him provost, an honorary post requiring him to sign and present diplomas at commencement, a ritual which, despite his token protests, he thoroughly enjoyed. Still, this was but a momentary diversion, and each evening as he made his customary entry in his journal, his thoughts turned to the crisis at Washington.

In July 1850 Kennedy's ambition was again awakened. President Taylor died July 9 in the midst of the struggle over the compromise, and Millard Fillmore, Kennedy's friend of the Twenty-Seventh Congress, succeeded to the Presidency. The Fillmores had shared a boarding house with the Kennedys and the Winthrops in 1841, and the three men had weathered the Tyler feud together as comrades in arms. Now that a new cabinet was to be formed of Union men, there was speculation that Kennedy was to be appointed. He left the decision to Elizabeth. "What am I to say? How could I go without you? How could you go without your father? How could he go without the factory?—and how could the factory go without the Patapsco? On the other hand, how could I refuse to mount such a platform, and throw away such a golden opportunity in my life?" [4] Both Elizabeth and Edward Gray urged him to accept.

Kennedy fumed as the issue hung fire in Washington. At last he left Baltimore for a tour of the western springs with Philip Pendleton. He worked hard to divert himself, bowling, swimming, fishing, and indulging himself in the interminable conversations which made up life at the springs, meanwhile assuring himself that the cabinet post really did not matter. By early August the Baltimore press was speaking confidently of his appointment.

But he was not invited. Bitterly disappointed, he hinted darkly that a "Maryland opposition" had cost him the post. From Baltimore he watched Congress laboriously hammer out the issues of the Great Compromise. Still another truce between the sections of the Union had been achieved. Kennedy turned back to his books and his pen.

In November 1850 an opportunity for travel suddenly presented itself. Kennedy found himself named executor of the estate of one John McDonogh, who had left his fortune to be divided between Baltimore, where he was born, and New Orleans, where he had made his money. Kennedy had never heard of the man, but he agreed to go to New Orleans to test the validity of the will. This duty was an excuse to journey to the Ohio and the Mississippi, which he had never seen. He found much to praise and little to censure in the West. At Pittsburgh ("this great busy workshop of a city") the leaden sky, murky even at midday, and the ubiquitous smoke and grime suggested no criticism to this prophet of an industrial America. In Louisville he frankly admired the boisterous, masculine Kentuckians with their "free and easy, bar room haunting, loud talking and indiscriminate associations," although his self-possession was occasionally ruffled by their "manifest want of refinement." He noted with detachment the heavy drinking which started before breakfast and the incessant whittling which pared down even the arms of the bar chairs. A report of an outbreak of cholera in New Orleans reached him in Louisville, and then came the frustrating news that the McDonogh fortune was greatly exaggerated and was being tied up in litigation by New Orleans lawyers, "buzzards circling around a dead horse." Abruptly Kennedy cut short his journey and hurried home to Baltimore in time for Christmas with Elizabeth. From his tour he concluded that "the West is yet fifty years too young to make it a desirable residence. After that lapse of time, it will be regarded the chief seat of empire." [5]

The new year, 1851, was for Kennedy one of leisurely retrospect and consolidation. The Compromise of 1850 had brought apparent calm to the political scene, and the Whig party could stand before the country as the proponents of peace and prosperity. Kennedy visited Washington in January and found the city full of talk for a Union party to be organized for the presidential contest of 1852, a party to be, he hoped, "nothing more than the reassertion of the fundamental principles of the real Whig Party." [6] His *Life of Wirt* was still selling; it received a boost by a laudatory review in the *National Intelligencer* in April. *Swallow Barn* reappeared in September amidst universal praise for book and author. The Gray Cotton Factory was having the most prosperous year in its history, and its management was absorbing more and more of Kennedy's time. Edward Gray was failing, and, although president in name, he made few decisions without the advice and approval of his son-in-law.

In August Gray was too feeble to travel north, so Kennedy went off alone to Berkeley Springs for a short vacation. He was surprised and alarmed to find the planters from South Carolina talking freely of disunion and "educated in the most settled hatred of the United States." President Fillmore arrived later in the month and the two friends spent a week lamenting the decline of Union sentiment. Fillmore complained that he did not know how to address himself to the various factions of his party. Kennedy, as always intensely nationalistic, urged him to say that he would stand for the Union. Fillmore could only answer, "I have spoken that resolve so often." [7] On his fifty-sixth birthday, October 25, Kennedy congratulated himself that he "had come to that age when nature takes charge of our virtue, by stripping us of the faculties for vice. I look back without regret and forward with pleasant hope and am quite content to notch my years as they run off the spindle."

Kennedy could congratulate himself on the serenity of his life in his beloved Baltimore, but the new year, 1852, was to be one of the most strenuous and satisfying of his career. In July he took Elizabeth to Saratoga Springs for a holiday. By chance Washington Irving was also vacationing there. Kennedy and Irving had first met in Baltimore in June 1832, just two weeks after the publication of *Swallow Barn*. Three years later Kennedy dedicated *Horse-Shoe Robinson* to Irving, and the same year, deep in stock market negotiations, Irving sought Kennedy's aid in assessing some Baltimore real estate speculations. This acquaintanceship had languished. Kennedy was preoccupied with politics, and Irving left in 1842 to assume his duties as minister to Spain. After

Cabinet Officer

Irving's return in 1846, the two men met occasionally in Knickerbocker literary circles, but the chance meeting in the summer of 1852 revived the friendship. Irving was so delighted with the reunion that he abandoned a Canadian tour to remain at Saratoga with the Kennedys.

Kennedy was flattered by the attentions of Irving, but his thoughts were on the capital. Early in July the Secretary of the Navy in Fillmore's cabinet, William A. Graham, resigned to run for Vice-President on the Whig ticket with the hero of the Mexican War, General Winfield Scott. July 12, the day Kennedy left Baltimore for Saratoga, he heard a rumor that he was to be invited to succeed Graham. By the time he reached New York, the newspapers had announced his appointment so confidently that official calls were tendered him by the naval officers in command. Fillmore, the most indecisive of men, had apparently consulted so many advisers that the news was known far in advance. Fillmore's invitation reached Kennedy July 20 at Saratoga. He accepted at once and hurried off to Washington leaving Elizabeth in the care of Irving and eliciting from him a promise to visit the capital during the winter season.

In appointing an author to head the Navy Department, Fillmore was following precedent, for James Kirke Paulding had held the post under Van Buren and George Bancroft had served under Polk. The Senate confirmed Kennedy's appointment by a unanimous vote without the usual form of reference to a committee. The choice seems to have been popular. Kennedy noted in his journal: "I find Joshua Jones of the Baltimore Patriot waiting to see me. . . . He tells me that he sees all the papers of the country nearly at the Patriot office and that he never knew an appointment to the cabinet that was received in all directions with a more kindly approbation by both parties than mine." [8]

Kennedy was eminently suited for the post. He enjoyed the ceremonial visits of naval officers, the tours of inspection, the seventeen-gun salutes, and the dispatching of ships hither and yon like a latter-day Gulliver manipulating the Blefuscu navy. "I like it," he told Elizabeth. "I like the stir and command and importance of the things—to be handling frigates like toys, and disposing of men and guns, as if I had them in my hands." [9]

Although the Whig party was traditionally identified with a strong naval policy, during the Taylor-Fillmore administration leadership gradually passed to Congress. The appropriations, larger than ever before in peacetime, were earmarked for pork barrel legislation such as additional navy yards, or doled out as subsidies to private steamship lines, presumably on grounds of national defense. The power of the navy gradually declined, and when Kennedy took office the fleet possessed not one vessel that could have given battle with prospect of victory against any first-class warship of the major European powers.[10] The navy had not one steamship in the Pacific Ocean even though California had been admitted to the Union in 1850. Eight months in office, four of them as the outgoing representative of a defeated party, gave Kennedy little opportunity to institute long-range reforms. Yet he was active in promoting the affairs of the navy during his brief tenure, and his name is associated with two famous expeditions: Commodore Matthew Perry's voyage to Japan and Doctor Elisha Kent Kane's search for the British explorer, Sir John Franklin.

Perry's mission was intimately bound up with the emotional surge of manifest destiny which swept America at mid-century. The vast territories acquired by conquest, purchase, or negotiation had made the United States a continental nation. The American whaling industry in the Pacific needed bases, and a railroad was begun across the Isthmus of Panama to expand the Pacific trade. The Whigs were naturally inclined to encourage commerce, and Commodore Perry himself opened the official account of the voyage by expressing his interest in "an extended field for commercial enterprise." [11] Perry was the obvious choice to lead a naval squadron to negotiate a commercial treaty with Japan. A career officer of forty-three years' service, he was well-informed and able, stern and inflexible, and motivated by an intense desire for fame.

The expedition, many months in preparation, sailed during Kennedy's term of office. His chief contribution was to add vessels to the squadron enabling Perry to make a more impressive show of force "upon a government and people who are accustomed to measure their respect by the array of power which accompanies the demand of it." [12] His responsibility did not go beyond these preliminaries. "My share in the Japan Expedition," he told a friend who was planning a book on the subject, "was in the fitting out, and arrangement of the force, and the details connected with that service, with occasional consultation with the President and the Secy. of State as to the mode of moving forward, which I embodied in some degree in my instructions to Commodore Perry." [13]

Kennedy was also influential in forwarding the expedition of Elisha Kent Kane. After taking a degree in medicine, Kane had traveled widely, dissatisfied with his profession and restlessly in search of a vocation. His imagination had been fired by the arctic frontier, and he had undertaken the ultimately futile quest for the British explorer, Sir John Franklin, who had failed to return from his search for the Northwest Passage. The vanishing of Sir John and his crew and the eloquent appeals of Lady Jane Franklin had stirred American chivalry. During Kane's first voyage to the north in 1850, he had found three graves, stark remains of Franklin's winter quarters. Planning a second voyage in 1852, he appealed to Kennedy for help. Kennedy ordered Kane on special duty, sent ten volunteers to his service on navy pay, and secured medical supplies, rations, and scientific equipment. Kane recognized Kennedy as the center of obligation: "Locofoco as I am, I cannot but feel that my little party belongs to another administration." [14] Kane remembered his benefactor while at sea, and on the charts of Greenland, Kennedy Channel flows past Cape Andrew Jackson into Kane Basin.

Kennedy's report on naval affairs for 1852 was a distinguished state paper. It called forth universal praise and resulted in his election to the American Philosophical Society and the Academy of Natural Sciences. Rufus Griswold wrote from New York: "You have become so accustomed to congratulations on your report since your entry into the Cabinet, that the subject wearies; but I doubt whether any cabinet paper ever received so much applause in this country." The report was a justification, on grounds of the government's responsibility to subsidize scientific research, of the Perry and Kane voyages as well as exploring and surveying expeditions Kennedy had organized to Liberia, the

River Plate, and the Northern Pacific. Kennedy suggested reorganization of the Naval Academy at Annapolis in order to bring it into harmony with the traditional four-year college program. He wanted a larger navy and asked for a re-examination of the problem of naval discipline. Congress in 1850 had responded to public demand by abolishing flogging in the navy and merchant marine. Kennedy reported that all evidence tended to show a most unsatisfactory result. Here, too, he was ready with a detailed plan to raise morale by increasing wage rates for seamen and by developing an equitable system of merit promotions. The report was enlightened, but, as Kennedy candidly admitted to Winthrop, it was full of "many impertinent suggestions and improbable reforms." [15]

The last Whig administration was drawing to a close, and Kennedy was caught up in a round of social obligations that left him no time to keep his journal. There were morning receptions, soirees, and as many as six formal dinners a week. John and Elizabeth found themselves obliged to decline two or three invitations a day. Three young and pretty Pendleton cousins came down from the Valley to sample the delights of official Washington society and to flirt with the naval officers who flocked each Monday to Elizabeth's levee.

In January 1853 Washington Irving arrived to make his promised visit to the Kennedys and to conduct research for his biography of George Washington. Irving was immediately caught up in the social life of the administration rushing to a close. Elizabeth had no intention of allowing her eminent author to burrow in the national archives out of sight of her guests. "I am in the midst of terrible dissipation," Irving wrote home to Sunnyside. "I have three young belles in the house on a visit; they are very pretty, very amiable, very lady-like, and one of them very musical; and I could make myself happy at home with them, if Tom, Dick, and Harry out of doors, would only leave me alone." [16] After one party Kennedy noted happily in his journal, "Irving a great lion tonight." [17]

Then, to complete Kennedy's social triumph, William Makepeace Thackeray arrived at Washington in February on his lecture tour. He brought a letter of introduction to Kennedy from Abbott Lawrence of Boston. Thackeray and Kennedy immediately became firm friends. Thackeray thought Kennedy "exceedingly pleasant, natural and good natured," while on his part, Kennedy believed Thackeray "a noble specimen of a real, fresh, true thinking and true speaking gentleman, whom I think honest fellows everywhere ought to love." Both men had undeniable social gifts, and in the making of fiction they shared a common interest in the ways of the historical imagination and the ironic portrayal of manners. "I gave him some hints," Kennedy noted, "to make a journey to California and to prepare some lectures adapted to the taste of that region. He received the idea with great deliberation—and on breaking up tonight told me I had made him a fortune." [18]

Kennedy basked in the sensation created by his two brilliant guests. It was a social coup that delighted all Whig society at Washington. Kennedy arranged for his two captive celebrities to accompany President Fillmore and President-elect Franklin Pierce, with a full complement of cabinet ministers, on a trial voyage of Captain John Ericsson's "caloric ship," which had been trumpeted as promoting a new era in naval propulsion. It turned out a bitter February day on the Potomac, and Irving and Thackeray huddled with the rest in the cramped quarters below deck, the Englishman obliged to keep his head poised perilously between the roofbeams. The party enjoyed a "sumptuous collation, beautifully served," and later Fillmore and Pierce resolved to attend Thackeray's lecture together. Thackeray made light of the compliment, but he was greatly flattered.[19]

The closing months of the Fillmore administration were the climax of Kennedy's public career. A popular and successful executive officer, the books written that established his reputation as a man of letters, and Thackeray and Irving his guests at Washington, the remainder of his life would be an anti-climax to this act being played out at the capital. His fortunes moreover were linked to the Whig party, and it was moribund. On November 2, 1852, the day of the presidential election, Kennedy went to Baltimore to vote for General Winfield Scott. In the afternoon he took the train back to Washington and found the cars full of roistering and drunken men shouting for Franklin Pierce. A stranger told him the crowd had been sent over from Washington to vote the Democratic ticket in Baltimore. That evening over an oyster supper, members of the cabinet sat with General Scott awaiting the telegraphic returns of the election. The first news from Baltimore was overwhelmingly for Pierce and it was prophetic. Scott however was in high good humor. He brewed a pitcher of whisky punch, and the men ate and drank heartily and laughed at the extravagance of the vote against them. At midnight Kennedy, having heard enough, went home to bed. It was a hurricane defeat, but the gloomiest prophets of doom did not realize the total consequences to the Whig party. Kennedy and his friends had been, however unwittingly, mourners at the demise of that party.

CHAPTER XII

Elder Statesman

AT THE CLOSE of his term as Secretary of the Navy John Kennedy returned to Baltimore reluctantly, for the final months had been exhilarating. The administration of Millard Fillmore had ended in such apparent concord that it seemed a new Era of Good Feelings had been ushered into existence. The transfer of government by the Whigs to the Democrats on a chill March morning in 1853 was so jovial and harmonious that the political calm seemed too deep to be disturbed by the faint tremors of civil war. Kennedy had been deeply impressed by President Pierce's inaugural address. He found it so sound and conservative that he told the new President there was nothing left for the Whigs to attack. Pierce, on his part, assured Kennedy that his innovations in the Navy Department would go forward without regard to partisan politics.[1]

Back in Baltimore Kennedy's days settled into a leisurely pattern. After breakfast with Elizabeth, her sister Martha, and Edward Gray, Kennedy spent the morning in his library poring over several newspapers, posting his journal, reading, or adding a few paragraphs to a lecture. He emerged for dinner at two, then hurried off to his club for billiards until tea. In the evening there was perhaps an hour or two for reading unless a friend came in for a game of besique. Saturdays were devoted to correspondence and Sundays to reading theology.

It was a tranquil life and, with the prosperity of the Gray Cotton Factory, an affluent one. To complete his comforts, Kennedy in 1854 added to the Grays' cottage on the Patapsco River a large library with a chamber above. The proximity to the river suggested "a Venetian fancy," and his design included a campanile tower with arched windows affording a view through the willow trees of a pretty waterfall. And in Baltimore, toward the end of the decade of the 1850's, he built his last town house, a handsome and spacious brownstone at 90 Madison Street.[2] Washington Irving, just returned from a visit to Kennedy, probably had him in mind when writing to Robert C. Winthrop of a new book, *Homes of American Authors:* "In commenting on that publication, a London critic observes, that 'the American authors seem to court the muse to some purpose.' He did not know that most of them, so well housed, had courted a rich wife into the bargain." [3]

If this thrust was aimed at Kennedy, it was not meant unkindly. The Kennedy domestic circle was exactly suited to Irving's temperament, and under such circumstances he was prone, as he said, to take root. At the age of seventy he discovered in Baltimore the "mill pond existence," Byron's phrase, which aptly described his ideal. "My intercourse with your family connection," he told Kennedy, "has been a great sweetener of the last few years of my existence, and the only attraction that has been able to draw me repeatedly from home." [4] With a splendid library at his disposal and Elizabeth Kennedy to pamper his whims, Irving found the home much like his own parlor at Sunnyside.

Irving left the Kennedys immediately after Pierce's inauguration in March 1853. He had made little progress on his biography of George Washington, so he returned to Baltimore in June to continue his researches. The friends set off for western Virginia ostensibly to examine manuscripts owned by members of the Washington family who had settled in Jefferson County. Irving was in a state of continual rapture, exclaiming over the scenery of the Shenandoah Valley and laughing aloud at the manifest contradictions of Harriet Beecher Stowe's picture of slavery which he discovered everywhere. Accompanied by Kennedy's brother Philip, who was about to publish his *Blackwater Chronicle,* and Kennedy's uncle, Philip Pendleton, the friends abandoned even the pretense of research and struck out for a tour of the western springs. The weather, unhappily for Irving, turned sizzling hot. Under the unceasing action of a fan, the portly Irving perspired, sulked in the arbor, and resolutely refused to be introduced to the company. The party escaped to Cassilis, the home of Kennedy's brother Andrew, where Irving revived in the company of Andrew's charming daughter Mary, to whom he later wrote a series of wistful, romantic letters.[5]

Irving left for Sunnyside early in July 1853 and Kennedy followed later in the month. In August the two men set out for a trip to Buffalo to visit Millard Fillmore. They sailed down Lake Champlain, voyaged up the St. Lawrence, and concluded their tour at Niagara. But "poor Irving was dissolving into train oil," and even Kennedy's imperturbable good humor was strained by his "disgruntled" companion. Irving returned to Virginia in October to visit the Valley in a more agreeable season. He came south for the last time at Christmas in 1854 to attend the wedding of Mary Kennedy at Cassilis.[6]

It was a curious friendship. Irving and Kennedy shared similar tastes, and there is every reason why they should have been intimate friends, yet the letters they exchanged are strangely impersonal in tone. There is scarcely an allusion to a subject that might conceivably have mattered: books, writing, foreign relations, or the American scene. That Kennedy was vitally alive to the currents of contemporary culture is clear from his notebooks of these years, but with Irving he exchanged only charmingly phrased platitudes. A day's visit at Sunnyside in 1853 Kennedy could describe as "one of the most agreeable days I have ever spent."[7] Yet, as his letters to Elizabeth make clear, traveling with the aging Dean of American Letters was largely an exercise in jollying him into good spirits. Irving was childishly delighted with his beginner's luck at bowling but shied when the conversation turned toward metaphysics or—much worse—politics. The Irving of seventy was no longer the Geoffrey Crayon whose writing had delighted the young Kennedy and stirred him to emulation.

When Irving returned to Sunnyside, Kennedy was thrown back on his own resources. He turned, predictably, to writing.

This desire seized him fitfully in his later years, then passed as suddenly as it had come. In a mood of disenchantment he began, toward the end of 1854, a work tentatively entitled "Mr. Ambrose: His Experiences, Opinions, and Philosophy." Kennedy wished to represent a philosopher who, through an honest pursuit of truth, incurred almost the universal enmity of the world, though gifted with every advantage of virtue, talent, wealth, and education. These, he wished to show, were insufficient to combat the "general sham, delusion, and imposture of the world." [8] Yet this plan, like so many others of his later years, was never realized. Fragmentary plots and jottings are sprinkled through the journals: "The Mysterious Dinner," "The Man of the Mountain," "The Spear of Ithuriel." Other subjects, "Mesmerism" and "Animal Magnetism," reached final drafts but were never published. He planned a magnum opus, a political and social history of the colonies from 1760 to 1776, designed to show the retrogression of republican principles since the days of the founders and to demonstrate that the country had "carried the universal suffrage to a point in which it has impaired free government." [9] This ambitious work, inspired by the success of Irving's *Life of George Washington*, was never carried beyond a reading of John Adams's diary.

Kennedy busied himself with civic duties. Each spring he performed the ritual connected with his post as provost of the University of Maryland. He exhorted the graduates, distributed the diplomas, and then, as he told Winthrop, "I took my dinner and went to billiards with an increased earnestness, by way of disabusing my mind of the humbug I had been practising before the world." [10] Kennedy was also chiefly responsible for the organization of Baltimore's Peabody Institute. This was the gift of Massachusetts-born George Peabody, who had known Kennedy in 1814 when both had served in the Maryland militia. Peabody had left Baltimore for London, where he made a fortune in finance. An expansive and vigorous man, he had his heart set on establishing a memorial in the city of his youth. At Peabody's request, Kennedy in 1854 drew up plans for a foundation to include a library, an art gallery, and an academy of music.[11] This rather grandiose project was sharply modified by a board of trustees who, he complained, wanted nothing more than "a respectable reading club house, where indolent and idle men may find the means of killing time." [12] Forced by petty jealousy and snobbery to compromise, he decided to resign but Peabody persuaded him to continue. Peabody, on his part, found that philanthropy embroiled him in the bickerings of men who grew officious when invited to spend his money. Kennedy was elected president of the board of trustees in 1860, a post he held until his death. The strife of civil war threatened to subvert the scheme, and when the Institute was formally dedicated in 1866, its successful realization was owing as much to Kennedy's tact and industry as to Peabody's generosity.

But Baltimore civic duties did not fill Kennedy's time, and he next turned his hand to business. He was a member of the boards of directors of three railroads threading the Susquehanna Valley and was active in negotiations which consolidated them into the Northern Central Railroad Company. In December 1854 he was offered the presidency of the new road. He accepted with characteristic enthusiasm. It was yet another opportunity, he wrote Winthrop, "to show the carping world how foolishly they talk when they say, what they do say, that a man of letters (not much of a man of letters, you say) is a mere blockhead in all matters of practical work." Washington Irving was not impressed. He wrote to Mary Kennedy at Cassilis: "Your Uncle John I understand is occupying himself very much with railroads. I wish he would put his mind on a better track and leave such everyday concerns to everyday people." Two years of "running up and down to and fro, amongst city councils, and Legislators, domestic and foreign, and Boards of Directors," brought Kennedy around to Irving's view. Although a prophet of an industrial America, he was content to leave business to others. "These men of business," he told Millard Fillmore, "are all tainted by that vice of refusing the pleasant appointments of life." [13] Nor was Kennedy temperamentally fitted to give battle to the breed of businessmen who, seeing the Northern Central prospering, cast covetous eyes upon it.

Meanwhile politics was not forgotten. During the winter of 1854 Millard Fillmore wrote from Buffalo to invite Kennedy to make a tour of the southern states. Kennedy accepted at once and suggested that Washington Irving be included. Although the men denied any political purpose, Irving was not deceived. He wrote to Elizabeth Kennedy:

> Heaven preserve me from any tour of the kind! To have to cope at every turn with the host of bores of all kinds that beset the paths of political notorieties. To have to listen to the speeches that would be made at dinner and other occasions to Mr. Fillmore and himself; and to the speeches that Fillmore and he would make in return. Has he not found out by this time how very bore-able I am? Has he not seen me sulk from bar rooms and other gathering places where he was making political capital among the millions? Has he forgotten how last summer a crew of blatant beasts of firemen, whose brass trumpets gave him so much delight, absolutely drove me into the wilderness? . . . I would as leave go campaigning with Hudibras or Don Quixote.[14]

In March 1854 Kennedy and Fillmore set out from Columbus down the Ohio River toward New Orleans. No sooner had they arrived at Cincinnati than the festivities began. At each city on their itinerary—Louisville, Memphis, Vicksburg, New Orleans—they were greeted by an official committee of city fathers, then wined and dined at sumptuous banquets. Fillmore was acclaimed as the architect of the Compromise of 1850 and the preserver of the Union. Then, as Irving had feared, the speeches began. Fillmore descanted on the values of Union and Moderation, and then Kennedy was called out. He was at the top of his speaking form. The newspaper reports of his wit preceded him, and when he tried to conclude, the crowd called out, "go on! go on!" His best efforts were greeted by shouts of "go it, old Horse-Shoe!"

The two friends returned eastward to Montgomery, Nashville, and Savannah. At Charleston a writer for the *Courier* observed that "wherever Mr. Kennedy has been, as the *compagnon du voyage* of Mr. Fillmore, in his welcome and almost triumphant march throughout the Western and Southern States, the former has distinguished himself by the continual play of wit and humor, so varied and exquisite and stored with the most polished weapons. The demure and dry manner, too, in which he says his best things, gives them the additional charm of surprise. . . ."[15] The role of court jester was a novel one for Kennedy, but he enjoyed it hugely. Back in Baltimore in mid-May he noted with pleasure reports current in the press linking his name with Fillmore as a Union ticket for the presidential contest in 1856.

In May 1855 Fillmore invited John and Elizabeth to accompany him on a European tour. They were obliged to refuse, for Edward Gray, in his seventy-ninth year, was in his last protracted illness. This proved a severe trial for his family, for Gray insisted that his daughters keep a constant vigil at his bedside. He lingered on until March 21, 1856. This ordeal left Elizabeth and Martha completely exhausted. At their father's death, neither had been outside the house for five months. The Kennedys' physician advised an immediate trip abroad, and in May they sailed from New York for Liverpool.

The journey was hastily arranged, and, in their shattered state of health, it was a joyless excursion. They spent several weeks in London, then journeyed to Ireland to make a pilgrimage to Edward Gray's birthplace in County Londonderry. A round of familiar tourist attractions followed: Paris, the Rhine journey, and Switzerland. Kennedy tirelessly cataloged the sights in his journal, but his thoughts were intent on the direction of politics at home. In February 1856 the newly formed American party, a conglomeration of old Whigs, temperance advocates, anti-Catholics, and nativists, had nominated Millard Fillmore for the Presidency. Before leaving for Europe, Fillmore had authorized Kennedy to speak for him in all political matters, and Kennedy knew that success for Fillmore would mean a cabinet appointment for himself. He insisted therefore on returning home in time for the fall elections. They came, and Fillmore carried only Maryland. The Democratic candidate, James Buchanan, won with the votes of fourteen slave and five free states. The Republicans, running nationally for the first time, carried eleven free states. The division revealed an ominous tightening of sectional lines.

Fillmore's defeat in the autumn of 1856 was the death knell of Whiggery as Kennedy had known it and defended it for a generation. At the age of sixty-one, he was a politician without a party. There was nothing now to keep him at home, and in August he and Elizabeth sailed again for Europe. They were gone fifteen months.

Kennedy was a zestful tourist. He enjoyed the "wheel-and-paddle life" of the traveler, and his capacity for sightseeing was boundless. Armed with a copy of John Murray's *Handbook for Travellers*, he followed a beaten track, and his travel journals, three closely written volumes, constitute a familiar chronicle. He gazed at the gothic cathedrals, exclaimed at the natural wonders, gaped at paintings of "Adam and Eve in Paradise in shocking nudity," tried to record it all, but broke off with the exclamation, "beautiful! beautiful! but is it not all described in the book of Murray?" His chief allegiance, naturally enough, was to England. He was in turn attracted and exasperated by its class system, admiring its stability but, being an American and therefore without status, stung by its hauteur. In London Charles Dickens was giving his readings, a public display of which Kennedy did not approve. It had been fourteen years since he had seen Dickens in Washington during his American tour. Kennedy thought "the change in his appearance is not favorable. He looks now too much like a blase'ed hero of the green room." This was a singular reversal of roles—an American finding an Englishman vulgar.

While visiting in Paris in September 1858, Kennedy renewed his friendship with Thackeray. The two men had last met in the winter of 1856 while Thackeray was lecturing in Baltimore. Although his health was failing, Thackeray had charmed Kennedy and his circle, and his visit lingered pleasantly for a half-century in the memory of those who met him. There were dinners of terrapin and Johannesberger and the inevitable introduction to Kennedy's conversation club. One morning in Kennedy's library Thackeray laid before him the plan for *The Virginians*, asked for information, and borrowed several books on the Revolution. Kennedy was at the time preparing a lecture on Maryland colonial history, and Thackeray offered to ask Macaulay's help in tracking down some documents in the British Museum.[16] This exchange of favors suggests an increased intimacy which was resumed in Paris in 1858.

An alleged literary obligation was the outcome of the Paris

meeting, and it has persisted as an indefinite footnote to literary history. On September 26, 1858, Kennedy recorded in his journal:

> Thackeray calls to see me and sits an hour or two. He is not looking well. He tells me he has need of my assistance with his Virginians—and says Heaven has sent me to his aid. He wants me to get his hero from Fort Duquesne where he is confined a prisoner after Braddock's defeat and to bring him to the coast to embark for England. "Now, you know all that ground," he says to me "and I want you to write a chapter for me to describe how he got off and what travel he made." He insists that I shall do it. I give him a doubtful promise to do it if I can find time in the thousand engagements that now press upon me on the eve of our leaving Paris. I would be glad to do it if circumstances would allow.

When John H. B. Latrobe came to write the Kennedy biography for *Appletons' Cyclopedia*, he rather fancifully embellished this core of fact and launched the myth that "Kennedy wrote the fourth chapter of the second volume of the 'Virginians' which accounts for the accuracy of the description of the local scenery about Cumberland, with which Kennedy was familiar, and which Thackeray had never seen." [17]

Thackeray's daughter, Mrs. Richie, wrote to James Grant Wilson, who was preparing his *Thackeray in the United States:* "I think it can be scarcely necessary to contradict the assertion that Mr. Kennedy wrote a chapter in 'The Virginians,' which is entirely in my father's handwriting. No doubt Mr. Kennedy gave him some facts about the scenery, but I am sure that my father wrote his own books, for no one could have written them for him." [18]

Further entries in Kennedy's journal indicate that the indebtedness extended only to suggestions.

> *September 30, 1858.* Thackeray calls. I tell him I am so much occupied with the engagements that press upon me, that I can do no more than give him a few hints for the description he wishes. I do this in conversation which he tells me is precisely what he wishes and I promise to repeat it in some notes which I shall prepare for him.

. . . . . .

October 3, 1858. I write nearly all the morning in preparing notes for Thackeray—an outline of the chapter he wants—and in making a rough map of illustration.
October 4, 1858. I send Thackeray the notes, &c.

Kennedy's remarks upon hearing of the death of Thackeray in 1864 are the last comment on a genial literary friendship: "The foreign papers bring us accounts of a great loss to the literary world in the death of Thackeray, the day before Christmas, at his home in London. I think this the extinguishment of the brightest light in the present literature in England. He was but little over fifty, with all the appearance of robust health, which I find however he had not. When I last saw him, it was at the Bristol Hotel in Paris, where he was sick in bed, and got me to write him a sketch for a chapter in 'The Virginians'—which I did and he afterwards partially incorporated in the book." [19]

These were prosperous years, free from financial worries, enriched by friendships with the great, and varied with travel. Kennedy's friends preserved the image of a benign and courtly gentleman of the old school, brilliant in conversation, youthful in outlook, a man wise and mellowed but otherwise untouched by time. Young writers who sought him out in Baltimore were captivated by his urbanity and wit. They found him still slender and erect and (in one of his favorite phrases) "quite a perpendicular person." He had allowed his beard to grow, and he seemed now in feature what he was in fact—the patriarch of the Pendleton family in America. "Your snow white beard," James Russell Lowell told him, "has a great advantage over us whom Time has only frostbitten and grizzled. I am impatient to be whitewashed." [20]

John Esten Cooke testified that he had "never heard finer humor or more vivid and dramatic descriptions of men, events, scenes—all passed before you like a living panorama. Those who listened went away under a charm. It was a rare entertainment to read his books, but a rarer one still to listen to him as he talked." [21] Lowell, once a guest of the Kennedys while lecturing in Baltimore, remembered his host with affection.

One could not be in his company for never so short a time, without being touched by that gentle consideration for others which is the root of all good breeding. His courtesy was not the formal discipline of elegant manners. There was a sense of benefaction in it. Whoever came near him felt the friendly charm which his nature radiated, so that his very house seemed steeped in it and welcomed you no less heartily than he. He was in the highest sense a genial man. He had a singular gift for companionship, for being something better than his books, and his finer qualities were lured out by the sympathy of the fireside. He was excellent in anecdote and reminiscence. His talk had just that pleasant suspicion of scholarship in it that befits the drawingroom, and never degenerated to the coarser flavor of pedantry. He could quote his bit of Horace and Virgil on occasion, which used to be the neck-verse of cultivated men. He had that somewhat rare excellence of being playfully earnest; and, though he had strong convictions, never made them the scourge of other men.[22]

Kennedy filled easily and naturally the role of elder statesman in the literary world. "I am a *quasi* lion," he told Elizabeth, "if not a lion out and out." [23] Yet his notebooks reveal that the face he turned to the world was but a mask which disguised an obscure malaise of the spirit which seemed to take hold of him after middle life. The first cause was his health. His old complaint, a severe inflammation of the skin, was liable to erupt unless he was rigidly abstemious. He was suffering annoying attacks of dizziness, and his eyes burned and smarted if he tried to read after nightfall. A painful lameness, the result of the injury to his hip when he was thrown from a horse in 1842, was exacerbated by even mild exercise.

Many of Kennedy's former diversions no longer amused. Chief among these was the theater. Its ancient magic had ceased to charm. He thought the audiences unfashionable and the productions crude. And Baltimore society, once so delightful, now wearied him. It had lost the courtly, elegant air that had lingered in the post-revolutionary generation. A new class had risen to power to dominate the city's social life. It was clearly defined, masterful, and complacent—a class at noonday—but it was only dimly aware that political power was slipping from its hands forever.

A society composed of wealthy merchants, manufacturers, and professional men, their reputations as sparkling conversationalists were founded on a few "good things" treasured up and reverently remembered. They formed a class intellectually slack, full of back eddies and placid coves, where a man could idle in talk as the time glided pleasantly away. They talked on and on: gossip at the Assembly Rooms, conversation over oysters and whisky punch at their clubs, or florid speeches in Monument Square. Towering figures in their time, they cared nothing for posterity, and posterity has repaid them in kind. Many could, and did, boast impeccable genealogies, and in their imaginations they saw themselves as latter-day cavaliers, descendants in spirit of the Lords Baltimore. Their accepted standard was commercial, and only current opinion passed for common coin, for ideas were not negotiable among them. Their surest test of a gentleman was his ability to distinguish between Chateau Margaux and Chateau Lafitte rather than between a volume of Swift and one of Sterne, for they set small value upon books that did not register accounts.

Kennedy divided these men into two classes, "the stupid, slangy young men who pretend to fashion—and the belly men who pride themselves upon their judgment in cookery, wines, &c. as a matter of study. They are both dressy, with an affectation of good society, and claim to be very knowing in all matters of taste." Both classes, he added, "I cordially detest." [24] After one particularly exasperating evening, he noted in his journal, "I must write an essay on Bores." He complained bitterly of the isolation in which he found himself: "I have nobody in the world to talk to. All my acquaintances are of the newspaper class. They weary me with prices and values and current news—and their discourse of material things. A spiritual man is unknown to me. The women have so much sentimental superstition which they think is religion, that I cannot fall in with it. If they have not that, they have such commonplaces and insipid platitudes, for the most part, that even their occasionally lively sallies on life and manners scarcely relieve it. Upon the whole, they are better, however, than the prosy, commonplace men. Conversation is a lost art." [25]

There was yet another cause for the gloom which overcame Kennedy at intervals and which he reserved for the pages of his notebooks—the threat of civil war. Although he had retired from the hurly-burly of active politics, he remained a close observer of events. During his own years in public life, he had fought to conserve the principles of a federal government formed through concession and compromise. But as sectional tensions increased during the 1850's and it became increasingly evident that he would be forced to take sides, his sympathies turned more and more toward the North. By 1860 there was little to distinguish him, politically speaking, from his Boston friend Robert C. Winthrop.

Kennedy's break with the South was foreshadowed in a variety of ways. Over the years a gulf seems to have widened between Kennedy and his brothers in western Virginia. Only John had chosen urban Baltimore rather than rural Virginia. Andrew in 1822 had taken his bride to the ancestral homestead, Clayton, near Charles Town, and settled down to a life of law and farming. Philip lived with his parents at The Bower and tried to imitate his eldest brother's success in literature. Anthony married his cousin, Sarah Dandridge, and turned to cultivating his wife's farm. Perhaps a tinge of envy estranged these established, if impecunious, country squires from their famous brother. Andrew was beset by a certain spirit of improvidence which made impediments of his best enterprises. Philip was a victim of intemperance. Anthony, according to John, "never thought a thought, read a book, or troubled his head with a serious application to a grave purpose a day in his life." [26] At one time or another all three owed John money, and they may have felt that their brother was more exacting in money matters than a Virginian, even an expatriate Virginian, ought to be. He was capable of blurting out in a blunt and annoying manner that he felt himself "scurvily treated" in a financial settlement, and in their eyes even the fact that he was right hardly justified the rebuke. Andrew Kennedy's eldest son made no secret of his dislike of his Uncle John and manifested it by an open indifference to commissions placed in his hands.

One by one Kennedy's ties with Virginia were severed. In 1836 his father died at The Bower following a long and crippling illness. His mother fell victim of a cholera epidemic in September 1854, and her son Andrew survived her but four years. Anthony's wife died in 1846. He came to Baltimore, married the daughter of the wealthy diplomat Christopher Hughes, and settled down to a life of elegant leisure. Therefore, when Kennedy chose the Union in 1860, it was an actual, as well as a symbolic, break with his Virginia heritage. The Dandridges at The Bower, the Cookes, and Andrew Kennedy's family ("the most venomous rebel stuff") all chose secession, and David Strother could write to Kennedy that he was "the only loyal gentleman in our district who has drawn the sword for the United States Government." When the fighting began, Kennedy noted in his journal: "I learn that our family connection in Virginia furnished over 60 men to the Confederate Army and that we had forty blood relations in one regiment on that side at Bull Run." [27]

At last Kennedy's only link with Virginia was his uncle, Philip Pendleton. And even this friendship cooled with the years. As doggedly loyal to Virginia as in the days when he had served as the model for Frank Meriwether of *Swallow Barn*, Philip Pendleton resented his nephew's summer excursions to Saratoga and Sharon. The old gentleman felt neglected and insisted that John accompany him to the western springs. Kennedy dutifully obliged, but he poured out his exasperation to Elizabeth.

> Uncle Phil and I are engaged all day long in disputes. We go at it hammer and tongs soon after breakfast and quarrel till night. He will not admit a single fact I state—to say nothing of opinions which are more debatable. For instance I said yesterday that from the porch of Sharon you could see over a space of fifty miles in extent. "How does it front?" he inquired. "North," said I. "Then," said he, "there is no view there—there can't be." "Why not?" "Because the Alleghany runs North and South and you would be looking along the line of its course." "There is no Alleghany there," said I. "That's a mistake," said he. "It was so and so." Well finally I had to give up and confess that there was no view at Sharon. This is a sample of our daily work. I go at billiards, to nine pins, to books to get out of the way of this constant wrangle, but Uncle Phil likes it and he is very apt to follow me.[28]

The degree of Kennedy's variation from extreme southern opinion is best seen in his relationship with the southern novelist,

William Gilmore Simms. Kennedy described to Elizabeth his first meeting with Simms in 1840.

> Who do you think dined here today? Guy Rivers [29] . . . . He is tall, well made, not handsome in feature, amazingly pedantic, Sir Oracle in conceit, a thorough Loco, and short sighted in every sense.* He talked *literary* but fortunately I had not read or believed I had not, any of the books he wanted me to criticize, and so shuffled off every imputation of scholarship he was pleased to presume in my favour. I abused Bryant to him for being *political*, and spoke of his editing a party newspaper as altogether derogatory to his fame. I was not overnice in my phrase in this matter, and after all, discovered that my new friend himself, who, by the by, claims to be a poet, was also, or had been, a party hack editor. I can't say I took very violently to him.[30]

Bryant's politics were condemned with tongue in cheek, for Kennedy at that moment was writing his political satire, *Quodlibet*. Notwithstanding the irony, the two men were unsuited for close friendship. Kennedy was more congenial with men like Irving and Thackeray, for among them a good deal of raillery concerning authorship eased the tension that might strain the relationship among gifted men. Simms, on the other hand, resembled Cooper in his positive manner and his readiness to suspect an affront. His impetuous temper was checked by Kennedy's habitual reserve. "We should judge the intellect of Mr. Kennedy," Simms wrote, "to be a strict and exacting one; perpetually at war with his sympathies, and perpetually counseling distrust when his affections would counsel confidence. With all his fancy, and his natural love of fiction—with all the necessity that prevails in the pursuit of an art which, over all requires geniality, there is that about the mind of Mr. Kennedy which constantly suggests the idea of calm, practical judgment, keen in its criticism and excessively slow to faith." [31] When the two men met in 1840, Kennedy had already won the political recognition that Simms, being southern to the core, so ardently desired; and Simms was living the literary life that Kennedy's public career denied him.

Simms and Kennedy were further separated by widely diver-

---

* Wears glasses [Kennedy's note].

gent views concerning their art. Like Poe, Simms tended to make his special gifts the norm of literary excellence. He was fond of praising "invention," the subordination of detail to epic largeness of conception, and the revelation of character through action rather than analysis. All were typical of his own work. Simms employed rapid-fire narration and headlong, unrevised composition, and he could defend his practice by citing the example of his countryman, Cooper, as well as Scott and Dickens. It is no wonder that he found *Rob of the Bowl* "rather a languid performance." [32] Yet Simms admired *Swallow Barn*, and Jay B. Hubbell has suggested that *The Golden Christmas*, published in 1852, was perhaps inspired by a reading of Kennedy's novel, which appeared in the revised edition a year earlier.[33]

In 1845 Simms dedicated *Count Julian* to Kennedy, but the author's private opinion of the novel reveals how empty was the compliment. Simms had been at work on the book as early as 1839, but a friend had misplaced part of the manuscript for two years, and when it finally turned up, it went the rounds of publishers until William Taylor brought it out in 1845. When Simms read the proofs, he found it "monstrous flat" and dubbed it a "wretched failure." It was so bad that he felt obliged to write Kennedy a letter of explanation.[34]

When Simms took over the editorship of the *Southern Quarterly Review* in 1849, he was eager to have Kennedy contribute. In connection with his crusade for southern literary independence, Simms wished Kennedy to prepare a memoir of his cousin, Philip Pendleton Cooke. Kennedy, absorbed with politics, delegated the task to his younger brother, Philip, who had grown up with Cooke in Martinsburg. But Simms would not be denied and next suggested that Kennedy prepare a political essay for the *Quarterly*. With sectional feeling running high, Kennedy was anxious to alleviate tension and wrote to Simms what was probably a sounding of the Charleston political depth.

> I detest the hypocrisy of abolitionism—the main feature of Northern politics—much more than I do its fanaticism; and I have quite a decided source of ridicule for the 'mutual admiration' principle which governs in the tribunals of our hyperborean literature. These good people—I mean north of our

Tweed, have no eye to look towards the equator. It is all Serbonian Bog to them—a great waste from Connecticut to Tallahassee. Now, there is a pleasant spur in the thought, that by a vigorous concentration of our critical forces here southward, we might startle the transcendentals with an occasional crack of the whip and teach them that we are not actually saurians yet —and I almost think I could do some work in it. The only difficulty that I can foresee is this that arises out of the unfortunate circumscription of your Carolina influence, by that net of metaphysical politics which you have thrown over your state—not you personally—for, I believe, that you are much more catholic than your contemporaries, and your *conlocales* (if you understand this coinage) and could do much more than you are permitted just now. Charleston is one of the great intellectual centres of the U. S. but it has unfortunately too small a circumference. My wish would be to remodel your endemic opinion and make it national. *You* could do it—but it would cost you much loss of present popularity and much tribulation—before it must succeed, which eventually, would be certain.[35]

Simms answered at once, explaining that the *Quarterly* was "against the Bank, the Protective Tariff, Int. Impro. &c. And in these respects your faith is not ours. We believe also that Negro Slavery is one of the greatest moral goods and blessings, and that slavery in all ages has been found the greatest and most admirable agent of Civilization." [36] Such a letter would only confirm Kennedy in his belief that below Baltimore the needle dipped more or less toward the pole of abstractionism. One thing was certain. He could not write for the *Southern Quarterly Review*. After this exchange, offers for political articles abruptly ceased, the intervals between letters lengthened, and with the coming of the war the correspondence stopped altogether.

As the country drifted toward disruption and civil war, Kennedy, like the chorus in a Sophoclean tragedy, warned but was powerless to change. He thought that "the conception and estimate of a *gentleman*" had been entirely obliterated from the popular mind. Political power had been usurped by "a miserable array of charlatans, and make believe statesmen, and little clap-trap demagogues and mock statesmen, manufactured out of blackguards." [37] Amidst the clamorous voices crying for disunion,

Kennedy joined with other old-line Whigs in a search for some middle ground upon which to erect a party platform dedicated to moderation and conciliation. In January 1860 Senator John J. Crittenden of Kentucky wrote to Kennedy inviting him to serve as chairman of the central committee of a new Constitutional Union party.[38] Kennedy returned briefly to active political duty to pen the party's call to arms and to serve as party chairman in Maryland. At a convention in Baltimore on May 9, 1860, the new party nominated John Bell of Tennessee and Edward Everett of Massachusetts. There was general agreement among moderates that the ticket was intellectually distinguished and eminently respectable. But everywhere they added that it was of no possible use. The opposition dismissed it derisively as the Old Gentlemen's party.

The Democrats met in Charleston in April 1860 and promptly split over the slavery issue. On June 18 in Baltimore the northern wing nominated Stephen A. Douglas of Illinois, and ten days later the southern wing, also meeting in Baltimore, named John C. Breckinridge of Kentucky to head the ticket. The Republicans assembled in Chicago in May and nominated Abraham Lincoln. In the election that brought Lincoln to power, the Constitutional Union party carried only Maryland and two other border slave states.

By the end of December 1860 South Carolina was out of the Union and six other states of the lower South were getting ready to follow. Maryland and Virginia and the other border states stood shivering on the brink of secession. Kennedy realized that some way must be found to keep them within the Union until Lincoln and the Republicans had the opportunity to show that they meant no harm to slavery within the states. In a pamphlet published in December 1860, *The Border States: Their Power and Duty in the Present Disordered Condition of the Country*, Kennedy called on the states forming a buffer zone between North and South to take the lead in effecting a compromise. At Washington Charles Francis Adams of Boston and Henry Winter Davis of Baltimore worked diligently to implement such a plan, but they were too late.

With the outbreak of hostilities at Fort Sumter, Virginia went over to the Confederacy and the cry went up in Baltimore that "Maryland must go as Virginia goes." On May 9, 1861, there appeared in the *National Intelligencer* a letter by Kennedy entitled "The Great Drama," an eloquent exposition of the practical and patriotic motives for Maryland to remain within the Union. Eloquence, however, would not suffice. In the crisis the federal government suspended habeas corpus in Maryland and arrested and imprisoned numerous state and local officials suspected of disloyalty. Under pressure Maryland held firm, but among the states of the borderlands, Arkansas, Tennessee, and North Carolina followed Virginia into secession. Kennedy placed the blame for the breakup equally on demagogues of both sections: "It is the mock-heroic of men who do not comprehend their own incapacity, who mistake passion for a just sentiment of honor, and who cannot perceive the desperate extremes of their own folly." [39]

The war years constitute a melancholy chapter in the life of John Kennedy. In the North it was easy to be loyal to the Union; it might even be profitable. In Baltimore loyalty meant ostracism. Kennedy complained to Winthrop that southern sympathizers had "voted our old-fashioned loyalty to be absolutely vulgar, and fancy themselves to be the true and lineal descendants of the Cavaliers who claimed to be on the gentlemanly side of the English civil war. This assumption has had a curious effect of throwing a very considerable amount of snobbery into the rebellion, to grace its other virtues. Many families here who have heretofore been permitted only to look over the fence of the elite, have, by their complaisance to secession, got free admission into the fold. Their absurdities will show you how very little a man of sense may lose in our city by the forfeiture of his privilege of fraternization with 'the Chivalry.' " [40]

When Kennedy presented the diplomas at the commencement of the University of Maryland, graduates known to be southern sympathizers were applauded and bouquets tied with red and white ribbons were thrown on the stage. Unionists were roundly hissed. Acquaintances of many years' standing rebuffed him by bellowing "No, sir! No, sir!" when he passed them on the street. When he entered a room, old friends hastened to leave by a side door. He might have spared himself this painful sundering of old friendships by the exercise of a prudent impartiality. But, as James Russell Lowell said, "he was a brave man, and chose the nobler privilege of danger." [41] Almost an outcast in his native city, he found himself honored in the North, and in 1863 Harvard College made specific mention of his loyalty to the Union in conferring upon him the degree of Doctor of Laws.

The saddest news of all came from the Shenandoah Valley. The neighborhood around Martinsburg was a no-man's land destined to witness the horrors of border warfare which Kennedy had graphically described years before in *Horse-Shoe Robinson*. News reached him of childhood friends arrested and imprisoned, and their homes and farms laid waste. Relatives, even the most disloyal, wrote him desperate and pathetic letters begging for provisions and money. The fate of The Bower, the prototype of Swallow Barn, and of its owner Stephen Dandridge, who had offered his home as headquarters for Confederate cavalry, was described to Kennedy by his brother Philip.

> With all his once fine estate, Stephen Dandridge has so little with which to feed and clothe him, that I have not the heart to take anything from him, beyond what he may think proper to offer. . . . I wonder if our friend and kinsman, who has many most excellent qualities, has not by this time some perception that he is one of these dupes and victims. Truly he has eaten an extra allowance of the insane root, if he does not now acknowledge this in his heart. Indeed when I think of the many firesides deserted, the poverty close bordering on want that has fallen upon so many, the ruin and wreck that is everywhere over the land, and what is worse than all, the defilement of soul that has fallen upon so many, both man and woman, that were once free from all touch of stain, I cannot but help think, that when our people entered upon this revolt, they were seized by an insane frenzy to become the dupes and victims they are, and that all that is wanted to make the manifestation of their madness complete, is to curse God and die—which I believe will yet be the fate of many a bitter and despairing heart.[42]

The war inspired Kennedy's last published writing, a series of eleven letters to the *National Intelligencer* in Washington which appeared in 1863 and 1864. The letters were a recapitulation of themes which had preoccupied him during his political life. He marshaled the historical evidence against state rights and secession, thus reaffirming his faith in a strong central government. The cause of the rebellion he believed was in part the heresy of "hair-splitting doctrinaires," in part the "shallow invention of a few Quixotes in politics." The letters were a lucid summary of the northern conservative position, conciliatory in tone, but unmarked by any special penetration or originality of conception. In 1865 they were collected into a volume entitled *Mr. Ambrose's Letters on the Rebellion*.[43] The letters are chiefly interesting for the added testimony they provide to Kennedy's unflagging political partisanship. He promised himself repeatedly that he would withdraw from all public controversy, but he was utterly incapable of either ignoring politics or remaining neutral. And his experience on the hustings had made him a realist. He wasted no pity on the Constitutional Union party. It was defunct. If the power struggle was to be between the Democrats and the Republicans, he would make a choice.

Kennedy had shared the southern suspicion of Lincoln, and he had been ready to believe, and to repeat, the tales of the new President's gaucherie. At first Kennedy bitterly criticized Lincoln for not prosecuting the war with sufficient vigor. But by 1862 he was writing to Winthrop that "old Abe has really, as he says, set down that great, broad, flat, and heavy-shod foot of his, in good earnest, and it will squelch the whole dozen reptiles who are now crawling across his path into an indistinguishable mass of slime." After Gettysburg, Kennedy supported Lincoln wholeheartedly. In the fall of 1864 while visiting Winthrop in Cambridge, Kennedy declined an invitation from Oliver Wendell Holmes to attend the illustrious Saturday Club in order that he might set out for Baltimore to be in time to vote for Lincoln in the national election. Lincoln's assassination was for Kennedy a shattering personal blow. He immediately grasped the symbolic force of the tragedy:

> The life of Lincoln seems like a heavenly mission. The simple, and shrewd, and honest woodman, thrown upon such a stage, with such a labor before him; the steady and almost inspired wisdom of his advance from each stage to the next, in the accomplishment of his task, and the final consummation of his

appointed work, in the end of the war, by which he has saved the Republic, and which has secured the complete and perfect liberation of four millions of slaves; and then, the duty done, the departure from the scene of his labors, a *sacrifice*, and on that great day of propitiation, when Christians were everywhere celebrating that greater sacrifice for sin which redeemed a world! [44]

This reference to Good Friday calls attention to one other effect of the war on the aging Kennedy—it turned his mind more and more to the subject of religion. Although a Presbyterian by heritage, he seldom attended religious services and was a severe critic of ritualism in the churches. He was as opposed to ultraism in religion as in politics, and was especially exasperated by "that particularly self-satisfied and complacent conglomerate—the religious public—very egotistical and very milk-soppy." Kennedy had no intense interest in grappling with theological subtleties. Indeed, he spoke scornfully of "metaphysics," whether alluding to John Calvin or John C. Calhoun. His library, which at his death contained over five thousand volumes and which he thought one of the best in the country, contained a rich collection of theology, but much of it he found, like Jonathan Edwards' dissertation on original sin, a "din of metaphysical jargon." "To me," he wrote, "it is written in an unknown tongue—I understand nothing of it. Poor dissolute bewildered man! What a destiny is yours if this be true—doomed to be compelled to believe all this which you can't understand—on pain of eternal torment." From the first Kennedy was more concerned with what man should do than with what he should believe. He had not, he said, "come into agreement with Rome or Geneva or with any other school of wranglers." But after a long period of soul searching, he determined to unite with the church. During the summer of 1864, he took his first communion in the Episcopal Church, the church of his devout Elizabeth.[45]

It would be pleasant to record that with the coming of peace the hatreds of the war years were forgotten. At least one Southerner, William Gilmore Simms, possessed the magnanimity of spirit to renew an old friendship. Kennedy made a brief trip to

Charleston, and Simms, true to the finest tradition of the code he had followed to its defeat, greeted him gallantly and cordially. And Simms's last letter to Kennedy, written in 1866 from New York, where he had gone to re-establish himself with publishers, requested a photograph and revealed that any estrangement owing to the war was forgotten: "I am making a collection of my friends' heads—i.e. where they have anything in them—for an album, which I design to keep for my children; taking for granted that they will learn to estimate & study the aspects of those whom I have known equally head and heart." [46] In Baltimore, however, Kennedy found himself isolated. "The Chivalry," having treated him with arrogance and contempt during the war, could not endure the fact that he had picked the winning side. Nor had Kennedy's attitude during the war made the resumption of old friendship easy. Unlike so many politicians, he had never formed the habit of speaking in a cautious and noncommital fashion. He spoke out what was in him, not fearing to utter what a more prudent temper would have left unsaid. He had prophesied doom for the South if it rebelled. And now, like many another prophet, he was without honor in his own country.

In July 1866, at the age of seventy, he left Baltimore in company with Elizabeth and Martha Gray for another tour of Europe. He resolutely made the rounds of tourist attractions, but his health was failing and with it his zest for new experiences. The reader of his travel journals is struck not by the fact that he became sated with sightseeing, but rather that, aged and ailing, he managed to sustain interest so long. Secretary of State William H. Seward named him a commissioner to the Paris Exposition of 1867, and for his services the French government conferred upon him the cordon of the Legion of Honor. But he had outlived his love of praise, and he was offended by Paris where he felt society existed for "the defiance of moral propriety." Paris was bad, but Rome was worse. He cataloged its wonders with an irony worthy of Jonathan Swift: "fleas, filth, beggars, extortionists, friars, priests, and soldiers." An audience with the Pope he thought "the dreariest, the dullest, the most unmeaning, and the most unsatisfactory, I imagine, of all the ceremonies of court presentations—always very stupid things—to be encountered anywhere in the great Vanity Fair of the World." He was weary and bored and homesick. And he had begun to fear, as had Jefferson, that too long a sojourn abroad unfitted an American for his native land. Kennedy eagerly searched the foreign papers for the scanty news of the United States, and he worried over the sad imbroglio of post-civil war politics at Washington. Back in Baltimore after an absence of twenty-seven months, he said to Elizabeth: "Number 90 Madison Street once more! I was afraid I would die abroad." [47]

Kennedy returned to the United States convinced of the superiority of the New World to the Old. "The American of the U.S.," he had written while abroad, "is the most genuine in his hospitality and the most genial and sympathetic in his intercourse with his fellow man, of all men in Christendom." He no sooner disembarked at New York than he inquired of friends about the chances of General Grant in the election of 1868, and once back in Baltimore he addressed a Republican mass meeting on October 31, 1868. Kennedy had been an articulate defender and eloquent prophet of an industrial society, but the triumph of his principles with the Republican party came too late for his personal reward. The new party welcomed him into the fold because his name lent substance and luster to its youthful exuberance, but to a new school of politicians, he was an anachronism, separated from them by the chasm of civil war.

His speech to the Republican mass meeting—a tribute to the federal Union "permanent, indissoluble, invincible"—was Kennedy's last public appearance. Even an hour's reading or writing brought on "a weariness of the brain," so he busied himself with besique, conversation, and his memories. His last official paper was his annual report as president of the Peabody Institute dated February 12, 1870. It provided one more opportunity to sound the note which was the central theme of his life: "I esteem it to be the peculiar excellence of Mr. Peabody's design [which was, of course, Kennedy's design] that he has given it pre-eminently this character of a *National* gift—a signally patriotic endowment —in the broad foundation he has laid for it."

Kennedy made his usual trip to the North during the summer of 1869. Millard Fillmore saw him at Saratoga Springs and re-

Elder Statesman 235

called that "he was there as joyous and hilarious as ever, the center of every social circle and the admired of all observers." [48] While visiting at Newport in August, he suffered a severe illness which was diagnosed as an abdominal tumor.[49] During the following winter in Baltimore, he was tormented by increasingly painful attacks. In July 1870 he again traveled north hoping to find relief.

During the last week of Kennedy's life, Oliver Wendell Holmes called twice to see him. Holmes found him "full of talk, so cheerful, so genial, so varied—sometimes on political and historical matters with which he was familiar, sometimes relating personal experiences of which he had such a fund in his memory, always lively, entertaining, graceful in his discourse,—that I have rarely sat in a company when one man did more to keep all the rest happy in listening to him. There was no look of warning, no tone that could suggest a melancholy foreboding; but, bright and brave in the face of fast gaining infirmity which he would not betray to sadden others, he shed sunshine about him to the last." [50] John Kennedy died Thursday, August 18, 1870, at Newport. Burial took place the following Sunday in the family lot at Greenmount Cemetery in Baltimore.

On October 25, 1854, Kennedy, in a nostalgic mood, had noted in his journal:

> My birthday. Fifty-nine. A clear balmy Indian summer day mild and beautiful. In some features a type of my life—sunshiny, peaceful, almost all I could wish. I say almost, it has had its drawbacks and its failures—enough to teach me my humanity. I have been prosperous in my modest way, and moderation is the best form of prosperity. I have had no extraordinary successes, no extravagant fortune, no pre-eminent good luck; but a temperate, fair and reasonable experience from day to day. I have lost many golden moments; I have committed many obvious errors; my faults have been carelessly weeded; these I confess with a penitent spirit . . . .

Perhaps this description is the most appropriate commentary on the life of John Kennedy. He was not a man of deeply philosophic mind, nor did he possess that uniquely original gift we call genius. Yet he was endowed with talents which he carefully improved and was earnest in the best truth he comprehended. And whatever he did, he did well, not always with the greatest distinction, but with integrity and courage and independence. If he subscribed to some of the fads and humbugs of his day such as mesmerism and phrenology, it was this same spirit of inquiry which led him to champion Morse's telegraph through Congress and, as Secretary of the Navy, to insist upon the responsibility of government to subsidize scientific research. He was a conservative by temperament as well as by conviction. His concept of the responsibility of public office and the manner in which it should be sought and accepted was formed in a school that during his lifetime became as outmoded as knee breeches and cocked hats. A most uncommon man, he was destined to live out his life in the Age of the Common Man, and he lacked the capacity for self-dramatization which might have carried him to greater political success.

Kennedy taught his countrymen that an American could mix politics and belles lettres and bring distinction to both. He never found it necessary, as did Poe, "to coin one's brain into silver, at the nod of a master," [51] and the fact accounts for his general indifference to public taste. He gave to literature only what it pleased him to give, and he has accordingly suffered in reputation for the narrowness of his range and the meagerness of his output. But since it was unnecessary for him to turn hack for dollars, he held himself to a consistently high standard of craftsmanship. While it is easy to indict him for not writing the books he planned, still he wrote with scarcely any sympathies to sustain or appreciation to encourage him. It was his fate to be born into a world that mistook provincialism for patriotism and found it eccentric, if not absurd, that a man should make literature more than a casual diversion or a dilettante enthusiasm. Kennedy's need to justify his role as novelist, like his desire for political fame, tells us as much about the world he lived in as it does about the man himself. It is in the lives of such men that we may hope to discover what Alfred North Whitehead has called "the inward thoughts of a generation." [52]

Acknowledgments

I HAVE BEEN assisted in the preparation of this study by the staffs of many libraries, especially those of the Peabody Institute Library in Baltimore, the University of Pennsylvania Library, and the University of Delaware Library. I am particularly indebted to Mr. Lloyd A. Brown, former director of the Peabody Institute Library, and to the present director, Mr. Frank N. Jones, for placing the Kennedy Papers at my disposal and for being generous with their assistance. I also wish to thank the librarians of the following institutions for their help and for permission to use material: the Boston Public Library, the Buffalo Historical Society, the Duke University Library, the Essex Institute in Salem, Massachusetts, the Historical Society of Pennsylvania, the Johns Hopkins University Library, the Library of Congress, the Massachusetts Historical Society, the Maryland Historical Society, the New York Historical Society, the New York Public Library, and the Rochester University Library.

I am deeply indebted to Professor Sculley Bradley, of the University of Pennsylvania, and to his colleague Professor Robert E. Spiller for their guidance and assistance in the early stages of this study. I should like to thank Mr. William B. Marye, corresponding secretary of the Maryland Historical Society, and Professor Francis C. Haber, of the University of Florida, for sharing with me their wide and detailed knowledge of the Baltimore scene.

Miss Elizabeth Taylor, of Ranson, West Virginia, grand-niece of John Pendleton Kennedy, graciously answered my inquiries. Mr. Cecil D. Eby, Jr., of Charles Town, West Virginia, skillfully guided me through those portions of Jefferson and Berkeley Counties which are associated with Kennedy.

I owe a debt of gratitude to Professor Arthur R. Dunlap, chairman of the English Department of the University of Delaware, for his kind interest and encouragement. A grant from the Faculty Research Committee of the University of Delaware enabled me to undertake additional research during the summer of 1959.

For permission to reproduce portraits of Kennedy and his wife I am grateful to Mr. J. Gilman D'Arcy Paul, Baltimore, Maryland; the Frick Art Reference Library, New York City; the Henry E. Huntington Library and Art Gallery, San Marino, California; the Peabody Institute, Baltimore; and Sleepy Hollow Restorations, Tarrytown, New York.

Portions of this work in somewhat different form have appeared in the *American Quarterly*, the *Maryland Historical Magazine*, the *Pennsylvania Magazine of History and Biography*, the *Virginia Magazine of History and Biography*, and the *William and Mary Quarterly*. I wish to thank the editors of these journals for permission to reprint material from their pages.

My greatest debt is to my sister, Kathryn B. Lawrence, who has with patience and good humor encouraged and assisted me in every stage of the preparation of this study.

SOURCES

THE INDISPENSABLE source for any comprehensive study of John Pendleton Kennedy is the John Pendleton Kennedy Papers in the Peabody Institute, Baltimore, a collection totaling 130 volumes. The most important segment of the collection is a

Sources

thirty-three-volume set of manuscript journals covering the period from 1847 to 1869. Two additional but fragmentary journals span the years from 1829 to 1847. In addition, there are seventeen supplemental volumes describing trips throughout the United States and Europe. Second in importance to the journals are thirty-four volumes of letters both by and to Kennedy from 1812 until the year of his death, 1870. There are also over three thousand pages of Kennedy's letters in press copy covering the years 1846 through 1869. Included in the Peabody collection are the manuscripts of all Kennedy's published works, a catalogue of his library, notebooks with hints and ideas for stories and essays, commonplace books, scrapbooks, and ephemera.

Of major importance for the first three chapters of this study are three autobiographical fragments, referred to in the notes as Fragment A (1847–1864), Fragment B (1834), and Fragment C (1825?). The first is a 143-page manuscript begun in 1847 (cf. Journal, April 18, 1847) and last added to in 1864. The entire manuscript is in the calligraphy of Kennedy's old age. The second fragment, dated by Kennedy January 1, 1834, is not carried beyond his school days, and a third, postdated "about 1825," is more fragmentary still. Taken together they reveal a decided mellowing of his memories over the years. The Kennedy Papers are described in some detail in Lloyd W. Griffin, "The John Pendleton Kennedy Manuscripts," *Maryland Historical Magazine*, XLVIII (1953), 327–36. A dozen other libraries holding Kennedy papers have given me access to them. These libraries are named in the footnotes in which their holdings are mentioned.

In his will Kennedy named Robert C. Winthrop, Josias Pennington, and Henry T. Tuckerman as his literary executors. He made provision for the publication of a uniform edition of his writings together with such portions of his private papers as his executors might direct. Tuckerman undertook the commemorative biography and performed the duty with unfailing tact and sympathy. He had a keen sense of what was permanently significant in the papers, and he preserved much contemporary evidence which would otherwise have been irrevocably lost. The biography is an authorized portrait but not conceivably to be taken as the last word.

The Collected Works of John Pendleton Kennedy (New York, 1871–72), ten volumes, includes the *Life* by Tuckerman and three volumes of miscellanies: *At Home and Abroad: A Series of Essays, with a Journal in Europe in 1867–68; Political and Official Papers;* and *Occasional Addresses.* These last three volumes were compiled and edited by Tuckerman from pamphlets and manuscripts among the Kennedy papers.

Swallow Barn was edited for the American Authors Series with an introduction by Jay B. Hubbell (New York, 1929). Ernest E. Leisy edited *Horse-Shoe Robinson,* with an introduction, chronology, and bibliography, for the American Fiction Series (New York, 1937).

Modern Kennedy scholarship begins with the essay by Vernon Louis Parrington, *Main Currents in American Thought* (New York, 1927), II, 46–56. "Few Americans of his day," Parrington wrote of Kennedy, "were so generously gifted; none possessed a lighter touch. He has been somewhat carelessly forgotten even by our literary historians who can plead no excuse for so grave a blunder." Four years later Edward M. Gwathmey published *John Pendleton Kennedy* (New York, 1931). This study was intended to emphasize the literary aspects of Kennedy's career. The book adds little not in Tuckerman's *Life,* and, unfortunately for the student of Kennedy, it is riddled with factual errors.

The best brief account of Kennedy's life and work is given in Jay B. Hubbell, *The South in American Literature* (Durham, 1954), pp. 481–95. Alexander Cowie has written penetrating criticism of Kennedy's novels in *The Rise of the American Novel* (New York, 1951), pp. 258–70. Van Wyck Brooks has drawn a graceful sketch of Kennedy in *The World of Washington Irving* (New York, 1944), pp. 218–21. The article in the *Dictionary of American Biography,* X, 333–34, is by Mary Wilhelmina Williams. Genealogical information may be found in Mary Selden Kennedy, *Seldens of Virginia and Allied Families* (New York, 1911).

References to manuscript materials and secondary sources consulted in the preparation of this study will be found in the notes. No attempt will be made here to duplicate the bibliographical information which appears in the notes or to furnish an inclusive

Sources

list of the sources that have been used in the preparation of this biography. Such a task would require a disproportionate amount of space and would not have sufficient value to justify it.

In the documentation all references to Kennedy manuscripts, unless otherwise noted, are to the Kennedy Papers in the Peabody Institute Library, Baltimore. When no depository is designated for a letter written by Kennedy to a correspondent other than his wife or Philip C. Pendleton, the letter is a copy in the Kennedy Papers.

Throughout the notes the following abbreviations have been used:

People

John Pendleton Kennedy	JPK
Elizabeth Gray Kennedy	EGK
Philip Clayton Pendleton	PCP

Libraries

Boston Public Library	BPL
Buffalo Historical Society	BuHS
Duke University Library	DUL
Essex Institute, Salem, Massachusetts	EI
Historical Society of Pennsylvania	HSPa
Johns Hopkins University Library	JHL
Library of Congress	LC
Massachusetts Historical Society	MassHS
Maryland Historical Society	MdHS
New York Historical Society	NYHS
New York Public Library	NYPL
Peabody Institute, Baltimore	PI
Rochester University Library	RUL

Notes

PREFACE

1. JPK to W. C. Rives, May 30, 1847.
2. Thomas Nelson Page, *The Old South* (New York, 1908), p. 84.

CHAPTER I: A Baltimore Boyhood

1. Baltimore *Federal Gazette*, Jan 2, 1800; Baltimore *Telegraphe and Daily Advertiser*, Jan. 3, 1800; Fragment A, p. 17.
2. Edmund Pendleton's Bible, owned by Colonial Williamsburg, Incorporated. Cf. David John Mays, *Edmund Pendleton* (Cambridge, Mass., 1952), I, 3–5.
3. Fragment A, p. 8; Martinsburg *Potowmac Guardian and Berkeley Advertiser*, Oct. 6, 1794.
4. Fragment B.
5. Mary Selden Kennedy, *Seldens of Virginia and Allied Families* (New York, 1911), II, 392–96; Fragment C.
6. Fragment C.
7. "Baltimore Long Ago," *At Home and Abroad* (New York, 1872), pp. 181–82.
8. *Niles' Weekly Register*, III (1812), 45.
9. Jared Sparks, "Baltimore," *North American Review*, XX (1825), 100, 115.
10. Fragment C.
11. E. P. Hunter to JPK, Dec. 24, 1812.
12. JPK to John Kennedy, Nov. 25, 1813; John Strother to JPK, Jan. 7, 1813; JPK to EGK, Aug. 28, 1828; Washington Irving to JPK, Aug. 31, 1854; Washington *National Intelligencer*, April 20, 1863.
13. Henry Howe, *Historical Collections of Virginia* (Charleston, 1845), p. 334; W. W. Blackford, *War Years with Jeb Stuart* (New York, 1945), pp. 154–60; H. K. Douglas, *I Rode with Stonewall* (Chapel Hill, 1940), pp. 192–93.

14. Fragment C.
15. Fragment A, p. 30.
16. *Ibid.*, pp. 42–43.
17. *Ibid.*, p. 44.
18. Fragment B.
19. Fragment A, p. 52.
20. E. P. Hunter to JPK, Dec. 24, 1812; Fragment A, p. 93.
21. Fragment A, p. 45.
22. Baltimore *American*, Dec. 5, 1812.
23. Fragment A, pp. 106–107.

CHAPTER II: Heroic Years

1. London *Evening Star* quoted in Baltimore *American*, March 30, 1813; Henry B. Fearou, *Sketches of America* (London, 1818), p. 344.
2. *Niles' Weekly Register*, II (1812), 376, 405.
3. J. P. Cranwell and W. B. Crane, *Men of Marque* (New York, 1940), p. 41.
4. "The Swiss Traveller," *The Portico*, II (1816), 147.
5. Fragment A, pp. 72–74.
6. *Ibid.*, pp. 105–106.
7. *Ibid.*, p. 119.
8. G. R. Gleig, *A Subaltern in America* (Philadelphia, 1822), p. 67.
9. "Colonel Joseph Sterett's Statement," *American State Papers, Military Affairs* (Washington, 1832), I, 568; "Winder's Narrative," *ibid.*, p. 558; "Pinkney's Statement," *ibid.*, p. 573; Fragment A, pp. 117–43.
10. JPK to PCP, Aug. 29, 1814.
11. William M. Marine, *The British Invasion of Maryland 1812–1815* (Baltimore, 1913), p. 165.
12. JPK to Rufus Griswold, Sept. 16, 1846.
13. JPK to Holmes Conrad, Sept. 14, 1854.
14. Lt. Col. Joseph Sterett to [Governor of Maryland], Feb. 1, 1815.
15. Cf. Kennedy's manuscript notes taken from Company Book, United Volunteers, and deposited with Fragment A.
16. *Niles' Weekly Register*, IX (1815), 1.
17. Fragment A, p. 97.
18. John E. Semmes, *John H. B. Latrobe and His Times* (Baltimore, 1917), p. 430.
19. Journal, June 11, 1831.
20. Samuel Tyler, *Memoir of Roger Brooke Taney* (Baltimore, 1872), p. 75.
21. John Neal, *Wandering Recollections of a Somewhat Busy Life* (Boston, 1869), p. 163.
22. Fragment A, p. 96.
23. *The Red Book*, II (1821), 139.

24. T. O. Mabbott and F. L. Pleadwell, *The Life and Works of Edward Coote Pinkney* (New York, 1926), p. 25.
25. John Neal, *Wandering Recollections*, p. 210. Neal has left an entertaining account of a Delphian meeting in his novel, *Randolph* (n.p., 1823), II, 316-20. Cf. MS minutes of the Delphian Club, IV, 214-16, MdHS.
26. *The Portico*, I (Feb. 1816), 141-45; I (March 1816), 240-44; I (April 1816), 315-21; I (June 1816), 494-501; II (Aug. 1816), 143-47.
27. Fragment B; JPK to Rufus Griswold, March 20, 1850.
28. JPK to Rufus Griswold, March 20, 1850.
29. Fragment A, p. 80.
30. Basil Hall, *Travels in North America* (Edinburgh, 1829), II, 394.
31. Henry M. Brackenridge, *Recollections of Persons and Places in the West* (Philadelphia, 1868), p. 118.
32. C. F. M. [?] to JPK, Feb. 12, 1819.
33. "Baltimore Long Ago," *At Home and Abroad* (New York, 1872), p. 172.
34. Fragment A, p. 60.
35. Edmund Pendleton to JPK, Oct. 23, 1821.

CHAPTER III: Apprentice Years

1. JPK to P. H. Cruse, Jan. 24, 1819, MdHS.
2. *Horse-Shoe Robinson* (New York, revised edition, 1852), Introduction, pp. vi-xii.
3. Fragment A, pp. 82-85.
4. [Peter H. Cruse], "Life of William Pinkney," *North American Review*, XXIV (1827), 68-92. A short description of Pinkney in this review, "from the hand of a gentleman, who, during a few years preceding his death, was on a footing of intimacy with him," is almost certainly by Kennedy.
5. Andrew Kennedy to JPK, March 11, 1821; H. T. Tuckerman, *The Life of John Pendleton Kennedy* (New York, 1871), p. 106.
6. John E. Semmes, *John H. B. Latrobe and His Times* (Baltimore, 1917), p. 222; "The Diary of Robert Gilmor," *Maryland Historical Magazine*, XVII (1922), 246; *The Red Book*, I (1819), 7.
7. Semmes, *Latrobe*, pp. 224-25; Josias Pennington to JPK, June 14, 1822, MdHS; JPK to EGK, Aug. 8, 1828.
8. Cruse to Philip R. Fendall, March 30, 1830, MdHS.
9. Joseph Robinson to JPK, Oct. 27, 1819; Robinson to Charles Dilworth, Oct. 18, 1819.
10. Joseph Robinson to JPK, Oct. 18, 27, 1819; Baltimore *Federal Gazette*, Nov. 18, Dec. 23, 1819; Jan. 22, 1820.
11. Baltimore *American*, Nov. 27, 1822; *The Red Book*, I (1819), 36; Joseph Robinson to JPK, Oct. 27, 1819; Baltimore *Federal Gazette*, March 16, 1820.

12. Paulding to JPK, June 10, 1832.
13. Andrews Norton to JPK, July 24, 1820; Edward Everett to JPK, June 26, 1820.
14. *Keep Cool* (Baltimore, 1817) was written by John Neal.
15. William Wirt to David Hoffman, Aug. 30, 1819. William Wirt Letter Book, LC.
16. Cruse to JPK, Jan. 9, 1821.
17. Baltimore *Federal Gazette*, Oct. 5, 1820.
18. Cruse to JPK, Jan. 9, 1821.
19. *Memoirs of the Life of William Wirt* (Philadelphia, 1849), II, 58.
20. Baltimore *Federal Gazette*, Sept. 24, 1821.
21. *Proceedings, House of Delegates, 1820 Session*, p. 26; Baltimore *Federal Gazette*, Jan. 16, 1821; Baltimore *American*, Dec. 21, 1820; Jan. 4, 6, 1821.
22. JPK to EGK, July 27, 1828.
23. Baltimore *Patriot*, Feb. 1, 1821; Baltimore *Federal Gazette*, Feb. 20, 1821.
24. Baltimore *Patriot*, Oct. 2, 1821; Baltimore *Federal Gazette*, Oct. 8, 1822.
25. *Proceedings, House of Delegates, 1821 Session*, pp. 106-109.
26. Owned by the Henry E. Huntington Library and Art Gallery, San Marino, California.
27. Edmund Pendleton to JPK, Oct. 23, 1821; Andrew Kennedy to JPK, March 11, 1821; Tuckerman, *Life of Kennedy*, p. 114.
28. Baltimore *Federal Gazette*, Feb. 12, 1823; Baltimore *American*, Feb. 14, 1823; Josias Pennington to JPK, Feb. 11, 1823.
29. Baltimore *American*, Feb. 14, July 18, 23, 26, Aug. 1, 1823.
30. *Ibid.*, Jan. 23, 1823.
31. John C. Calhoun to JPK, May 12, 1822.
32. John C. Calhoun to JPK, Jan. 21, 1823; William Wirt to James Monroe, April 18, 1822.
33. William Wirt to JPK, Jan. 26, 1823; John C. Calhoun to JPK, June 10, 1823.
34. MS copy in Cruse Papers, MdHS.
35. Baltimore *American*, Oct. 20, 1824.
36. Journal, May 31, 1852.
37. Isaac McKim to JPK, March 2, 1825; Samuel Smith to JPK, March 1, 1825; MdHS. John C. Calhoun to JPK, March 9, 1825.
38. "I lost no time in procuring the Signature of all the Maryland delegation [in Congress] in your favor for the appointment you wished." Isaac McKim to JPK, March 2, 1825, MdHS.
39. Broadside signed "John P. Kennedy," 1826, JHL.
40. Baltimore *American*, July 18, 1823.
41. *Ibid.*, Oct. 5, 1826.
42. JPK to Nancy Kennedy, June 18, 1826; Feb. 12, 1827.

Notes

CHAPTER IV: "A Right Merry Young Lawyer"

1. Fragment A, p. 94.
2. Jay B. Hubbell, *The South in American Literature* (Durham, 1954), p. 492n.
3. JPK to Robert C. Winthrop, Jan. 3, 1850, Robert C. Winthrop Papers, MassHS.
4. Journal, May 31, 1852; Feb. 5, 1848.
5. JPK to EGK, Aug. 8, 11, 1828.
6. JPK to EGK, April 6, 1844.
7. JPK to EGK, April 25, 1832.
8. *Memoirs of the Life of William Wirt* (Philadelphia, 1849), II, 150.
9. Allan Nevins, ed., *Diary of Philip Hone* (New York, 1927), I, 303.
10. JPK to EGK, March 7, 1835.
11. JPK to EGK, Aug. 10, 1834.
12. H. T. Tuckerman, *The Life of John Pendleton Kennedy* (New York, 1871), pp. 246–52; Journal, Oct. 28, 1847; Jan. 29, 1851.
13. Journal, Dec. 25, 1843.
14. *Ibid.*, Dec. 17, 1848; Feb. 28, 1850. Cf. JPK to Richard Pakenham, May 6, 1849.
15. "A Review of Mr. Cambreleng's Report from the Committee of Commerce . . . ," *Political and Official Papers* (New York, 1872), pp. 9–86; Journal, April 13, 1830.
16. Pierre Irving, *The Life and Letters of Washington Irving* (New York, 1864), IV, 125.
17. V. L. Parrington, *Main Currents in American Thought* (New York, 1927), II, 48–49.
18. JPK to Edward Gray, Aug. 9, 1833.
19. Journal, Nov. 19, Dec. 10, 1829; Nov. 11, 1833.
20. JPK to Nancy Kennedy, Feb. 12, 1827; JPK to Harriet Douglass, Jan. 4, 1851.
21. Josiah Quincy, *Figures of the Past* (Boston, 1884), pp. 296–97.
22. "Address . . . on the Occasion of the Opening of the Collegiate Department in the University of Maryland . . . , *Occasional Addresses* (New York, 1872), p. 24; Baltimore *American*, Jan. 3, 1831; Journal, Dec. 28, 1830.
23. *Occasional Addresses, passim.*
24. Journal, April 9, 1835; W. D. Hoyt, "The Monday Club," *Maryland Historical Magazine*, XLIX (1954), 301–13; James Wynne, "John P. Kennedy," *Harper's New Monthly Magazine*, XXV (1862), 336.
25. JPK to PCP, Oct. 17, 1844.
26. Journal, Dec. 11, 1833.
27. Kennedy Papers, Vol. XLI.

CHAPTER V: Virginia Revisited

1. Journal, Oct. 19, 1829; Dec. 31, 1831; JPK to EGK, Aug. 28, 1828.
2. H. C. Carey to JPK, Oct. 2, 1832; H. C. Carey to P. H. Cruse, April 14, 1832.
3. *Swallow Barn, eller en sommar pa Laudet i Virginien* (Stockholm, 1835).
4. [G. H. Calvert], "Swallow Barn," Baltimore *Times*, III (June 2, 1832), 78; J. K. Paulding to JPK, June 10, 1832; M. C. Simms Oliphant, *et al.*, *The Letters of William Gilmore Simms* (Columbia, South Carolina, 1952-1956), III, 122; Jay B. Hubbell, *The South in American Literature* (Durham, 1954), p. 492. Professor Hubbell notes, as did Simms, that this is true only of a certain class. Cf. Francis Pendleton Gaines, *The Southern Plantation: A Study in the Development and Accuracy of a Tradition* (New York, 1924).
5. JPK to EGK, Aug. 23, 1828.
6. JPK to EGK, Aug. 28, 1828.
7. *Ibid.*
8. Fragment A, pp. 37-41.
9. MS Swallow Barn, Vol. LVI. In my discussion of the novel, I have used extensively the unbound and unpaged sheaf of preliminary notes included in the bound manuscript.
10. JPK to EGK, Aug. 19, 1828.
11. JPK to EGK, May 21, 1830.
12. JPK to George P. Putnam, May 3, 1851.
13. [A. H. Everett], "Swallow Barn," *North American Review*, XXXVI (1833), 532-33; James A. Harrison, ed., *The Complete Works of Edgar Allan Poe* (New York, 1902), VIII, 4.
14. JPK to Rufus Griswold, Sept. 16, 1846.
15. Washington Irving, *The Sketch Book* (New York, 1860), p. 497.
16. Journal, Oct. 19, 1829; Sept. 21, 1830; Thomas Nelson Page, *The Old South* (New York, 1908), p. 84; John E. Semmes, *John H. B. Latrobe and His Times* (Baltimore, 1917), p. 430.
17. Journal, Sept. 10, 1850. For Kennedy's efforts to have *Swallow Barn* republished, see H. C. Carey to JPK, Feb. 8, 1833; Carey and Lea to JPK, March 25, 1839; Lea and Blanchard to JPK, Nov. 2, 1845.
18. Fragment A, p. 38.
19. JPK to John Kennedy, Nov. 25, 1813.
20. Fragment C.
21. *Ibid.*
22. H. T. Tuckerman, *The Life of John Pendleton Kennedy* (New York, 1871), pp. 402-403. See above, Chapter I, pp. 8-9.
23. H. C. Carey to JPK, Jan. 15, 1834. The Cooper passage is transcribed by Carey.

Notes 249

24. Hubbell, *The South in American Literature*, p. 492n.
25. William Wirt to JPK, May 23, 1832.
26. Fragment C.
27. H. C. Carey to JPK, Feb. 29, 1832.
28. Harrison, ed., *Works of Poe*, VIII, 4.
29. [A. H. Everett], "Swallow Barn," *North American Review*, XXXVI (1833), 519.
30. "Swallow Barn," *New England Magazine*, III (1832), 77.
31. *Ibid.*, p. 79.
32. [John H. B. Latrobe], "Kennedy's Novels," *New York Review*, XIX (1842), 147; J. K. Paulding to JPK, June 10, 1832.
33. John Esten Cooke, *Virginia: A History of the People* (Boston, 1883), p. 496; V. L. Parrington, *Main Currents in American Thought* (New York, 1927), II, 52.

CHAPTER VI: The Novelist as Historian

1. *Memoirs of the Life of William Wirt* (Philadelphia, 1849), I, 125.
2. "A Legend of Maryland," *At Home and Abroad* (New York, 1872), p. 37.
3. Journal, Dec. 13, 1832; July 13, 1833; MS notes for *Horse-Shoe Robinson*, Vol. XXXIII.
4. Henry James, "Hawthorne," *The Shock of Recognition*, Edmund Wilson, ed. (New York, 1955), p. 436.
5. Fragment A, p. 57.
6. MS notes for *Horse-Shoe Robinson*, Vol. XXXIII.
7. Richard Bentley to JPK, May 14, 1834; Feb. 6, 1836.
8. Irving to JPK, June 5, 1835; James A. Harrison, ed., *The Complete Works of Edgar Allan Poe* (New York, 1902), VIII, 4; *Southern Literary Journal*, I (1835), 206; *New England Magazine*, IX (1835), 390-91; *Knickerbocker*, VI (1835), 71; *American Quarterly Review*, XXXV (1835), 240-41; George S. Bryan to JPK, June 19, 1835.
9. Henry C. Carey to JPK, Oct. 4, 1835; Journal, May 5, 1856.
10. JPK to Rufus Griswold, Sept. 16, 1846; MS chronology, Vol. LVIII; MS notes for *Horse-Shoe Robinson*, Vol. XXXIII; Cf. John Robert Moore, "Kennedy's Horse-Shoe Robinson: Fact or Fiction," *American Literature*, IV (1932), 160-66.
11. Rhoda Coleman Ellison, "An Interview with Horse-Shoe Robinson," *American Literature*, XXXI (1959), 329-32; see the same author's "Early Alabama Interest in Southern Writers," *Alabama Review*, I (1948), 107-108.
12. *Revolutionary Pension Roll, Vol.* XIV, Senate Document 514, 23rd Congress, 1st session, 1833-34.

13. John E. Semmes, *John H. B. Latrobe and His Times* (Baltimore, 1917), p. 430.
14. Ellison, "An Interview with Horse-Shoe Robinson," p. 332.
15. This excerpt from a letter written from the House of Representatives [c. 1839] from Kennedy to Mrs. Henry Vernon Somerville of St. Mary's County appears in an article on St. Mary's in the Baltimore *Sun*, May 28, 1910.
16. MS notes for *Rob of the Bowl*, Vol. xxxv.
17. Henry C. Forman, *Jamestown and St. Mary's* (Baltimore, 1938), *passim*.
18. "A Legend of Maryland," p. 51.
19. MS minutes of the Maryland Historical Society, v, 367–69, 403–404, MdHS.
20. JPK to Rufus Griswold, Sept. 16, 1846.
21. "A Legend of Maryland," p. 51; Kennedy Papers, Vol. lv.
22. John V. L. McMahon, *An Historical View of the Government of Maryland* (Baltimore, 1831), pp. 210–14.
23. *Archives of Maryland*, ed. William Hand Browne *et al.* (Baltimore, 1883——), xv, 192–93, 244–47.
24. *Ibid.*, xv, 388–91; xvii, 31, 48, 65.
25. *Ibid.*, xv, 402–12; xvii, 67.
26. *Ibid.*, xv, 388–92; McMahon, pp. 215–16n.
27. *Rob of the Bowl* (Philadelphia, 1838), i, 70, 76–77; *Archives*, xvii, 50.
28. *Rob of the Bowl*, ii, 274–75; *Archives*, xvii, 53, 87.
29. *Rob of the Bowl*, i, 228–53; *Archives*, xvii, 71, 78, 85–87.
30. *Rob of the Bowl*, i, 71; *Archives*, xv, 54–55; xvii, 22.
31. *Archives*, xvii, 400–401.
32. *Rob of the Bowl*, ii, 80–81.
33. MS notes for *Rob of the Bowl*, Vol. xxxv.
34. JPK to EGK, Aug. 1, 1838; [John H. B. Latrobe], "Kennedy's Novels," *New York Review*, xix (1842), 150; JPK to PCP, Dec. 12, 1838.
35. [Latrobe], "Kennedy's Novels," p. 150.
36. V. L. Parrington, *Main Currents in American Thought* (New York, 1927), ii, 53.
37. Carey and Lea to JPK, March 25, 1839.
38. Bryan to JPK, Feb. 21, 1839.
39. Bryan to JPK, Aug. 19, 1861.
40. Parrington, *Main Currents in American Thought*, ii, 54; Alexander Cowie, *The Rise of the American Novel* (New York, 1951), p. 267.
41. Kennedy Papers, Vol. ii; *Knickerbocker*, vi (1835), 71.
42. "Swallow Barn," *New England Magazine*, iii (1832), 78.
43. JPK to Rufus Griswold, Oct. [?], 1851, BPL.
44. "Appendix to the Discourse on the Life and Character of George Calvert," *Occasional Addresses* (New York, 1872), p. 166.
45. JPK to Philip Pendleton Kennedy, April 10, 1851.
46. JPK to George S. Bryan, Oct. 1, 1854.

47. "Tributes to the Memory of John Pendleton Kennedy," *Proceedings, Massachusetts Historical Society*, XI (1870), 366.
48. James Russell Lowell to JPK, April 26, 1860.

CHAPTER VII: "A Man of All Work"

1. MS on Laws, Vol. LVIII, unpaged.
2. JPK to PCP, June 5, 1841.
3. James A. Harrison, ed., *The Complete Works of Edgar Allan Poe* (New York, 1902), XV, 155.
4. *Niles' Weekly Register*, XXVI (1824), 245.
5. Journal, Oct. 8, 1829.
6. *Ibid.*, Sept. 28, 1830.
7. Baltimore *American*, Nov. 18, 1833.
8. JPK to EGK, Feb. 10, 14, 1832.
9. R. M. McLane, *Reminiscences 1827-1897* (n.p., 1903), p. 96.
10. JPK to EGK, Jan. 31, 1833.
11. Journal, Oct. 25, 1830; JPK to EGK, Feb. 11, 1832.
12. John E. Semmes, *John H. B. Latrobe and His Times* (Baltimore, 1917), pp. 399-401; Journal, Dec. 10, 1833.
13. Journal, Dec. 10, 11, 21, 1833.
14. Journal, April 23, 1834; Baltimore *American*, April 24, 1834.
15. Baltimore *Republican*, April 25, 1834; Journal, Dec. 19, 1839.
16. "Defense of the Whigs," *Political and Official Papers* (New York, 1872), p. 317.
17. McLane, *Reminiscences*, p. 96.
18. Journal, Sept. 28, 1830.
19. JPK to EGK, Feb. 11, 1832; Journal, Nov. 7, 1833; JPK to EGK, Oct. 18, 1833; Baltimore *American*, Nov. 18, 1833.
20. Baltimore *Republican*, July 1, 6, 25, 26, 1837; Baltimore *Patriot*, July 8, 27, 1837.
21. Baltimore *Sun*, April 27, 1838; Baltimore *Patriot*, April 14, 26, 27, 1838; JPK to PCP, May 1, 1838.
22. EGK to JPK, May 14, 1838.
23. JPK to PCP, July 22, 1838.
24. Scrap Book, Vol. XLI, unpaged.
25. "Speech . . . on the Sub-Treasury Bill," *Political and Official Papers*, p. 225.
26. JPK to PCP, April 18, 1839.
27. JPK to PCP, July 22, 1838.
28. JPK to PCP, Sept. 29, 1839; Baltimore *American*, April 26, 1838, Oct. 3, 1839.
29. Journal, Dec. 14, 1839.

30. "Baltimore Long Ago," *At Home and Abroad* (New York, 1872), p. 179.
31. Journal, Dec. 15, 1839.
32. *Ibid.*
33. V. L. Parrington, *Main Currents in American Thought* (New York, 1927), II, 55.
34. Journal, Dec. 6, 1840.
35. Jared Sparks, "Baltimore," *North American Review*, xx (1825), 100.
36. Lea and Blanchard to JPK, Nov. 29, 1843.
37. [William Gilmore Simms], "Kennedy's Horse Shoe Robinson," *Southern Quarterly Review*, XXII (1852), 203.
38. [John H. B. Latrobe], "Kennedy's Novels," *New York Review*, XIX (1842), 151.
39. John Esten Cooke, "The Author of Swallow Barn," *Appletons' Journal*, X (1873), 205-206.
40. JPK to PCP, Oct. 10, 1840.

CHAPTER VIII: A Whig in Harness

1. *Niles' Register*, LVIII (1840), 152-59; Baltimore *American*, May 2, 3-5, 1840.
2. Baltimore *American*, May 8, 1840; Journal, Dec. 6, 1840.
3. JPK to PCP, Oct. 10, 1840.
4. Journal, Jan. 26, Feb. 22, March 22, 1841.
5. John Quincy Adams, *Memoirs* (Philadelphia, 1875-77), X, 366.
6. Journal, Feb. 7-8, 1841.
7. *Ibid.*, April 20, 1841.
8. Baltimore *American*, April 20, 1841.
9. Baltimore *American*, May 20, 1841; Journal, May 17-18, 1841.
10. Adams, *Memoirs*, x, 457.
11. Journal, April 3, 1841.
12. JPK to EGK, June 22, 1841.
13. JPK to PCP, June 5, 1841.
14. *Congressional Globe*, 27th Congress, 1st session, p. 22.
15. JPK to PCP, July 13, 1841.
16. JPK to EGK, Aug. 13, 1841.
17. *Ibid.*
18. JPK to EGK, Aug. 18, 1841.
19. Journal, Sept. 17, 1841.
20. *Niles' Register*, LXI (1841), 35.
21. Unidentified newspaper clipping, Vol. LXV, unpaged.
22. Journal, Sept. 26, 1841.
23. Baltimore *Republican*, Feb. 1, 10, 1844.
24. *Memoirs of the Life of William Wirt* (Philadelphia, 1849), I, 344.

Notes

25. Journal, Sept. 1, 1842.
26. Robert Gilmor to Jonathan Meredith, March 30, 1844, MdHS.
27. JPK to EGK, June 15, 1844.
28. JPK to EGK, Sept. 1, 1844.
29. Greeley to JPK, Jan. 16, 1844.
30. JPK to EGK, Sept. 1, 1841.
31. Carleton Mabee, *The American Leonardo: A Life of Samuel F. B. Morse* (New York, 1944), p. 253.
32. *Ibid.*, pp. 251–53.
33. *Congressional Globe*, 27th Congress, 3rd session, p. 317.
34. *Ibid.*, p. 323.
35. *Ibid.*, 28th Congress, 1st session, p. 313.
36. H. T. Tuckerman, *The Life of John Pendleton Kennedy* (New York, 1871), p. 181.
37. N. P. Willis to JPK, n.d. [1842?].
38. JPK to PCP, June 5, 1841.
39. JPK to EGK, Nov. 16, 1838.
40. Robert C. Winthrop, Jr., *A Memoir of Robert C. Winthrop* (Boston, 1897), *passim*.
41. Winthrop to JPK, Nov. 13, 1841.
42. Adams, *Memoirs*, x, 24, 321, 495, 512; Journal, Nov. 20, 1847.
43. Adams, *Memoirs*, xi, 105.
44. Louisa Catherine Adams to JPK, Oct. 6, 1843, MdHS.
45. Journal, Dec. 24, 1843.
46. Allan Nevins, ed., *Diary of Philip Hone* (New York, 1927), I, 179.
47. *Ibid.*, II, 445.
48. "Work," *At Home and Abroad* (New York, 1872), p. 121.
49. Adolph Bacourt, *Souvenirs of a Diplomat* (New York, 1885), p. 281.

CHAPTER IX: "New Men, New Measures, New Country"

1. Robert C. Winthrop to JPK, Jan. [?], 1844.
2. JPK to PCP, Feb. 10, 1844.
3. Baltimore *American*, Feb. 15, 1844.
4. Journal, Oct. 13, 1844; JPK to EGK, May 30, 1844; Allan Nevins, ed., *Diary of Philip Hone* (New York, 1927), II, 711.
5. Journal, Oct. 13, 1844.
6. JPK to Robert Gilmor, Dec. 18, 1844, MdHS.
7. New York *Tribune*, Nov. 29, 1844.
8. *Discourse on the Life and Character of George Calvert* (Baltimore, 1845).
9. Bernard U. Campbell, *Review of the Hon. John P. Kennedy's Dis-*

course . . . (Baltimore, 1846); *Reply of John P. Kennedy to the Review of his Discourse* . . . (Baltimore, 1846).
10. Kennedy Papers, Vol. LVIII.
11. "Letter on the Annexation of Texas, May 15, 1844," *Political and Official Papers* (New York, 1872), pp. 604–614.
12. Journal, Oct. 13, 1844; Baltimore *American*, May 22, 1844, quoting Philadelphia *American*.
13. Journal, Dec. 16, 1830.
14. JPK to EGK, Aug. 30, 1844.
15. "My Notebook," Vol. XL, unpaged.
16. JPK to Robert C. Winthrop, Jan. 19, 1848. Winthrop Papers, MassHS.
17. JPK to EGK, June 13, 1844.
18. JPK to Robert C. Winthrop, May 31, 1845. Winthrop Papers, MassHS.
19. Journal, "autumn of 1845."
20. *Ibid.*
21. Baltimore *American*, Oct. 2, 1845.
22. JPK to Robert C. Winthrop, Sept. 21, 1845. Winthrop Papers, MassHS.
23. "Notes and Hints," Vol. XXXI, unpaged.
24. Baltimore *American*, Oct. 9, 1846; R. C. McGrane, *Foreign Bondholders and American State Debts* (New York, 1935), pp. 86, 89–101; H. S. Hanna, *Financial History of Maryland* (Baltimore, 1907), pp. 105–25.
25. JPK to EGK, Dec. 15, 1846; Jan. 13, 1847; McGrane, *Foreign Bondholders*, p. 101.
26. "Journal of a Tour to Canada," Vol. VI, *passim;* JPK to EGK, May 3, 1847.
27. Baltimore *American*, Sept. 27–30, Oct. 1–2, 1847; JPK to Robert C. Winthrop, Oct. 11, 1847, Winthrop Papers, MassHS; Baltimore *American*, Oct. 7, 1847.
28. Journal, Nov. 13, 1848.

CHAPTER X: The Literary Life

1. JPK to William Gilmore Simms, Feb. 29, 1852.
2. "Literature Considered as a Profession," *New York Mirror*, XIII (1836), 285; Baltimore *American*, Oct. 21, 1852; Journal, Sept. 26, 1841.
3. JPK to EGK, June 28, 1840.
4. JPK to EGK, Dec. 28, 1832.
5. Irving to EGK, Feb. 1, 1855.
6. V. L. Parrington, *Main Currents in American Thought* (New York, 1927), II, 30.
7. "A Discourse on the Life and Character of William Wirt," *Occasional Addresses* (New York, 1872), pp. 78–110.
8. Journal, Dec. 24, 1843.
9. "Notes on Life of William Wirt," Vol. XXIV, *passim*.
10. JPK to C. J. Faulkner, Jan. 6, 1850.

Notes

11. JPK to Mrs. Alexander Randall, Dec. 20, 1849.
12. Journal, July 23, 1846.
13. JPK to EGK, Nov. 6, 1849.
14. *United States Magazine and Democratic Review*, xxv (1849), 480.
15. William Gilmore Simms, *Southern Quarterly Review*, xvii (1850), 192–236; *North American Review*, lxx (1850), 255–59; JPK to Philip Hone, Nov. 28, 1849.
16. James R. Thompson to JPK, Feb. 8, 1850; "Kennedy's Life of Wirt," *Southern Literary Messenger*, xvi (1850), 206–209.
17. JPK to Blanchard and Lea, Jan. 11, 1851; JPK to Park Benjamin, Nov. 25, 1849; Lea and Blanchard to JPK, Jan. 18, 1850.
18. Journal, April 13, 1851. This accounting was apparently compiled from letters and contracts still preserved among the Kennedy Papers (Vols. xx, xxi). An examination of these data reveals the statement to be correct. Kennedy actually received $568.50 for the first edition of the *Life of Wirt*, but he divided the profits with Wirt's widow.
19. See above, Chapter v, note 17.
20. Journal, Oct. 29, 1850.
21. *Ibid.*, Sept. 12, 1850; JPK to G. P. Putnam, March 29, 1851.
22. John E. Semmes, *John H. B. Latrobe and His Times* (Baltimore, 1917), p. 430.
23. JPK to W. G. Simms, March 8, 1851; JPK to Philip Pendleton Kennedy, Feb. 6, 1852; Robert C. Winthrop to JPK, June 5, 1852.
24. Italics supplied.
25. Jay B. Hubbell, ed., *Swallow Barn* (New York, 1929), pp. xxvii, xxviii.
26. New York, 1854, p. 7.
27. Vol. xxviii.
28. JPK to Calvin Wiley, Nov. 18, 1848.
29. New York, 1853.
30. Journal, Nov. 13, 1853.
31. John D. Allen, *Philip Pendleton Cooke* (Chapel Hill, 1942), p. 27.
32. JPK to EGK, June 4, 1839.
33. "Business Memoranda," Vol. lxxiv, May 29, 1846.
34. JPK to PCP, Sept. 28, 1845; P. P. Cooke to R. W. Griswold, Oct. 15, 1845, Griswold Papers, BPL; Joy Bayless, *Rufus Wilmot Griswold* (Nashville, 1943), p. 128.
35. Cooke to JPK, Oct. 3, Nov. 15, 1845.
36. Cooke to JPK, Dec. 1, 1845; JPK to Rufus Griswold, Jan. 6, 1846, Griswold Papers, BPL; Cooke to E. A. Poe, Sept. 16, 1839, Griswold Papers, BPL.
37. Cooke to Griswold, Nov. 8, 1846, Griswold Papers, BPL; Cooke to JPK, Nov. 23, 1846.
38. "I have written nothing at my book since I came to the country, for with all the apparent leisure of my life I lead here, it is true that I am really too busy in idleness." JPK to EGK, Aug. 11, 1828.

39. Journal, Dec. 8, 1846; JPK to Cooke, Nov. 26, 1846; JPK to Griswold, April 10, 1847.
40. Cooke to Griswold, Jan. 20, 1847, Griswold Papers, BPL.
41. John Esten Cooke, *Virginia: A History of the People* (Boston, 1883), p. 481; J. E. Cooke to JPK, Dec. 27, 1860; cf. JPK to J. E. Cooke, Nov. 12, 1851, DUL.
42. Journal, June 29, 1848; JPK to G. P. Putnam, April 5, 1851; Strother to JPK, Aug. 9, 1862; Strother to JPK, Oct. 29, 1862; JPK to William H. Seward, Aug. 16, 1862, Seward Papers, RUL.
43. Journal, Nov. 2, 1833.
44. James A. Harrison, ed., *The Complete Works of Edgar Allan Poe* (New York, 1902), XVII, 3.
45. J. W. Ostrom, ed., *The Letters of Edgar Allan Poe* (Cambridge, Mass., 1948), I, 56-57.
46. *Ibid.*, I, 81.
47. *Ibid.*, I, 73.
48. JPK to Poe, Sept. 19, 1835, Griswold Papers, BPL.
49. Ostrom, ed., *Poe Letters*, I, 81.
50. *Ibid.*, I, 299; JPK to Poe, Dec. 1, 1845, Griswold Papers, BPL.
51. Ostrom, ed., *Poe Letters*, I, 172, 190.
52. JPK to George W. Fahnestock, April 13, 1869.
53. Journal, April 20, 1850.

CHAPTER XI: Cabinet Officer

1. R. C. Winthrop to JPK, Jan. 1850.
2. JPK to EGK, Jan. 20, 1850.
3. Journal, March 8, 1850.
4. JPK to EGK, Aug. 9, 1850.
5. Journal, Nov. 19-Dec. 24, 1850.
6. *Ibid.*, Jan. 16, 1851.
7. *Ibid.*, Aug. 13, 1851.
8. *Ibid.*, July 29, 1852; JPK to Millard Fillmore, July 20, 1852, BuHS.
9. JPK to EGK, July 28, 1852.
10. Harold and Margaret Sprout, *The Rise of American Naval Power 1776-1918* (Princeton, 1939), p. 138.
11. M. C. Perry, *Narrative of the Expedition of an American Squadron to the China Seas and Japan*, Sidney Wallach, ed. (New York, 1952), p. 1.
12. "Report as Secretary of the Navy," *Political and Official Papers* (New York, 1872), p. 500.
13. JPK to Brantz Mayer, June 20, 1855, MdHS.
14. E. K. Kane to JPK, May 17, 1853.
15. Rufus Griswold to JPK, Feb. 5, 1853; JPK to R. C. Winthrop, Dec. 6, 1852, Winthrop Papers, MassHS.

Notes

16. Pierre Irving, *The Life of Washington Irving* (New York, 1864), IV, 126.
17. Journal, Jan. 21, 1853.
18. Gordon N. Ray, ed., *The Letters and Private Papers of William Makepeace Thackeray* (Cambridge, Mass., 1946), III, 543; JPK to W. W. Follett-Synge, Dec. 16, 1853; Journal, Feb. 27, 1853.
19. Ray, ed., *Letters of Thackeray*, III, 212, *passim*. Eyre Crowe, *With Thackeray in America* (New York, 1894), p. 116; Journal, Feb. 27, 1853.

CHAPTER XII: Elder Statesman

1. Journal, March 4, 1853.
2. Now 12 Madison Street.
3. Pierre Irving, *The Life of Washington Irving* (New York, 1864), IV, 146–47.
4. Irving to JPK, March 22, 1856.
5. S. T. Williams and L. B. Beach, "Washington Irving's Letters to Mary Kennedy," *American Literature*, VI (1934), 44–66.
6. JPK to EGK, June 29, 1853; JPK to Robert C. Winthrop, Sept. 27, 1853; Journal, Oct. 2–25, 1853, Dec. 28, 1854–Jan. 8, 1855; JPK to EGK, Jan. 1, 1855.
7. Journal, Aug. 30, 1853.
8. Vol. XXXVII, unpaged.
9. Vol. XLVI, unpaged.
10. JPK to Robert C. Winthrop, March 24, 1850. Winthrop Papers, MassHS.
11. Journal, Dec. 8, 1854; cf. JPK to W. E. Mayhew, Feb. 5, 1857, Peabody Papers, EI.
12. Journal, April 27, 1857.
13. JPK to Winthrop, Dec. 25, 1854, Feb. 19, 1854, Winthrop Papers, MassHS; S. T. Williams and L. B. Beach, "Washington Irving's Letters to Mary Kennedy," *American Literature*, VI (1934), 58; JPK to Millard Fillmore, Feb. 5, 1854.
14. Irving to EGK, Feb. 21, 1854.
15. Charleston *Courier*, May 25, 1854.
16. Journal, Jan. 8, 1856.
17. J. G. Wilson and John Fiske, eds., *Appletons' Cyclopedia of American Biography*, III, 517.
18. James Grant Wilson, *Thackeray in the United States* (New York, 1904), I, 348.
19. Journal, Jan. 17, 1864.
20. J. R. Lowell to JPK, May 7, 1870.
21. John E. Cooke, "John Pendleton Kennedy," *Appletons' Journal*, X (1873), 205.

22. "Tributes to the Memory of John Pendleton Kennedy," *Proceedings, Massachusetts Historical Society,* XI (1870), 365.
23. JPK to EGK, March 29, 1854.
24. Vol. XXXVII, unpaged.
25. Vol. XXXI, p. 88.
26. JPK to Robert C. Winthrop, Feb. 21, 1856. Winthrop Papers, MassHS.
27. Journal, Nov. 1, 1863; D. H. Strother to JPK, Aug. 9, 1863; Journal, Nov. 21, 1861.
28. JPK to EGK, Aug. 2, 1850.
29. The title of the first of the Border Romances, published in 1834.
30. JPK to EGK, June 28, 1840.
31. William Gilmore Simms, "Kennedy's Life of Wirt," *Southern Quarterly Review,* XVII (1850), 200.
32. William Gilmore Simms, "Kennedy's Horse-Shoe Robinson," *ibid.,* XXII (1852), 204.
33. Jay B. Hubbell, *The South in American Literature* (Durham, 1954), p. 593.
34. M. C. Simms Oliphant, *et al.,* eds., *The Letters of William Gilmore Simms* (Columbia, South Carolina, 1952–1956), I, 366, 382; II, 12n.
35. JPK to Simms, Feb. 29, 1852.
36. Oliphant *et al.,* eds., *Letters of Simms,* III, 173–74.
37. JPK to PCP, May 11, 1859.
38. Cf. JPK to John J. Crittenden, Jan. 25, 1862. Crittenden Papers, NYHS.
39. Journal, July 5, 1861.
40. JPK to Robert C. Winthrop, Jan. 21, 1862. Winthrop Papers, MassHS.
41. "Tributes to the Memory of John Pendleton Kennedy," *Proceedings, Massachusetts Historical Society,* XI (1870), 366.
42. Philip P. Kennedy to JPK, Jan. 30, 1864.
43. New York, 1865.
44. JPK to Robert C. Winthrop, Feb. 16, 1862, Winthrop Papers, MassHS; JPK to Goldwin Smith, June 8, 1865.
45. Vol. XL, unpaged; "Theological," Vol. LVIII, unpaged; Journal, Aug. 7, 1864.
46. Oliphant *et al.,* eds., *Letters of Simms,* IV, 558–59.
47. Travel Journal, *passim;* H. T. Tuckerman, *The Life of John Pendleton Kennedy* (New York, 1871), p. 459.
48. Millard Fillmore to Robert C. Winthrop, Nov. 12, 1870, Winthrop Papers, MassHS.
49. Tuckerman, *Life of Kennedy,* p. 464.
50. "Tributes to the Memory of John Pendleton Kennedy," *Proceedings, Massachusetts Historical Society,* XI (1870), 368.
51. J. W. Ostrom, ed., *The Letters of Edgar Allan Poe* (Cambridge, Mass., 1948), I, 172.
52. A. N. Whitehead, *Science and the Modern World* (New York, 1926), p. 100.

Index

Abbot, Edward, 106
Abolition. *See* Slavery
Academy of Natural Sciences, 207
"Adam's Bower," 8, 9–10, 76, 223
Adams, Charles Francis, 228
Adams, Henry, 169
Adams, John, 214
Adams, John Quincy: as Secretary of State, 52; as President, 55; and JPK, 64, 154, 159–60; *Quodlibet* attributed to, 136; on W. H. Harrison, 142–43; on Tyler, 144; and copyright law, 157; tours West, 160; and Texas, 169; declines to write Wirt biography, 181; mentioned, 25, 180
Addison, Joseph, 13, 29, 41
Airs of Palestine (Pierpont), 28
American party, 217
American Philosophical Society, 12, 207
American Revolution. *See* Revolutionary War
American System, 66, 121–23
Antietam, Battle of, 23

Bacourt, Adolph, 162
Baltimore: honors Washington's memory, 1–2; in 1800, 4–7; mob rule, 17, 62–63, 131, 165; in 1820, 31–32, 46–47; described in *The Red Book*, 40–41; society in 1826, 68; shift in political temper of, 130–31; and *Quodlibet*, 136–37; antebellum society, 221–22; during Civil War, 229–30, 233
Baltimore College, 12, 13
Baltimore Phrenological Society, 68
Bancroft, George, 205
Bank of Maryland, 120, 131
Bank of the United States, 119–20, 126–27, 146–48
Barrow, Isaac, 13
Bell, John, 228
Belles Lettres Society, 30–31, 32
Benjamin, Park, 184
Bentley, Richard, 96
Biddle, Nicholas, 160
Blackwater Chronicle, The (P. P. Kennedy), 190, 212
Bladensburg, Battle of, 20–21, 24
Border States: Their Power and Duty in the Present Disordered Condition of the Country, The, 228
Bracebridge Hall (Irving), 78, 92
Brackenridge, Henry Marie, 28, 31
Braddock, General Edward, 8
Brandt, Captain Randolph, 105
Breckinridge, John C., 228
Brooks, Van Wyck, 240
Bryan, George S., 97, 111, 113
Bryant, William Cullen, 30, 225
Buchanan, James, 217
Bull Run, First Battle of, 224
Burke, Edmund, 13

Calhoun, John C.: as Secretary of War, 53; as Secretary of State, 168; and state rights, 199; mentioned, 64, 153, 232
Calvert, George, first Lord Baltimore, 166
Calvert, George Henry, 73
Calvin, John, 232
Carey, Henry C.: publishes *Swallow Barn*, 72–73, 86, 89; publishes *Horse-Shoe Robinson*, 97; and Poe, 195
Carlyle, Thomas, 90
Carr, Dabney, 84
Carroll, Charles, 31, 56
Caruthers, Robert L., 155
Chase, Samuel, 27
Chicheley, Sir Henry, 107
Civil War, 10, 154, 227–32
Clay, Henry: and "corrupt bargain," 55, 123; and JPK, 64, 65, 115, 125, 146, 200; his character, 122–23; at Convention of Whig Young Men, 141; and Tyler, 144–48; and copyright law, 157; nominated for Presidency in 1844, 164; the conciliator, 199; mentioned, 66, 118, 171
Clemm, Maria, 194
Cockburn, Sir George, 19
Compromise of 1850, 199, 202–203
Constitutional Union party, 228, 231
Coode, Colonel John, 105
Cooke, George Frederick, 32
Cooke, John Esten: on *Swallow Barn*, 88, 193; on *Quodlibet*, 138–39, 193; his *Leather Stocking and Silk*, 188–89; influenced by JPK, 193; on JPK, 220
Cooke, Maria Pendleton, 190
Cooke, Philip Pendleton, 190–93, 226
Cooper, James Fenimore: defines gentleman, vii; and Bread and Cheese Club, 31; on *Swallow Barn*, 84, 89; and New York frontier, 93; and JPK, 172, 191; and George P. Putnam, 186; compared with Simms, 225; mentioned, 30, 32, 90, 92, 103, 189
Copyright Law. *See* International Copyright
Count Julian (Simms), 226
Cowie, Alexander, 111, 240
Cox, James H., 137
Crittenden, John J., 228
Crockett, Davy, 136
Cruse, Peter Hoffman: his character, 36–37; and JPK, 53–55; professor, 69; and *Swallow Barn*, 72; tours Virginia, 77; writes introduction for *The British Spy*, 180

Dana, Richard Henry, 193
Dane, Clarence, 97
Darnall, Henry, 106
Davis, Charles Augustus, 160
Davis, Henry Winter, 228
Davis, Warren R., 98
Debore, Clause, 106
Defense of the Whigs: political history, 149–51; and Tyler, 152; reception of, 152–53; style of, 153; its nationalism, 166
Defoe, Daniel, 13
Delphian Club, 28–31 *passim*
Democratic party: under Jackson, 116–21; and independent treasury, 126; satirized in *Quodlibet*, 133–34, 136; nominates Van Buren, 141; election of 1852, 209–210, 211; election of 1860, 228
DeQuincey, Thomas, 113
Dickens, Charles, 218
Digges, William, 106
Dorsey, Judge Walter, 27
Douglas, Stephen A., 228
Dulany, Grafton, 36, 54

Ellicott, Thomas, 119–20, 137
Ellison, Rhoda Coleman, 100

Index

Era of Good Feelings, 30, 45-46, 211
Ericsson, Captain John, 209
Everett, Alexander H., 78, 87
Everett, Edward: on *The Red Book*, 43-44; and JPK, 175-76; and Constitutional Union party, 228

Fahnestock, George W., 197
Federalist party: and P. C. Pendleton, 8; criticizes JPK, 47; its history, 149-51; mentioned, 5, 45
Fendall, Captain Josias, 103-107 *passim*
Fillmore, Millard: and JPK, 159, 213; succeeds to Presidency, 202; his nationalism, 204; and John Ericsson, 209; tours West, 215-17; and American party, 217; on JPK, 234-35
Fort McHenry, 1, 19
Franklin, Sir John, 207
Friends of Domestic Industry, 118
Froissart Ballads (P. P. Cooke), 192, 193

Gales, Joseph, 200
Gates, General Horatio, 95
Ghent, Treaty of, 24, 27
Gilmor, Robert, 70
Golden Christmas, The (Simms), 226
Goldsmith, Oliver, 13
Gone With the Wind (Mitchell), 74
Graham, William A., 205
Granger, Francis, 159
Grant, Ulysses S., ix, 234
Gray, Edward: his character, 63-67; and American system, 121; illness and death, 204, 217
Gray, Martha, 63, 102, 217, 233
"Great Drama, The," 229
Greeley, Horace, 152, 153
Green, Duff, 67

Greene, General Nathanael, 3
Griswold, Rufus Wilmot: and Philip P. Kennedy, 190; his *Poets and Poetry of America*, 191; assists Philip P. Cooke, 191-93; on naval report of JPK, 207; mentioned, 78, 98, 102, 112
Gulliver's Travels (Swift), 5, 41, 205

Hamilton, Alexander, 63, 122, 150
Handbook for Travellers (Murray), 218
Harper, General Robert Goodloe, 25-26, 130
Harrison, William Henry, 64, 129, 137, 144
Harvard College, 230
Hawthorne, Nathaniel, 90, 179
Heath, James E., 184
Hollingsworth, Zebulon, 35
Holmes, Oliver Wendell, 231, 235
Hone, Philip: and JPK, 62, 164, 170, 191; on *Horse-Shoe Robinson*, 161; on American society, 161; on *Life of Wirt*, 184
Horace in London (Smith), 42
Horse-Shoe Robinson: historical accuracy of, 90-91; structure of, 91-93; chauvinism of, 95, 166; style of, 95-96; Canadian edition, 175; dedicated to Irving, 180, 204; revised edition, 189; and border warfare, 230
Houston, George S., 156
Howard, Benjamin Chew, 123-24, 136-37
Howard, John Eager, 18, 68, 123
Howe, Henry, 9
Hubard, William James, 59, 67
Hubbell, Jay B., 73, 188, 240
Hume, David, 13

Internal Improvements, 47, 49, 117, 173-74, 227

International Copyright, 157-58
Irving, Washington: on Philip C. Pendleton, 9; member of "The Nine Muses," 28; on Edward Gray, 65-66; influenced *Swallow Barn*, 78; and *Horse-Shoe Robinson*, 96-97; compared with JPK, 111, 113; on literary life, 180; his biography of Columbus, 181; declines to write Wirt biography, 181; friendship with JPK, 204-205, 208-209, 212-13, 216; on *Homes of American Authors*, 212; mentioned, 30, 32, 89, 186, 189, 225

Jackson, Andrew, 55-56, 66, 116-120 *passim*, 129, 151
James, Henry, 95
Jefferson, Joseph, 32
Jefferson, Thomas, 2, 12, 45, 151, 169
Johnson, Cave, 155-56
Johnson, Samuel, 13
Johnston, Mary, 74
Jones, Joshua, 205

Kane, Elisha Kent, 207
Kean, Charles, 62, 175
Kennedy, Andrew (uncle of JPK), 4
Kennedy, Andrew (brother of JPK), 7, 74, 213, 223
Kennedy, Anthony (uncle of JPK), 4, 12, 58
Kennedy, Anthony (brother of JPK), 13, 74, 171, 223-24
Kennedy, Elizabeth Gray (second wife of JPK): her character, 59-63, 72; death, 102; advises JPK, 125; her pessimism, 128; at Baltimore, 144; at Washington, 159; visited by Bacourt, 162; urges JPK to join cabinet, 202; at Saratoga Springs, 205; and Irving, 212; mentioned *passim*

Kennedy, John (father of JPK): as soldier, 1-2; his character, 4; bankruptcy, 11-12, 49; antipathy to British, 16; re-establishes business, 34; moves to Virginia, 74; and Henry Clay, 123; and slavery, 169; death, 223
Kennedy, John Pendleton: birth, 4; boyhood in Baltimore, 5-7; Virginia vacations, 7-10; education, 10-14; in War of 1812, 16-24, 169; his nationalism, 17, 24, 29-30, 43, 94, 165-67, 200-202, 204, 236; studies law, 24-27; practices law, 34-35, 58, 62; in House of Delegates, 45-52, 173-75; diplomatic mission to Chile, 51-52, 124; marries Mary Tenant, 53-54; in House of Representatives, 55-56, 123-25, 143, 163-64, 172-73, 176; marries Elizabeth Gray, 59-61; and University of Maryland, 69, 202, 214; his literary credo, 111-14, 179-80; and Jacksonism, 116-21 *passim*; his political credo, 122, 130-31, 160-62; his ill-health, 125-26, 160, 163, 221, 235; breaks with South, 153-54, 169-71, 223-24; as literary patron, 189-98; tours West, 203, 215-17; Secretary of the Navy, 205-10; railroad president, 215; tours Europe, 217, 218, 233-34; during Civil War, 229-31; his religion, 232; death, 235
Kennedy, Mary (niece of JPK), 213, 215
Kennedy, Mary Tenant (first wife of JPK), 53-56
Kennedy, Nancy Clayton Pendleton (mother of JPK): her character, 3-4; visits Virginia, 7; during War of 1812, 22; death, 223; mentioned, 139, 190
Kennedy, Philip Pendleton (brother of JPK): birth, 13; and Vir-

Index

ginia, 74, 223-24; and JPK, 112, 189-90, 223; criticizes *Swallow Barn*, 187; publishes *The Blackwater Chronicle*, 190; during Civil War, 230
Kennedy, Tenant Pendleton (son of JPK), 54
Kent, James, 181
Knowles, Sheriden, 62
Knox, Samuel, 12, 14

Landor, Walter Savage, 113
Latrobe, John H. B.: on JPK, 25, 36, 219; on *Swallow Barn*, 79, 88, 186; on *Horse-Shoe Robinson*, 99; on *Rob of the Bowl*, 109; on *Quodlibet*, 138; and Greenmount Cemetery, 158; and Poe, 194
Lawrence, Abbott, 160, 209
Lea and Blanchard, 111, 138, 184, 186
Leather Stocking and Silk (J. E. Cooke), 188-89, 193
Letters of Jack Downing, Major, The (Davis), 160
Letters of the British Spy (Wirt), 28, 180
Lincoln, Abraham, 228, 231-32
Lionel Lincoln (Cooper), 103
Locke, John, 13
Log Cabin and Hard Cider campaign, 129-30, 140-43
Longfellow, Henry Wadsworth, 175
Longstreet, Augustus Baldwin, 193
Lord Ashburton, Alexander Baring, 161
Lord Morpeth, George Howard, 161
Louisiana Purchase, 151, 169
Lowell, James Russell, 113, 114, 220-21, 230

McDonogh, John, 203
McKim, Isaac, 124
McMahon, John V. L., 104
Madison, James, 2, 16, 17, 151
Marion, General Francis, 94, 95
Marshall, John, 181
Martin, Luther, 18
Martineau, Harriet, 62
Maryland Historical Society, 166, 175
Maryland, State of: grants Baltimore charter, 4; internal conflicts, 46; and internal improvements, 49, 173-74; its colonial history, 102-108 *passim;* during Civil War, 229
Maryland, University of, 48, 202, 214, 229
Meek, Alexander Beaufort, 99
Memoirs of the Life of William Wirt: research for, 181-82; structure of, 182-83; reception of, 183-84, 205; profits from, 185
Mesmerism, 156, 236
Mexican War, 176
Miller, James H., 194
Millerism, 156
Mills, Robert, 67-68
Minor, Benjamin B., 192
Missouri Compromise, 46
"Mr. Ambrose: His Experiences, Opinions, and Philosophy," 214
Mr. Ambrose's Letters on the Rebellion, 230-31
Mitchell, Charles, 26
Mitchell, Margaret, 74
Monday Club, 69-71
Monroe, James, ix, 2, 25, 46, 52, 180
Morse, Samuel F. B., 154-57, 236
Murray, John, 218

National Republican party, 45, 55-56
National Road, 51, 117
Neal, John: at Baltimore, 26, 28, 32; and Delphians, 28-29; his chauvinism, 111

Niles, Hezekiah: on Baltimore commerce, 6; on privateers, 17; on national character, 24; and American system, 66
North Point, Battle of, 22
Norton, Andrews, 43

Old Bachelor, The (Wirt), 28, 41, 180

Page, Thomas Nelson: on JPK, ix; and plantation tradition, 74, 88; on authorship, 79
Pakenham, Sir Richard, 161, 175
Parrington, Vernon Louis: on Edward Gray, 66; on *Swallow Barn*, 88; on *Rob of the Bowl*, 110, 111; on *Quodlibet*, 131; on William Wirt, 180
Paulding, James Kirke: and "Nine Muses," 28; on American imitativeness, 43; on *Swallow Barn*, 73, 88, 89; Wirt's opinion of, 84; and Dutch Knickerbockers, 93; his chauvinism, 111; Secretary of the Navy, 205; mentioned, 32, 189
Peabody, George, 214, 234
Peabody Institute, 214-15, 234, 238-39
Pendleton, Agnes Patterson, 3
Pendleton, Edmund, 26, 32, 50
Pendleton, General Nathaniel, 3
Pendleton, Henry, 3
Pendleton, Philip, 3
Pendleton, Philip Clayton: his character, 8-9; and *Swallow Barn*, 82-83; estranged from JPK, 224; mentioned, 21, 108, 124, 128, 139
Pennington, Josias, 36, 53, 127
Perry, Commodore Matthew, 206-207
Pickens, Andrew, 94
Pierce, Franklin, 209, 210, 211
Pierpont, John, 28
Pinkney, Charlotte, 35, 36, 47

Pinkney, Edward Coote, 28
Pinkney, William: his character, 25, 35, 130; his political clique, 46-47; mentioned, 52, 180
Plantation tradition, 73-74, 88, 114
Poe, Edgar Allan: on Edward Coote Pinkney, 28; and *Swallow Barn*, 78, 87, 89; on *Horse-Shoe Robinson*, 97; and JPK, 116, 178, 189, 194-97; and Philip Pendleton Cooke, 192; on literary life, 236
Poets and Poetry of America, The (Griswold), 191
Polk, James Knox, 164, 205
Porte Crayon. See Strother, David Hunter
Portico, The, 29, 30
Potomac Canal, 50-51, 117, 124
Power, Tyrone, 62
Prescott, William Hickling, 175
Priestly's Academy, 10-11
Privateers, 17
Purchas, Samuel, 186
Putnam, George Palmer, 78, 186, 189

Quincy, Josiah, 68
Quodlibet: as political satire, 120, 133-34; structure of, 132-34; as social satire, 135-36; Baltimore as prototype of, 136-37; reception of, 138-39; mentioned, 225

Rainbow, The (Wirt), 180
Randall, Alexander, 143
Red Book, The: collaboration of JPK and Cruse, 36-38, 42-43; its publication, 38-40; reception of, 38, 43-45; as social satire, 41-42; mentioned, 56, 69, 71, 111, 180
Revolutionary War, 5, 90-92, 98-100
Ridgely, Charles Sterett, 123
Ridgely, David, 101
Robertson, James. See Robinson, James

Index

Robinson, James ("Horse-Shoe"), 34, 98–100
Robinson, Joseph, 38–40, 45
Rob of the Bowl: research for, 101–108, 175; structure of, 109–10; reception of, 111; mentioned, 128, 158
Ross, General Robert, 19, 21, 22
Rousby, Christopher, 105

Sakell, Launcelott, 106
Salmagundi, 40, 41
Saturday Club, 31, 231
Scott, Walter, 90, 94
Scott, Winfield, 205, 210
Sewall, Nicholas, 106
Seward, William H., 233
Shakespeare, William, 109–10
Simms, William Gilmore: and *Swallow Barn,* 73, 187, 226; on *Quodlibet,* 138; edits *Southern Quarterly Review,* 178; on *Life of Wirt,* 184; and JPK, 113, 189, 225–27, 233; on *Rob of the Bowl,* 226
Sinclair, William, 12, 14, 28, 81
Sketches of the Life and Character of Patrick Henry (Wirt), 180
Slavery: attitude of JPK toward, 47–48, 169–71, 200, 201, 226–27; in *Swallow Barn,* 86–87, 187–88; and abolitionists, 199; attitude of Simms toward, 227
Smith, John, 186
Smith, Samuel, 24, 130
Smithson, James, 154
Sparks, Jared, 7
Spy, The (Cooper), 90, 92
Stanly, Edward, 156, 157
Steele, Richard, 13, 41
Sterne, Laurence, 11, 13, 136
Stowe, Harriet Beecher, 212
Strother, David Hunter, 190, 193, 224
Stuart, General James E. B., 10

Sumter, Thomas, 94
Swallow Barn: reception of, 71, 73, 87–88, 89, 189; publication of, 72–73; and Virginia, 73–78, 187–89; and Irving, 78; characterization in, 80–83; style of, 83–84; profits from, 185; revised edition, 186–89, 204; mentioned, 113, 115, 147, 193
Swann, Carruthers, 82
Swift, Jonathan, 87, 136
"Swiss Traveller, The," 29–30, 166

Talbot, George, 105
Taney, Roger Brooke, 26, 119–20
Tariff, 117–18, 122, 176, 227
Tarleton, Colonel Banastre, 91
Tayleure, C. W., 97
Taylor, Zachary, 177, 200
Tenant, Colonel Thomas, 58, 62, 70, 121
Texas, State of, 168–69
Thackeray, William Makepeace, 208–209, 218–20, 225
Thompson, John Reuben, 178, 184
Tilyard, Philip, 50
Tocqueville, Alexis de, 25
Tristram Shandy (Sterne), 5, 13
Tucker, Henry St. George, 190
Tucker, Nathaniel Beverley, 190
Tuckerman, Henry T., 82, 240
Tyler, John, 129, 146–49, 152, 183

Uncle Tom's Cabin (Stowe), 187
Union Bank of Baltimore, 66, 119–20, 137
United States Naval Academy, 208
United Volunteers, 18–24 *passim*
Upshur, Abel P., 168

Van Buren, Martin, 124, 130, 132, 141–42, 155, 205
Virginians, The (Thackeray), 218

Warner, William Burke, 32

Washington, George, 1, 29, 63-64
Watkins, Tobias, 30
Waverley (Scott), 31
Waxhaw Creek, Battle of, 91
Webster, Daniel: and JPK, 64, 65, 118, 142, 176; at Convention of Whig Young Men, 141; and copyright law, 157; opposed to admission of Texas, 168; spokesman for North, 199; Seventh of March speech, 201-202
"Whig Manifesto," 148-49
Whig party: in Baltimore, 120-21; and English Whigs, 121; campaign of 1840, 129-30, 140-43; its history, 149-51; under Tyler, 144-49; its philosophy, 160-62; election of 1844, 164; and Texas, 176; election of 1848, 209-10
White, Thomas W., 178, 194, 195

Willis, Nathaniel Parker, 157-58, 175, 179-80
Wilmot Proviso, 171
Wilson, James Grant, 219
Winder, William, 21
Winthrop, Robert C.: his character, 159; and JPK, 163, 200, 223; criticizes *Swallow Barn*, 187; and Philip P. Kennedy, 190; mentioned, 175, 177, 212
Wirt, William: JPK's biography of, viii, 180-85; his character, 25; as man of letters, 28; on *The Red Book*, 44; and JPK, 52-53, 59; on Washington Monument, 61; and *Swallow Barn*, 81, 84-85; mentioned, 65, 130, 143
Wynne, James, 70

Yeo, John, 105

DATE DUE

GAYLORD | PRINTED IN U.S.A.